RESPONSIBLE TECHNOLOGY
A Christian Perspective

BY THE FELLOWS OF THE CALVIN CENTER FOR CHRISTIAN SCHOLARSHIP CALVIN COLLEGE

STEPHEN V. MONSMA	ARIE LEEGWATER
CLIFFORD CHRISTIANS	EGBERT SCHUURMAN
EUGENE R. DYKEMA	LAMBERT VAN POOLEN

William B. Eerdmans Publishing Company
Grand Rapids, Michigan

Copyright © 1986 by William B. Eerdmans Publishing Company
255 Jefferson SE, Grand Rapids, Mich. 49503
All rights reserved
Printed in the United States of America

Library of Congress Cataloging-in-Publication Data

Responsible technology.

Bibliography: p. 245
1. Technology—Moral and religious aspects.
I. Monsma, Stephen V., 1936–   .   II. Calvin Center for
Christian Scholarship.
T49.5.R47   1986   261.5′6   86-11676

ISBN 0-8028-0175-7

Contents

Preface

THE SIX AUTHORS AND TWO STUDENTS WHO WORKED ON THIS BOOK were frequently reminded of the old saw that a camel is a horse made by a committee, and we wondered which animal our efforts would most resemble. We leave it to the reader to judge which of these creatures is the more apt simile, but all of us working on this project had three basic commitments that we trust have led to an integrated product.

First, we were committed to writing a book for the general reader, not primarily for the scholar specializing in the philosophy of science or technology or in other academic subfields. Early on we concluded that our most important contribution would be to give the broad Christian community greater insight and guidance in relation to technology. Even though technology plays a crucial role in everyday life, the Christian community has given it short shrift. The church has devoted much time and effort to questions of social justice, evolution and creation, and war and peace, and comparatively little time and effort to studying and reflecting upon modern technology and its implications for the Christian life. We hope this book can help the general reader begin this task.

This leads to our second basic commitment: that doing technology is not a neutral activity but one that involves valuing of a profound, fundamental nature. The value-ladenness and the pervasiveness of technology in modern societies make it clear that all Christians—whether as consumers, citizens, and formers of culture, or as technological designers or others pursuing occupations and callings that involve them directly in technology—need to confront the issues raised by the nature of modern technology.

Third, we are firmly committed to the belief that technology, as one form of human cultural activity, must be done under the Lordship of Jesus Christ. We had lengthy—sometimes heated—debates over exactly what this means in concrete situations, yet we never wavered from the truth of this commitment.

It is our hope and prayer that these three commitments live on every page of this book.

A word should be said about the joint authorship of this work. Each of the six authors was responsible for drafting one or more chapters, and these drafts were then subjected to intense review and discussion by the entire team. The editor then reworked all of the chapters to assure stylistic consistency and an orderly flow of concepts. These revisions were then subjected to additional reviews and discussion. Thus the final product is truly a joint venture. This does not mean that each author would endorse every idea exactly as it is stated, with the same nuance and emphasis it is given. Yet we were able to reach agreement on the basic concepts and conclusions set forth here.

The six authors wish to acknowledge the many debts we incurred in the pursuit of this project. First of all, we wish to thank the governing board of the Calvin Center for Christian Scholarship and the broader Calvin community for their support, which enabled us to pursue this project on a nearly full-time basis for eleven months. We owe a particular debt of gratitude to Rodger Rice, Calvin College's academic dean and secretary of the governing board of the Calvin Center for Christian Scholarship, for his constant encouragement and support. Also heading our list of acknowledgments are the two students—Katherine Wable (now Katherine Schreur) and Scott Grit—who served as research assistants and as participants in our numerous discussions. We also wish to thank Shirley Roels of Calvin College's Department of Economics and Business, who worked with the authors during the January interim. She gave us valuable insights into the processes by which businesses promote and adopt technological innovations. Finally, we also express our appreciation to Mary Hietbrink of Eerdmans Publishing Company, who performed a skillful job of improving the wording and flow of the manuscript, and Nelle Tjapkes, who increased the efficiency of the team by providing us with excellent secretarial services.

STEPHEN V. MONSMA
CLIFFORD CHRISTIANS
EUGENE R. DYKEMA
ARIE LEEGWATER
EGBERT SCHUURMAN
LAMBERT VAN POOLEN

CHAPTER ONE

Understanding Technology

TECHNOLOGY IS OMNIPRESENT IN MODERN SOCIETY. FROM THE HOME computers we use, to the clothes of synthetic fibers we wear, to the cars we drive, the fruits of technology are all around us. In fact, technology and its results are so much with us that, like the air we breathe, their presence and effects often go unnoticed and unanalyzed. As a result, modern technology and all it entails are often accepted by default, with few questioning what life would be like if humankind performed tasks and attained goals by other means.

This is not as it should be. We need to focus attention on technology and try to understand it. We should do so because the beliefs that infuse technology, the processes that mark it, and the outputs that flow from it are not inevitable, neutral, or necessarily benign. And God calls us to live responsible lives before him: "Whatever you do, whether in word or deed, do it all in the name of the Lord Jesus, giving thanks to God the Father through him" (Col. 3:17). Given these considerations, it is clear that we must understand technology in order to live responsibly before the Creator because, although most of us are not directly involved in doing technology, we are all consumers of the fruits of technology and live in a society suffused with modes of thought shaped by technology. To understand technology, we need to be aware of it, to comprehend its nature, and to recognize the role it plays in culture.

This understanding must, however, be more than merely rational; it must be an understanding we reach with our hearts as well as our minds. We already have many facts; we can use technology to achieve seemingly miraculous ends. We send human beings to the moon and back again; we build missiles of remarkable accuracy; we put complex, powerful computers in incredibly small packages. But do we truly understand what we are doing? Four considerations strongly suggest that to live responsibly before God in modern society requires us to understand technology with both heart and mind.

IMPORTANT REASONS TO UNDERSTAND TECHNOLOGY

The Pervasiveness and Power of Technology. It is hard to overstate technology's pervasiveness and power in modern, technologically oriented societies such as those found in Western Europe, North America, and Japan. A little reflection reveals that no area of human life in modern societies is left untouched by today's technology. People move themselves and their goods about by cars, trucks, trains, and planes; use energy such as electricity and various oil and gas products that have been produced or processed by highly complex technological means; live in a world of technologically produced materials such as plastics and synthetic fibers; and process, manipulate, store, and transmit information by using calculators, computers, and satellites. Even entertainment often depends on technology: witness video games, powerboats, and television.

But this is only the beginning of the story. Less obvious but more important are two additional aspects of the pervasiveness of technology. First, the artifacts of a modern, technologically sophisticated society are developed and manufactured by very large, complex structures and institutions. The firearms used in the Revolutionary War in the eighteenth century were largely produced by scattered craftsmen working in small workshops. Compare this means of production with today's armaments industry. It is an understatement to say that the structures and institutions that develop and manufacture earth satellites, computers, cars, electrical appliances, sophisticated medical equipment, and many other technological objects[1] are large and complex. One immediately thinks in terms of giant corporations such as General Dynamics, AT&T, and General Motors with their tens of thousands of employees, research and testing laboratories, and worldwide support systems. The very size of these institutions means their presence is felt everywhere in society.

Second, many technological objects need complex support systems if they are to function as intended. Take the family car, for example. To be used effectively and safely, it requires support systems stretching from faraway oil fields to giant refineries to a vast network of local gas stations. In addition, it needs a network of maintenance and repair facilities, plus a network of streets and highways that in turn require maintenance (pothole repair, snow removal, etc.) and traffic-control systems.

---

1. As explained more fully in the following chapter, throughout this book we use the term "technological object" to refer to any device or organism produced or transformed by the technological process, while we use the term "technological tool" to refer to technological objects that are primarily used in some other technological activity, and the term "technological product" to refer to technological objects that are not primarily used in some other technological activity.

A law enforcement system of police and courts is necessary to maintain driving safety and order. The car, which almost every one of us considers commonplace and uses daily, illustrates the point. Modern technological objects do not simply exist; often they can be used only in the context of large, interconnected support systems that pervade society.

The sheer pervasiveness of technology implies that its effects have penetrated deeply into the fabric of society—into its political, economic, and social processes and institutions, and into its cultural attitudes and values. In fact, the rise of institutions and structures dedicated to the development and manufacture of today's technological objects and to their support and maintenance has remade the political, social, economic, and entrepreneurial landscape of modern societies.

Technology affects, among other things, the ways societies look at and think about themselves and their world; it shapes cultural attitudes and values. In the nineteenth century the Industrial Revolution and the resulting urbanization deeply affected attitudes and values. Today television has changed politics, affected child-rearing practices, altered the economic system, shaped the development of language, influenced religious evangelism, and molded a host of ideas. Similarly, earth satellites, automated industries, and changing medical technologies are having social, economic, and political impacts that are difficult even to imagine. In the process, human culture is transformed.

The Value-Ladenness of Technology. Adding to the need to understand technology is the fact that it is not neutral. Engaging in technological activities inevitably and necessarily means valuing; there is no escaping this fact. At times the argument is made that technology and its tools and products are neutral, and that only the uses to which they are put involve valuing. But there can be no such neat division. Of course valuing affects how technological tools and products are used, but valuing begins long before the use stage. Technology itself is value-laden. (This point is so important and yet so seldom recognized that much of Chapter Three is spent explicating it.) Thus responsibility in a technological society necessarily means that we must have insights into the valuing that is reflected in the technology with which we are surrounded. Only then can we make responsible choices.

Conflicting Opinions Regarding Technology. To greater or lesser extents we all use technological objects and experience the consequences of doing so, but we have not decided if they are a blessing or a curse. We have not agreed on what is technological progress and what is not. If technology has been regarded by some as a god, worthy of allegiance and even worship, it has been regarded by others as a demon, or at the very least as a god that has failed, a crippled god—"the god that limps," to borrow the title of Colin Norman's book.[2]

Some are concerned that technology has not delivered its apparent promise: a cornucopia of goods without the labor of producing them, and a "high-tech" culture in which to enjoy the resulting leisure. To these observers, the failed promise is in the lack of beneficial results in the hoped-for magnitude; happiness—if, indeed, it has to do with less work and more leisure—still eludes us. The primary complaint of others is that the cost is too high: the very technology that was to bring freedom and improvement seems to have brought slavery and decline instead, in the form of such things as a numbing uniformity and impersonality, the threat of nuclear destruction, and a despoiled creation.

Such concerns have led to an examination of technology—one that looks not only at its results but also at the path it takes to those results. The question then is not merely what objects will be produced, but what will be the consequences of the process by which they are produced. What effects will technology have on the whole of life? How will work, leisure, religion, and culture be changed? To many of us it seems that technological prowess has somehow outstripped the other aspects of human life. The works of minds and hands seem to have outstripped those of the heart; the technological appears to loom large in our lives while the spiritual languishes. Some fear that the facts of technology have outshone and perhaps in some sense "done in" the values by which we can measure and control technology. These distinctions are, as we will see, far too simple, yet they get at a fundamental cause of the malaise of our times. There is widespread worry that, as E. F. Schumacher put it, "Man is far too clever to be able to survive without wisdom."[3]

Thus, although some praise technology for bringing about human progress—dreaded diseases are conquered, the drudgery of work is relieved, distances are shrunk, and new opportunities are opened up[4]—others damn technology for depersonalizing human relationships, wasting precious natural resources, polluting the earth, and threatening the

2. See Colin Norman, *The God That Limps: Science and Technology in the Eighties* (New York: Norton, 1981).

3. E. F. Schumacher, *Small Is Beautiful: Economics as if People Mattered* (New York: Harper & Row, 1973), p. 30.

4. See, for example, Samuel C. Florman, *The Existential Pleasures of Engineering* (New York: St. Martin's Press, 1976); and Emmanuel G. Mesthene, "Technology and Wisdom," in *Philosophy and Technology: Readings in the Philosophical Problems of Technology*, ed. Carl Mitcham and Robert Mackey (New York: Free Press, 1983), pp. 109–15.

very existence of human life with weapons of mass destruction.[5] Some therefore seek life-styles as far removed from modern technology as possible, believing that what is smaller and simpler is also better; others—with equal sincerity and equal conscientiousness—study to be engineers in order to live and work in a world of high technology.

Even those writing about technology from a Christian perspective often differ markedly in their assessment of it. Some, such as Jacques Ellul, see modern technology as being in tension with a Christian understanding of humankind and society;[6] others, such as Harvey Cox and Friedrich Dessauer, see modern technology as being fully in keeping with Christianity.[7]

The confusing variety of opinions about technology results in a lack of direction for modern technological society and reveals the need for a deeper, more earnest understanding of technology. And this understanding must move beyond a mere amassing of more facts about technology—it must be an understanding of the mind *and* the heart. Such an understanding sees what technology rests upon, the valuing integrated into it, the ways in which it shapes and is shaped by culture, and what all this means. Only as we gain such an understanding can we hope to find our way in today's trackless technological forest of conflicting claims.

The Divergent Nature of Today's Technologies. A fourth reason why understanding technology is crucial can be seen in the fact that modern technologies have the very real potential to be oppressive—even demonic—social forces and the equally real potential to be positive, liberating forces. And sometimes both positive and negative forces are present in the same technology. Thus divergent pictures emerge.

On the one hand, there is the picture of a technology in keeping with the biblical vision of God's kingdom, a kingdom of shalom. According to this vision, technology is a liberating force that helps people live in a responsible, harmonious relationship with God, each other, and nature. Shalom is a state of harmony and order that leads to a society at peace. It is not a peace born of quietude and rest, but a peace of dynamism. In this vision society is alive, moving, and pulsating, but also at peace

5. See, for example, Barry Commoner, *The Closing Circle* (New York: Bantam Books, 1972); and Theodore Roszak, *Where the Wasteland Ends* (Garden City, N.Y.: Doubleday, 1973).

6. Jacques Ellul, *The Technological Society*, trans. John Wilkinson (New York: Knopf, 1965).

7. Harvey Cox, *The Secular City* (New York: Macmillan, 1965); and Friedrich Dessauer, *Streit um die Technik*, 2nd ed. (Frankfurt: Verlag Josef Knecht, 1958).

because its vibrancy and dynamism exist in a context of right relationships. It is a peace born of active harmony, not a peace born of stagnation.

Philosopher Nicholas Wolterstorff has described shalom as consisting of three right relationships:

> Shalom in the first place incorporates right, harmonious relationships to *God* and delight in his service. . . . Shalom is perfected when humanity acknowledges that in its service of God is true delight. . . .
>
> Secondly, shalom incorporates right, harmonious relationships to other *human beings* and delight in human community. Shalom is absent when a society is a collection of individuals all out to make their own way in the world. . . .
>
> Thirdly, shalom incorporates right, harmonious relationships to *nature* and delight in our physical surroundings. Shalom comes when we, bodily creatures and not disembodied souls, shape the world with our labor and find fulfillment in so doing and delight in its results.[8]

Responsible technology done in keeping with God's will for humankind supports shalom. When technology progressively frees humankind from dreary, arduous labor and long-combatted diseases, enables men and women to move about and to exchange goods and ideas, and creates tools and products of beauty and usefulness, it is fully in keeping with the vision of shalom. This earth—a planet full of beauty and bountiful treasures—could be a place of fear and barrenness. A world without technological objects would be a world of rampant hunger and disease, life-threatening fluctuations in weather, impassable rivers and oceans, and resources deeply buried and unusable in their natural forms. There would be little shalom in a life shaped by such severe threats and lacks. It would be life lived in constant fear and devoid of security, joy, and pleasure.

Technology in keeping with shalom is represented by a white-coated scientist developing a vaccine that will banish from this planet a dreaded disease that previously tore husband from wife and child from parent, leaving shalom trampled in its wake. It is represented by a graceful bridge spanning a previously uncrossable river, a bridge that fits in with its natural setting, is in itself a thing of beauty and grace, and brings together in mutual delight and benefit two previously separated peoples.

But today's technology is often not in keeping with shalom—indeed, it is impossible for it to be fully so in this imperfect, fractured world.

---

8. Nicholas Wolterstorff, *Until Justice and Peace Embrace* (Grand Rapids: Eerdmans, 1983), p. 70.

Technology does not often appear as a knight in shining armor. Instead, it all too often sweeps through societies like an avenging Hun, raping, pillaging, and destroying. One has only to think of entire species of plants and animals wiped off the face of the earth, of young children laboring twelve hours a day under dangerous, unhealthy conditions in nineteenth-century English mills and mines, of the efficient gas chambers of Auschwitz and Buchenwald, of napalm raining down upon villagers in Vietnam, of persons growing fat and sleek on haute cuisine while others die from the lack of a crust of bread. Then shalom lies dead under the avalanche of technology. The world of difference between these two pictures of technology—of a society of shalom with its peace and delight, and of a society of repression, fear, and exploitation—could not be clearer or starker.

Between these two pictures lies a host of technological processes and objects that are neither wholly good nor wholly evil. Each may be both a blessing and a curse. A new strain of rice developed at an agricultural research laboratory, for example, may increase the yield of rice by forty percent, thereby feeding additional millions and reducing starvation in the world. But it may also require the heavy use of chemical fertilizers and pesticides, thereby raising long-term health and safety problems. Should the technological process providing such a result be placed on the credit or the debit side of the ledger? On the side of peace and delight, or the side of repression and fear? The answer is not obvious. There is a tension difficult to resolve as one contemplates certain advantages that must be traded off in order to gain other advantages.

How can one explain the fact that humankind develops technological objects as congruent with shalom—as beneficent—as a polio vaccine and as vicious and demonic as a neutron bomb, which leaves buildings standing and dooms human beings to terrible, agonizing deaths? In the Book of James we find the rhetorical question, "Does a fountain gush with both fresh and brackish water from the same opening?" (James 3:11, NEB), but modern technological processes seem indeed to bring forth both fresh, reviving water and brackish, poisonous water. How is it possible that what appear to be the same mind-sets, the same processes, and the same educational-research structures give society such great good and such great evil? And how can they sometimes produce good and evil tightly interlocked in the same process or object?

A partial answer to these questions lies in the broken, fallen nature of humankind and the world. It is clear that when humankind fell into sin, human nature was not the only thing fractured; the natural creation and humanity's relationship to it were also changed and broken (see Gen. 3:14-19). Henceforth the creation was in "bondage to decay" and "groaning as in the pains of childbirth" (Rom. 8:21–22). As a result, we ought not to expect that a society of perfect shalom will be created through humankind's technology or any of its other works. Human work—technological or otherwise—will always be incomplete, imperfect, and impermanent. No doubt our frequent need to make cruel choices when we confront good and evil intertwined in the same technological process or object results in part from the brokenness of our world.

But this is not the whole story. Even in this world progress as well as regression is possible. And by God's grace we can tell the difference. A polio vaccine is indeed different from a neutron bomb. And God's call to "seek first his kingdom" (Matt. 6:33) includes seeking technologies in keeping with his kingdom of shalom and rejecting those in keeping with Satan's kingdom of pride and inordinate self-love.

Yet often humankind seems to choose wrongly, irresponsibly. Why does technology so often seem to be fearsome and destructive? The answer lies in the nature of modern technology itself and the way in which society goes about doing technology. Much of the rest of this book will be needed to develop this answer. Certainly technology's capacity for both good and evil—sometimes intermixed—speaks to our need to examine it and understand it, so that we may act responsibly in seeking good and opposing evil.

THE TASK AT HAND

To truly understand modern technology, we must move beyond simply looking at the technological objects produced, the uses to which those objects are put, and the steps taken to develop and manufacture them.

When we do so, we find that technology is not a neutral, discrete entity isolated from societal institutions, historical traditions, and cultural beliefs and attitudes. Underlying modern technology is a set of beliefs, assumptions, and values—a faith. This faith is rooted in the Renaissance and the Enlightenment, which declared human autonomy from God and from his will for human beings and the rest of creation. The fact that this faith is often not clearly formulated or self-consciously articulated only makes it less easily seen, not less powerful—or less dangerous.

A crucial problem is that this faith sets its adherents on the wrong path and blinds them to the fact they are on it. As a result, technological processes and objects time and again are molded not in response to God's normative will but in response to human pride and selfishness.

Sometimes God, by his grace, brings forth good out of evil. Sometimes the natural consequences of humankind's false faith are restrained by God, and all of their potential for evil is not realized. Sometimes men and women of conscience and love respond in faith to God's will in their lives. Thus technology sometimes brings joy and harmony—the characteristics that define shalom—among human beings and the creation. But at other times the natural consequences of humankind's following a false faith result in the exploitation of fellow human beings, the earth, and its creatures, which leads to fear and alienation. Sometimes technological change is benign or beneficial; sometimes it is harmful, even fatal; sometimes it brings both good and evil.

The authors of this book—all of whom are committed Christian scholars—are convinced that Christianity provides a basis for a faith that gives proper direction to modern technology. God the Creator has made known his will for human beings and all their activities, including the technological. God's will supplies us with normative principles that should guide the doing of technology. Employing these principles will lead to a technology in keeping with the joy, peace, and harmony of shalom. Indeed, this entire book is an explication of this basic thesis.

This explication has several parts. The following chapter completes the introduction to our topic by defining technology and further developing the focus of our study. Chapter Three argues against the claim that technology itself is neither good nor evil, thereby strengthening the case that technology can be done either responsibly or irresponsibly. Chapters Four and Five lay the groundwork for a Christian approach to doing technology, analyzing the false faith by which technology is usually done today and developing certain normative principles for doing technology based on God's will. Chapters Six, Seven, and Eight consider the scientific, economic, and political relationships of technology, deepening our understanding of technology by contrasting these relationships as they are with what they should be if technology is done in keeping with God's normative will. Chapters Nine and Ten consider the technological design process itself, showing how it should be shaped by the normative principles developed in Chapter Five. The last two chapters focus on the responsibilities borne by those involved in technology. Since all of us are involved in technology in one way or another, the last two chapters are in essence a call to everyone to live responsibly in an increasingly technological world.

CHAPTER TWO

Technology Examined: Definitions and Distinctions

TECHNOLOGY PLAYS SO CENTRAL A ROLE IN MODERN SOCIETY THAT IT IS impossible to live responsibly without understanding it and its role in human affairs. This much was established in the first chapter. But in order to get on with the task of understanding technology and the meaning of responsible technology, we must answer a fundamental but difficult question: What is technology?

Chapter One used such terms as "technology" and "technological processes" with purposeful ambiguity. But now more precision is called for. "Technology" and related terms have been used in almost every conceivable way to describe almost every conceivable phenomenon, from the designing of nuclear power plants ("Modern technology's answer to the energy crisis is nuclear power") to the way a ballet dancer performs ("Her vitality was great but her technique was off"). This confusion in language indicates that modern societies have not thought self-consciously about technology. The confusion in popular language is paralleled by equal confusion among scholars, who disagree on such basic questions as whether or not technology refers only to physical reality and whether or not consumer products such as television sets and cars should be identified as technology.

This chapter seeks to clear away this terminological underbrush, thereby delineating the meanings we attach to various terms. The following discussion assesses technology from a Christian view of humankind and society, explores a Christian concept of technology in the context of alternative approaches others have taken, and explains the validity of that concept.

DEFINITIONS: CONFUSION AND CONFLICTS

The Historical Development of the Word Technology. The starting point for understanding the confusing array of meanings that have been attached to the word *technology* is the origin of the word. It comes from the Greek word *technologia,* meaning "the systematic treatment of an art." In his *Rhetoric* Aristotle used it more specifically to refer to a systematic treatment of grammar or speech.

A form of the word *technology* first appeared in English in the seventeenth century, and by the early eighteenth century it was being used to describe the arts generally—taken broadly as any skill or craft—and the mechanical arts in particular.[1] Gradually its usage in English came to focus on industrial and practical arts as distinct from the fine arts. Using a term that in the original Greek had referred to the systematic use or "crafting" of words to refer to the systematic use or "crafting" of the physical world reflects the fact that Galileo, Descartes, and other seventeenth-century thinkers had led their age to think in terms of dominating and manipulating nature.[2]

In the nineteenth century the word *technology* underwent further evolution. It gradually came to refer primarily to the mechanical and industrial arts as distinct not only from the fine arts but also from crafts and more general skills. The word also acquired a second meaning: "a systematic or scientific study of the mechanical and industrial arts." In this sense technology referred to the study or systematic organization of the knowledge of machines, tools, and industries, particularly those of the Industrial Revolution—which, in the nineteenth century, was at its zenith.

In short, by the twentieth century the word *technology* was being used to refer both to the systematic study of the mechanical and industrial arts and to the mechanical and industrial arts themselves. This duality is seen in the definition of the word given in the Oxford English Dictionary: "1. a discourse or treatise on an art or arts; 2. by transference, the practical arts collectively." Many languages other than English have two separate terms for these two meanings. French, for example, uses the word *technologie* for the study or systematic knowledge of the mechanical and industrial arts and the phrase *arts et métiers* for the industrial, mechanical, and practical arts themselves.

In the twentieth century the popular English usage of the word *technology* is no longer limited to these two meanings. Increasingly, *technology* is used to refer to a complex range of techniques, organizations, and knowledge in addition to tools, machines, and utensils. Often no distinction is made between a particular technology and its products—between, say, computer technology and a computer—or between consumer products of technology such as cars and the technological tools or

1. See Carl Mitcham, "Philosophy and the History of Technology," in George Bugliarello's *The History and Philosophy of Technology,* ed. Dean B. Doner (Urbana, Ill.: University of Illinois Press, 1979), p. 184.

2. See Mitcham, "Philosophy and the History of Technology," p. 187.

machines such as industrial robots used to make cars. The word is now so broadly used that, according to one scholar, "Technology is everything and everything is technology."[3]

According to N. Bruce Hannay and Robert E. McGinn, this broad-ranging usage has resulted in "persistent, mistaken and misleading identification of technology with science, applied science, hardware (material artifacts), or with all the products of technology (material artifacts and procedural systems)."[4] The first step in our way out of this trackless jungle of blurred distinctions, double meanings, and undiscriminating terms is to look at how others who have reflected on the nature and definitive characteristics of technology have sought to find their way.

Ways of Defining Technology. As one moves from popular usage of the word *technology* to its more scholarly usage, the level of confusion does not decrease. Some would even say it increases. Engineers, for instance, tend to give narrower, more restrictive definitions to technology than do social scientists. Engineers are inclined to identify technology with the actual process of constructing material artifacts, while engineering—viewed as a discipline—develops the knowledge required to design those artifacts. Social scientists, who usually have a more pronounced concern for the consequences of technology, tend to develop broader definitions of it. In the *International Encyclopedia of the Social Sciences,* for example, sociologist Robert S. Merrill defines technology very broadly:

> Technology in its broad meaning connotes the practical arts. These arts range from hunting, fishing, gathering, agriculture, animal husbandry, and mining through manufacturing, construction, transportation, provision of food, power, heat, light, etc., to means of communication, medicine, and military technology. Technologies are bodies of skills, knowledge, and procedures for making and doing useful things. They are techniques, means of accomplishing recognized purposes.[5]

Harvey Brooks, another sociologist, has reacted against efforts to define technology "in terms of physical embodiment" and has argued that "technology must be socio-technology rather than technical, and a tech-

3. Langdon Winner, *Autonomous Technology: Technics-out-of-Control as a Theme in Political Thought* (Cambridge, Mass.: MIT Press, 1977), pp. 9–10.

4. N. Bruce Hannay and Robert E. McGinn, "The Anatomy of Modern Technology: Prolegomenon to an Improved Public Policy for the Social Management of Technology," *Daedalus* 109 (Winter 1980): 26.

5. Robert S. Merrill, "Technology," in *International Encyclopedia of the Social Sciences,* vol. 15, ed. David L. Sills (New York: Macmillan, 1968), pp. 576–77.

nology must include the managerial and social supporting systems necessary to apply it on a significant scale."[6]

Underlying the many struggles to acquire an adequate definition of technology are three broad approaches: (1) the anthropological approach, which considers technology a making activity intrinsically related to the nature of humankind; (2) the epistemological approach, which considers technology to consist of certain procedures and the knowledge of the making process; and (3) the sociological approach, which views technology and its pervasive effects as the defining mark of thought and action in modern society.[7]

Each of these three approaches partially captures the complex manifestations of modern technology, but each tends to evolve into a one-sided view. All have their shortcomings and introduce their own distortions. The rest of this section considers each of these three approaches and indicates why they offer insightful yet ultimately inadequate means of working toward an understanding of technology.

The anthropological approach sees technology as an expression of human beings' very nature. According to this view, technology lies at the heart of what it means to be human: doing technology is the defining mark of human beings. Melvin Kranzberg and Carroll W. Pursell, Jr., two historians of technology who take an anthropological approach, assert that technology is "the most fundamental aspect of man's condition," which leads them to define technology as "nothing more than the area of interaction between ourselves, as individuals, and our environment, whether material or spiritual, natural or man-made."[8]

Lewis Mumford—the well-known American historian of technology and culture—also takes the anthropological approach to technology. Mumford thinks that human beings are different from other vertebrates because they possess very large, superior brains that permit them to gain increasing control over their social and psychological environment by creating culture. Making or developing tools or machines is, then, simply a part of humankind's broader capacity to create culture. Thus Mumford urges the development of what he calls "polytechnics"—technologies that are broadly life-oriented or people-oriented—rather

6. Harvey Brooks, "Technology, Evolution, and Purpose," *Daedalus* 109 (Winter 1980): 65.

7. These three approaches were first delineated by Carl Mitcham and Robert Mackey in "Introduction: Technology as a Philosophical Problem," in their *Philosophy and Technology: Readings in the Philosophical Problems of Technology* (New York: Free Press, 1983), pp. 1–7.

8. Melvin Kranzberg and Carroll W. Pursell, Jr., eds., *Technology in Western Civilization*, vol. 1 (New York: Oxford University Press, 1967), p. 11.

than the development of "monotechnics," technologies that are centered on work and mechanical power.[9]

Those who take an anthropological approach correctly emphasize technology as a human activity, and those like Mumford are certainly correct in emphasizing technology as a human cultural activity. But this approach is, in the end, inadequate. It is weak first of all because it sees technology as *no more than* a human cultural activity. The perspective stays on a wholly horizontal plane, with no conception of technology done in response to God's normative will. This approach is also weak because it fails to emphasize technology as merely one aspect of various kinds of culture formation. It often leaves one unsure of how to distinguish technical culture formation from nontechnical culture formation.

The epistemological approach sees technology as a special form of knowledge. This approach is often taken by three kinds of people: philosophers of science who wish to compare the knowledge claims and the methodology of technology with those of the natural sciences; social scientists who are concerned with the societal consequences of technology transfer and innovation; and representatives of the engineering disciplines who see the knowledge required to make or control technological tools and products—not the making activity itself—as central to technology. All of these view technology as a methodology and as a body of knowledge that is developed and used in a way that tends to emphasize rationality, experimentation, and the application of scientific knowledge.

Like most of those taking the epistemological approach to defining technology, Mario Bunge sees what he calls the "conceptual kernel" of technology in its methodology, defined by the way it uses and organizes knowledge in order to gain desired ends. He asserts that a body of knowledge is justifiably called a technology "if and only if (i) it is compatible with science and controllable by the scientific method, and (ii) it can be employed to control, transform or create things or processes, natural or social, to some practical end deemed to be valuable."[10] This statement presumes that a certain type of knowledge is at the heart of technology and the only question to be asked is what distinguishes that type of knowledge from other kinds.

Bernard Gendron also takes an epistemological approach. He defines

9. See Lewis Mumford, "Technics and the Nature of Man," in Mitcham and Mackey, *Philosophy and Technology*, pp. 77-85.

10. Mario Bunge, "The Philosophical Richness of Technology," in *Philosophy of Science Association 1976*, vol. 2, ed. F. Suppe and P. D. Asquith (East Lansing, Mich.: PSA, 1977), p. 154.

technology as "any systematized practical knowledge, based on experimentation and/or scientific theory, which enhances the capacity of society to produce goods and services, and which is embodied in productive skills, organization, or machinery."[11] Gendron sees technology as "practical knowledge" that is distinguished from other kinds of practical know-how by its scientific basis. Robert Merrill's definition of technology (quoted earlier) also has an epistemological emphasis: "Technologies are bodies of skills, knowledge, and procedures for making and doing useful things."

Emmanuel Mesthene defines technology "as the organization of knowledge for the achievement of practical purposes." He goes on to characterize technology as "tools in a general sense, including the machine, but also including such intellectual tools as computer languages and contemporary analytical and mathematical techniques."[12] This definition is designed to cut two ways: to broaden the concept of technology by freeing it from a fixation on machine-centered definitions of technology, and to limit the concept of technology by keeping it from identifying technology with rationality in its broadest sense.

Those taking an epistemological approach tend to see technology as characterizing many human activities in addition to the manipulation of materials. According to this view, technology, because it is a certain type of knowledge, often characterizes social, political, and psychological activities. Persons taking this approach usually stress that inquiries into technology ought not to be limited to exploring material products and the processes by which these products are made. Intellectual tools, practical knowledge, and bodies of knowledge: these are the stuff of technology.

The epistemological approach to defining technology—at least *modern* technology—puts proper emphasis on the importance of methods and procedures in the doing of technology. Modern technology is in fact marked by distinctive procedures, procedures related to the use of scientific and technical knowledge and to the use of means self-consciously chosen in order to attain desired ends. But the epistemological approach goes wrong in emphasizing technology as a body of knowledge or a group of certain procedures to the virtual exclusion of the proper ends that technology is to serve. Those taking the epistemological approach usually ignore humankind's relationship and responsibility to its Creator. As a result, there is no firm basis on which to consider the

11. Bernard Gendron, *Technology and the Human Condition* (New York: St. Martin's Press, 1977), p. 23.

12. Emmanuel Mesthene, *Technological Change* (Cambridge: Harvard University Press, 1970), p. 25.

proper ends of technology. It is a procedure, a body of knowledge, a methodology, but to what end or ends it should be put is left vague and uncertain. Bunge wrote of "some end deemed to be valuable," but without God and his will, how is the valuable to be distinguished from the nonvaluable? Viewing technology as no more than a body of knowledge or a group of certain procedures also leads to seeing technology wherever one looks in modern society. A certain crispness or focus is thereby lost. Greater analytical clarity is maintained if a sharper, more limited focus is given technology, one that separates technology itself from its effects.

A third approach to defining technology is *the sociological approach,* which sees technology as the definitive characteristic of modern society. The effects of technology on society are emphasized.

Jacques Ellul, a Christian sociologist, is representative of this approach. He believes that technology is a pervasive manifestation of what he calls technique: "In our technological society, technique is the *totality of methods rationally arrived at and having absolute efficiency* (for a given stage of development) in *every* field of human activity."[13] Technology has predominantly become a question of method, of technologically rationalized action in which means have become ends in themselves. This emphasis on technology as a "totality of methods" would seem to make Ellul's approach an epistemological one, and his approach certainly has strong epistemological characteristics. Yet the heart of his message is that technology has transformed the modern world into a thoroughly "technological society" or a "technological system" (to use the titles of two of his books).

Those taking the sociological approach, in short, see modern society as being technologically conditioned and molded—some would even say determined. They believe that the defining characteristic of modern technology is its pervasive, dominating influence in society.

The sociological approach is commendable to an extent. As Chapter One emphasized, technology has permeated the very warp and woof of society. It extends beyond society's means of production and tools, beyond the products of technological processes; it permeates cultural values and attitudes, economic and political systems, and the way science is done. But to reduce the technological to its societal impact is to ignore other important dimensions of technology. Two problems in particular emerge. One is that concentrating on the effects or impact of technology makes it more difficult to ask what technology itself really

---

13. Jacques Ellul, *The Technological Society* (New York: Vintage Books, 1964), p. xxv.

is. More seriously, the emphasis on technology's impact gives little insight into how to evaluate and judge that impact, how to gain insight into the reasons behind it, and how to alter it. A certain fatalism tends to pervade the sociological approach to defining technology; it does not do much more than point to the enormous impact of what it takes as a given. Without a deeper understanding of technology, humankind, and the relationship between the two, one is left without a solid basis for understanding and evaluating technology's impact on society.

What is needed is a definition of technology—an approach to understanding technology—that incorporates the strengths of the three commonly used approaches to defining technology but avoids their weaknesses. One final note is needed to lay the proper groundwork for such a definition. It concerns the question of whether or not the making of physical objects should be central to an appropriate definition of technology. Carl Mitcham, a philosopher of technology, argues that it ought to be:

> The tension between the narrow, engineering usage and the broad social science usage given to the word "technology" seems to point, first, toward the conceptual primacy of the making of material artifacts, then, second, toward a large number of elements and influences that go into and arise out of the primary process, determining its different forms.[14]

Mitcham thereby limits and focuses his concept of technology by tying it to "the making of material artifacts."* At the same time he recog-

14. Carl Mitcham, "Types of Technology," in *Research in Philosophy and Technology*, vol. 1, ed. Paul T. Durbin (Greenwich, Conn.: Jai Press, 1978), p. 231.

*The use of the word *artifact* in technological discourse is often very confusing. Most dictionary definitions relate *artifact* in one way or another to artistic activities. Clearly we would not want to use the word in this sense. Scholars of technology have used the terms "artifact" and "technological artifact" to refer to a confusing variety of things that appear to be linked only by the fact that they are made by human endeavor.

For the sake of clarity, this book will use three terms, each with its own distinct meaning, in place of the term "artifact": "technological object," "technological tool," and "technological product." A *technological object* is any physical device or organism produced or transformed by technological activity. There are two kinds of technological objects. A *technological tool* is a technological object that is intended to be used primarily in some other technological activity. "Tools" include hand tools and implements as well as contemporary fabricative assemblies—integrated systems of tools—such as machine tools, robots, and entire factories and energy-transforming assemblies such as electricity-generating plants.

Tools can be distinguished from a second type of technological object—*technological products*. We will use this term to refer to technological objects the primary use of which is not in some other technological activity. The vast majority of consumer products are of this nature: synthetic fibers, flowerpots, lamps, can openers, washing machines, cars, paints, and toothpaste. The list is endless.

The distinction between technological tools and technological products is sometimes

nizes technology's broad, expansive role and impact. He recognizes the many "elements and influences" that affect technology and by which technology affects society.

This approach is fruitful if the phrase "material artifacts" is used in a broad sense. Technology today encompasses a diversity of complementary technologies involving natural aspects of reality other than physical artifacts, at least as that term is usually understood. Besides involving those processes that form or transform materials, technology involves energy processes. The energy of wind and water flow, for example, has long been captured and transformed into the mechanical motions of windmills and waterwheels, which generate power. Today modern electrical plants transform solar energy, the energy of water flow, the energy of nuclear fission, and the energy generated by the combustion of fossil fuels into electrical forms of energy. There are also information-processing technologies such as those used by the mass media to collect and transfer data to various audiences. Some areas of technology such as brewing, food production, and sewage treatment have long used processes dependent on living organisms. The newer biotechnologies involve the alteration of microscopic gene structures and thereby seek to modify the characteristics of organisms such as plants, animals, and even (potentially) human beings. Our understanding of technology encompasses all of these types of technologies. Thus, if "the making of material artifacts" is to lie at the heart of our definition, the term "material artifacts" must include more than physical objects.

TECHNOLOGY DEFINED

Because of the very nature of definitions and because the word *technology* encompasses so much, any definition we might formulate will have to be tentative. Yet it is important to define this word to clarify exactly what we are including and excluding in this discussion, and to set us on the right path toward an appropriate Christian understanding of technology and persons' appropriate responses to it. The definition should do three things: (1) enable one to distinguish technical activity from other human activities; (2) provide a basis for analyzing the relationship between premodern and modern technology; and (3) follow

---

difficult to maintain. A computer, for example, can be used to guide and control making processes through procedural systems embedded in its memory—in which case it is a technological tool—and it can function as a video game in a domestic setting—in which case it is a technological product. Whether a technological object is considered a tool or a product depends on its intended purpose or end use.

from a Christian understanding of reality and humankind's role in technology.

The Definition. In essence we can define technology as a distinct human cultural activity in which human beings exercise freedom and responsibility in response to God by forming and transforming the natural creation, with the aid of tools and procedures, for practical ends or purposes.

There are five key elements in this definition. The first is that technology is a *human cultural activity.* Technology is an activity; it is not essentially certain products or hardware. This distinguishes our definition from many that stress the objects produced by technology. Nor is technology in essence certain procedures or knowledge. This further distinguishes our definition from that of the epistemological approach.

Technology is an activity of human culture. In this respect, our definition is like that of the anthropological approach. We are here using the word *culture* according to the definition of it in Webster's (eighth edition): "the integrated pattern of human behavior that includes thought, speech, action, and artifacts and depends upon man's capacity for learning and transmitting knowledge to succeeding generations." As formers of culture, human beings shape materials into new forms, process information, raise and harvest crops, establish families, states, political parties, and businesses, craft words into novels, produce radio and television programs, develop languages, taboos, and customs—and much more.

These cultural forms and expressions are not simply a random, unconnected assortment but are formed into an "integrated pattern" of activities and results: an extremely complex network of human activities, customs, beliefs, traditions, institutions, and products. These patterns or networks differ widely from one society to another, from so-called "primitive" tribal societies to modern, industrialized Western societies. But all societies possess culture.

God calls his children as his image bearers to be formers of culture. As such, we purposefully take what is given in God's creation and creatively form it into art, language, laws, social mores, societal institutions—and technological tools and products.

The second key element in our definition of technology is that this cultural activity involves persons *exercising freedom and responsibility in response to God.* This is already implied in our view of technology as a cultural activity. Cultural formation generally—and the doing of technology in particular—is purposeful activity in which human beings make choices, choices for which they are held responsible. This is not to deny that often there are very strong forces that limit human choice and, if given free rein, would even determine it. But we view such situations as distortions or aberrations, not the standard by which technology should be defined. Technological activity, as a form of cultural activity, is to be done in response to God's calling us to be formers of culture. This response can be either one of joyful, loving obedience or one of prideful rejection and disobedience. But whether one responds to God and his normative will in a positive or a negative manner, one is still responding to him. Those who respond in obedience thereby serve him. This does not, of course, exclude service to one's fellow human beings, other creatures, or the rest of God's natural creation. Service to God implies and includes serving his creation.[15]

The third key element in our definition is that technology involves *forming or transforming the natural creation*. This phrase is the first of three that distinguish technology from other cultural activities. Technology deals with the natural creation, not primarily with the worlds of ideas, thoughts, or symbols. Doing technology is thereby distinguishable from such cultural activities as developing language, telling stories, and writing laws. The natural creation includes both the physical and the biological worlds created by God. Technology thereby deals with both the living and the nonliving worlds. Examples of technological activities that utilize aspects of the living creation include brewing, some baking processes, and certain sewage treatment and biotechnology processes. Ideas, religious beliefs, and other nonphysical realities deeply influence and guide the doing of technology, of course, but technology itself is limited to the natural creation.

Technology deals with the natural creation in order to form or transform it. Forming refers to shaping or making something out of existing materials, while transforming refers to changing objects or processes from one form to another, like changing the energy of water flow into electricity. Both forming and transforming consist of two separate processes: design and fabrication. Design is the process that specifies the means by which the actual forming or transforming is to be done. Fabrication is the process that carries out the design.

The fourth key element in our definition of technology is that this forming or transforming is done *with the aid of tools and procedures*. The word *tools* is used very broadly here to encompass everything from simple hand tools to complex, automated machines composed of thousands of integrated parts electronically controlled by computers. Tech-

15. On the concept of humanity being called to serve God's creation, see Wesley Granberg-Michaelson, *A Worldly Spirituality* (New York: Harper & Row, 1984), pp. 65-67.

nology is also done by following certain procedures. Here an aspect of the epistemological approach to defining technology comes into play. Technology is an activity that is not done randomly or whimsically. It is done by following certain known, set steps or procedures. These procedures may consist of unwritten, almost unconsciously held ideas in the mind of the person doing technology, or—as is the case with modern technology—consist of very detailed, lengthy procedures that have been carefully and self-consciously designed. The use of tools and procedures sets technological activity apart from other cultural activities that are pursued more unself-consciously or in largely nonphysical areas of human existence—activities such as the development of patterned social relationships, religious practices, and many recreational and leisure activities.

The fifth and final key element in our definition of technology is that it is done *for practical ends or purposes*. This is a key to the distinction between technological endeavors and artistic endeavors. Technology is done for the sake of utility; its products have practical uses. One does not use products of technology by contemplating them for their own beauty or grace—one uses them by engaging in some activity with them. Art, on the other hand, is appreciated for what it is, not used to perform a task. This is what distinguishes practical use from aesthetic or contemplative use, and thereby distinguishes technology from art. This does not mean that the products of technology should not be aesthetically pleasing, but only that artistic quality is not the definitive characteristic of technology.

The Definition and the Criteria for Definition. Earlier we posited three criteria that a definition of technology should meet. The first was that the definition should enable one to distinguish technological activity from other human activity. In our definition, technological activity is distinguished from nontechnological activities by its last three key phrases or elements.

The second criterion was that the definition should provide a basis for analyzing the relationship between premodern and modern technology. Technology, as a making or forming/transforming activity, is fundamental to human capacities. We cannot find any period in history in which humankind did not both do technology and use its results. The skilled making of artifacts from natural resources, the harnessing of energy processes, and the utilization of living organisms in, say, fermentation processes undergirds both premodern and modern technology. The forming and transforming of the natural creation is the common element of continuity between the technology of the past and that of the present.[16] In addition, both premodern and modern technology are marked by the use of tools and procedures and by the making of objects for practical ends or purposes.

But there are also elements of discontinuity between premodern and modern technology that our definition allows us to address. In modern technology the skills and knowledge required for technological activity—the procedures for forming and transforming—have taken on an increasingly scientific, methodological cast. In fact, persons often speak loosely of modern technology as being a science-based technology. One reason why so many of the definitions are epistemological in approach— are knowledge-centered and methodologically oriented—is due to the intrusion and seeming dominance of scientific forms of knowledge in technology.

A second element of discontinuity between premodern and modern technology is the explicit, crucial role of design in modern technology. To a very large extent, the design activity as an expression of human creativity has come to be separated from the fabricative activity both in time sequence and work assignment. Usually one group of persons is involved in the designing and engineering aspects of technology, and another group is involved in the fabricating aspects. In premodern technology, by contrast, the procedures to be followed were usually in the mind of the craftsman doing the forming or transforming—or at the very least the fabricating activity was closely related to the designing activity.

The third criterion we established for a definition of technology is that it follow from a Christian understanding of reality and human beings' role in technology. Because our definition concentrates on the making process, one could question whether our definition perhaps neglects the point made by C. S. Lewis: "What we call man's power over nature turns out to be a power exercised by some men over other men with nature as its instrument."[17] In other words, are we minimizing the fact that the creation of technological objects and their integration into culture entails a certain forming or controlling of fellow human beings, either explicitly or implicitly? This is a valid question, but the answer is no.

We certainly recognize that human nature and human society, as well as the natural creation, are affected by technological developments. The sociological approach places proper emphasis on the societal impact of technology. One's perspective on technology must display a fundamen-

16. See Egbert Schuurman, *Technology and the Future* (Toronto: Wedge Publishing, 1980), pp. 5, 351–52.
17. C. S. Lewis, *The Abolition of Man* (New York: Macmillan, 1947), p. 69.

tal respect for the integrity of human beings as made in the image of God and created to respond in freedom to his calling and direction. If humankind's freedom and responsibility are not respected, technology will invariably turn into a demonstration of power for purposes of domination, manipulation, and self-aggrandizement. The decisive question in technology will always concern the direction in which its power is applied. That is why our definition stresses technology as a *cultural* activity done in freedom and responsibility in response to God. This is a crucially important perspective that enables us to speak against the use of technology for dominance and exploitation.

CHAPTER THREE

Is Technology Neutral?

LIVING A FAITHFUL, RESPONSIBLE LIFE BEFORE ONE'S CREATOR IN-
cludes living responsibly in relation to technology. This is so because, as
pointed out in Chapter One, technology is a pervasive, powerful, value-
laden force that presents modern society with a highly ambiguous
situation.

There is, however, a contrary position, one that asserts that technology
is neutral and therefore that technology itself need not be considered in
living responsibly. According to this position, only the uses to which
technology are put involve human valuing. Technology itself is thereby
value-free: it is merely a tool that can be used for good or for evil. One
scholar, for example, has written, "Technology in itself is neutral and
should not be labeled 'good' or 'bad.' It is the uses to which we put new
scientific developments that enhance or degrade personal well-being and
prosperity."[1] Another has written that technology is "essentially amoral, a thing apart from values, an instrument which can be used for good or
ill."[2]

According to this view, if the cancer rate goes up because of the
indiscriminate use of pesticides, if whales become extinct because of
modern methods of hunting them, if catastrophic climatic changes occur
because too much carbon dioxide is being released into the atmosphere,
and if a remote tribal society is devastated by social disruptions that occur
because of the introduction of new technologies, we are not to blame the
persons who created the technological tools, products, and processes
involved. Instead we should blame politicians, corporations, and individual consumers for misusing technology. One is reminded of the slo-
gan used by many gun enthusiasts opposed to further regulation of guns:
"Guns don't kill people, people do." Technology is not at fault; certain

---

1. Richard R. Landers, *Man's Place in the Dybosphere* (Englewood Cliffs, N.J.: Prentice-Hall, 1966), p. 207.
2. R. A. Buchanan, *Technology and Social Progress* (Oxford: Pergamon Press, 1965),
p. 163.

users of technology are. To many the truth of such a statement appears self-evident.

But technology is not actually neutral. The belief that it is spreads confusion and points the search for the meaning of technological responsibility in a fundamentally false direction. Thus we need to explore the supposed neutrality of technology.

Before doing so, however, we need to clearly understand the meaning of valuing, a human activity that is widely done and acknowledged but the meaning and content of which are in dispute. Unfortunately, the most common view of valuing is that it does nothing more than express preferences for outcomes. In essence, this view, known as an emotive view of values, holds that to value something is to say nothing more than that one likes it.

This book argues for a wholly other grounding for valuing: the normative will of God. The contrast between the man-centered source of emotive values and the God-centered view of normativity is of fundamental importance. This is true in all areas of life, of course, but it strikes at the heart of modern technological hubris. When human beings set themselves up as masters of their fate, they set themselves up not for an ascent to freedom, as they imagine, but for a descent into slavery. The sad stories of fashioning golden calves and of building the Tower of Babel are being repeated on larger and larger scales.

Avoiding the man-centered view of valuing while at the same time acknowledging the human responsibility to value things comes from accepting God's will as the ground for human valuing. Human valuing, imperfect though it is, must be judged by whether it comports well with God's revealed normative standards. The judgment is not based on human logic or empirical observations; the testimony of God's Spirit is the final proof. This stance asserts that God's normative standards are facts as firm and as real as anything else in the universe. Because God has taken special care to reveal his divine *oughts*—his divine norms—to humankind, they are preeminent facts worthy of all trust.

Valuing, then, is a human activity, one properly done in response to God's revealed normative standards, but done nevertheless as an act of human choice. So valuing is an activity both common and unique to human experience: all human beings engage in valuing, and only human beings do so. The presence of human will in the doing of technology inevitably intertwines valuing and technology.[3] But a specific examination of the points at issue is required.

3. Carl Mitcham, for example, especially emphasizes this connection between "technology-as-volition" and human values. See Carl Mitcham, "Types of Technology," in *Research in Philosophy and Technology*, vol. 1, ed. Paul T. Durbin (Greenwich, Conn.: Jai Press, 1978), pp. 229-94.

THE SUPPOSED NEUTRALITY OF TECHNOLOGY

The Supposed Neutrality of Means. Those who see technology as neutral usually make a distinction between means and ends: they see technology as an ethically neutral means to reach a predetermined, ethically chosen end in which human valuing plays a salient role. Judgments are made concerning the worth to be attached to the end use to which technology is put. But many claim that the best means to reach that end is only a technical matter. Herbert Schnadelbach summarizes this position:

> Only the discussion of ends is commonly regarded as ethically relevant, and if ethically relevant decisions have been made, the remaining problems seem to be only technical problems. "We only dealt with the technical problems and had no influence on the determination of goals"—this is a type of excuse frequently advanced in order to separate technical from ethical responsibility after political and moral catastrophes.[4]

The presumption is that once the policy decision has been made to attain a certain end—whether that decision was made by government, corporate leaders, or the demands of the market—decisions related to the best means of designing and fabricating the technological object to meet the end are neutral, involving no valuing. They are only technical matters.

But this perspective is fundamentally and profoundly inaccurate. The argument that technology is a means does not dismiss the issues of valuing and normative principles. There are normative principles that should guide the choice of means as well as the choice of ends. Sometimes the attempt is made to limit the evaluation of means to no more than the issue of efficiency. But this is entirely too narrow an approach, and one that in itself involves valuing. Also, in evaluating a number of possible means to reach a desired end, many questions beyond that of efficiency arise—questions of aesthetics, economics, social impact, justice, resource use, and more.

The Supposed Neutrality of Science. The supposed neutrality of technology rests in part upon a view that sees science as neutral, and since science is closely linked with modern technology, technology is also seen as a neutral activity. The neutrality of science and the neutrality of technology are seen as twin truths.

There are two flaws in this position. The first is that the link between modern science and modern technology is far less close than is popularly assumed. This point is fully discussed in Chapter Six, but at this stage it

4. Herbert Schnadelbach, "Is Technology Neutral?" in *Ethics in an Age of Pervasive Technology,* ed. Melvin Kranzberg (Boulder, Colo.: Westview Press, 1980), p. 28.

will suffice to note that technology is not simply applied science. But there is a second, even more basic flaw in the view that sees the neutrality of technology as following from the supposed neutrality of science. Science is not in fact neutral, and its very non-neutrality points to the non-neutrality of technology.

The desacralization of nature—the rejection of the belief that spirits pervade natural objects such as trees and streams—is intertwined with the emergence of modern science. While the desacralization of nature is commonly regarded as a condition for the flowering of science—in the sense that humankind no longer risked offending the gods by investigating nature—it is also true that the emergence of scientific explanations influenced desacralization. As desacralization progressed, God was presumed to be no longer needed as hypothesis or helper.[5] Religion was seen neither as a necessary component to a human explanation nor as a problem-solver; instead it was seen as a source of bias, an extraneous, nonrational factor for which no proof could be offered.

The perspective that sees science as value-free and able to stand on its own without reference to God or revealed truth rests in part on a supposed distinction between *is* and *ought*. According to this view, science—and, by implication, technology as well—deals with concrete, observable facts, with that which is. Science rests upon empirical facts, facts discoverable through observation by the human senses. An entirely different category of propositions, and one alien to the methods of science, is that of "oughtness." That which ought to be, in distinction from what is, rests upon valuing, preferences, and presuppositions; it cannot be proved or confirmed by the senses. Because of the apparent concreteness of scientific knowledge, there is a further presumption that "is" propositions are real, while "ought" propositions are ethereal, subjective, and—because they are based on individual preferences—optional. On the basis of this distinction, science, and, by extension, technology, have been seen as concrete, sure—and neutral.

But now the heyday of such scientific hubris and simplistic dichotomies seems to be drawing to a close, and to the extent that the argument for neutral technology is based on a view of science as neutral, it is seen to be built on false premises. Although the idea of fact purged of all valuing and presuppositions and wedded to pure logic may once have captured the imaginations of the philosophers of science, it no longer does.[6] They now commonly concede that scientific under-

5. See Ian Barbour, *Technology, Environment, and Human Values* (New York: Praeger, 1980).

6. For a useful treatment of this recent trend in science, see *The Structure of Scientific Theories*, 2nd ed., ed. Frederick Suppe (Champaign: University of Illinois Press, 1977).

standing depends on something that comes before it, something that is
prescientific: namely, a confession about the nature of life and the
world. Valuing underlies the supposedly objective, presuppositionless
facts. Some think that this admission puts science on shaky ground and
threatens fondly held notions of objectivity and universality. Others—
including the authors of this book—believe that it puts science on surer
ground than ever before, for only when it is recognized that science is
based on such presuppositions can it be founded on the truth about God,
humankind, and nature that is revealed to human beings outside of their
own powers. In either case, the admission that science involves valuing
puts an end to the neutrality notion, for it admits that one's scientific
knowledge is dependent on one's beliefs.

The Role of Precommitments. Putting aside the question of the neutrality of science and its impact on technology, there is an even more
direct way to demonstrate that doing technology can never be neutral
but inevitably involves presuppositions, valuing, and normative principles. There are three facets to this demonstration. First, any definition
of what factual situations constitute ''problems'' or what constitute
''solutions'' clearly comes from some source outside of the factual situation itself. Problems never present themselves in a self-defined way.
Whether or not a rainy day is a problem depends on conditions outside
the factual situation—such as whether one is a farmer with parched
crops or a tourist hoping for pleasant weather for sight-seeing. Similarly, any set of standards for determining what does or does not constitute
a solution to a problem must clearly lie outside the problem itself. The
solution to broken troth in a marriage, for example, can range from
reestablishing troth to divorce to the stoning of the offending party (a
solution once employed in certain societies). The factual situation does
not carry within it a single clear solution. Varying contexts and commitments offer a variety of solutions.

This point may seem obvious, but the second factor involved is less
so. For the truth is that not even ''factual situations'' speak for themselves in a presuppositionless way. Human perception is involved, and
this perception is always something more than the observation of ''bare
facts.'' In general, human beings perceive the objects they encounter *as*
something—as a family, a house, a democracy, an animal. This
''seeing as'' is preconditioned, and involves subjectivity.

We should also note that there is a third and final way in which
precommitments enter into supposedly presuppositionless situations.
Persons do not look randomly for problems—or for facts, for that matter. They do not have enough time and energy to do that. Instead, persons make a selective investigation of certain problems to which they

deem certain facts—and not others—to be relevant. The principles of selection that someone follows are themselves largely external to one's investigation and are influenced by one's precommitments. Some problems or facts capture a person's attention because of a certain interest he or she has in them, and this interest usually arises from one's deepest loyalties, from one's heart.

In summary, all of us come to selected situations, defined as problematical and in need of solution, with a structured set of preconceptions. These preconceptions help us make sense out of the situations we face. Our observations, the meaning and significance that we assign to them, even our declaring something to be a fact—all are dependent on this structure of preconceptions.

The Role of One's World and Life View. The next point concerns the source or nature of the structure of preconceptions on which observations, interpretations, and conclusions rest. This returns us to the earlier point that we are preconditioned to see things *as* something. The basic source of one's structure of preconceptions is one's world and life view. Many of the elements of such a view owe their existence to the heart as well as the mind; they are confessional or religious in nature. This is what makes human understanding truly human.

It may be helpful to link up the idea of a worldview—with its very broad scope and content—with the narrower viewpoints we usually draw upon when approaching a particular problem. One such link is what philosopher Nicholas Wolterstorff refers to as "control beliefs." The context for Wolterstorff's discussion is that of theory construction and evaluation. He argues that control beliefs are those beliefs that govern the requisite or necessary structure of a theory, or those beliefs that are about the sorts of patterns in reality to which a theory may correctly commit us. Among Wolterstorff's examples is the infamous relationship between the church and Copernicus. The theologians who sat in judgment of Copernicus's theory held two kinds of control beliefs that led them to view his theory as unacceptable. First, they held to the authority of the Scriptures over all domains, including science; and second, they held to particular beliefs about the content of the Scriptures regarding the relative motion of the sun and the earth. Although the latter beliefs were later seen as erroneous, the fact remains that such control beliefs are common and undergird all scientific work. At any given point in theory development, Wolterstorff argues, only theories that comport well with these control beliefs will be deemed acceptable.[7]

---

7. See Nicholas Wolterstorff, *Reason Within the Bounds of Religion* (Grand Rapids: Eerdmans, 1976).

This same concept can be applied to the definition of technological problems and to the acceptability of solutions. Control beliefs govern such factors as what sorts of situations are perceived to be problems and which ones may properly be subjected to technological manipulation. These control beliefs link one's broad understanding of the nature of reality with the particular issue at hand.

Control beliefs must in turn comport well with the religious base or, broadly speaking, with the heart commitments of their holders. If they do not, the holders of these beliefs will be torn apart, for they will attempt to develop conceptual understandings and technological solutions that are at odds with their fundamental confessions about the nature of reality. Persons can maintain this dichotomy for some time by setting it aside—for example, by attempting to assert that such beliefs are irrelevant to science and technology (the neutrality argument)—but the persistent presence of the belief component and its link to their world and life view will eventually create internal conflict. The result may be struggles labeled "value crises" or "crises of relevance," and the consequent attempt to regain harmony will spur revision of either one's scientific-technological approach or one's beliefs. Which of these is revised depends, unfortunately, not only on which is true or false but also on such things as the comparative cultural strength of each. In a technological society, the deck is stacked against belief. The dominant presumption is that belief—with its connotations of anachronism—must give way to the "advances" of science and technology. Throughout this book the case will be made for correcting such distortion.

At this point some might object that thus far the doing of technology has been treated as too explicitly a cognitive act. One objection might be that not all technological results can be construed as rationally rigorous, as has sometimes been implied. A case in point is invention, which is sometimes characterized by accident: the thing found was not the thing sought after. A second objection might be that this argument does not consider that some technological forming may be more a product of intuition, or even characterized as more a product of the unconscious hand than the conscious mind. The first objection is not entirely valid: even in the event of accidental discovery, there must be some basis for recognition, or there would not in fact be a discovery in the usual sense—what is revealed would go unmarked and unutilized. This recognition is dependent on the very same framework of presuppositions examined above. In the second case—that of intuitive or unconscious forming—there is no need to link the technological result to the preconceptions via a supposedly rational process. Here the heart is more directly and holistically involved from the outset, and so our case for linking heart commitment to technology is justified.

THE VALUE-LADENNESS OF TECHNOLOGY

Thus far it has been argued that technology is not neutral: problems, solutions, and concepts do not exist in a presuppositionless vacuum. Technology proceeds out of whole human experience and is affected by the confessional, religious commitments unique to human beings. As a result, technology is value-laden, the product of the inevitable valuing activities of human beings. Clearly, the non-neutrality and the value-ladenness of technology are two sides of the same coin.

Valuing penetrates all technological activity, from the analytical framework used to understand technological issues through the processes of design and fabrication to the resulting technological objects—tools and products. Although valuing is also involved in the uses to which people put these technological objects, it begins long before the use stage.

Before considering the value-ladenness of technology directly, however, we need to clarify the meaning we attach to the term "value-laden." There are those who argue that technology is value-laden because it is intertwined with various social structures. The development of the private car, for example, has altered transportation patterns, and thereby affects human interrelationships at work and play. Confronted with new choices and new ways of interaction, people may alter how they value things, processes, and even other people. In this view, technology is seen as an instrument or agent that affects not only material things but also social organization and values. While such effects are both demonstrable and important, they do not fully encompass the value-ladenness of technology. The value-loading of technology is far more intrinsic to its own nature and structure than this view implies. Indeed, it is embedded in technology; it does not arise only as technology interacts with political and social factors.

A proper view of the value-ladenness of technology emerges from two basic characteristics of technological objects: they are unique, not universal; and they are intertwined with their environments, not isolated.[8]

Technological Objects Are Unique. Technological objects—both tools and products—are unique. They combine specific resources—know-how, materials, and energy—into unique entities with unique sets of properties and capabilities. Any technological object, therefore, embodies decisions to develop one kind of knowledge and not another,

---

8. The first of these points owes something to H. van Riessen's "The Structure of Technology," trans. Herbert D. Morton, in *Research in Philosophy and Technology,* vol. 2, ed. Paul T. Durbin and Carl Mitcham (Greenwich, Conn.: Jai Press, 1979), pp. 313–28.

to use certain resources and not others, to use energy in a certain form and quantity. There is no purely neutral or technical justification for all these decisions. Instead, they involve conceptions of the world that are related to such issues as permissible uses, good stewardship, and justice: they involve, in other words, human valuing.

Technological objects are also unique in that to a certain extent they impose on the user the way in which they are to be used. There is frequently some degree of latitude in their use, but obviously there is not complete freedom. A nuclear bomb, for example—like many other objects of modern warfare—has an extremely limited use. In general, each object is designed to function in a certain way, utilizing certain kinds of inputs and producing certain kinds of outputs. Even a simple technological product such as a can opener must be used in a certain way if it is to fulfill its function effectively.

Generally speaking, the more complex a technological object, the more strictures govern its use. A quote from George Grant about computers illustrates the point:

> Abstracting facts so that they may be stored as "information" is achieved by classification, and it is the very nature of any classifying to homogenize what may be heterogeneous. Where classification rules, identities and differences can only appear in its terms. [This means] that the "ways" that computers can be used for storing "information" can only be ways that increase the tempo of the homogenizing process in society, [and that computers'] very capabilities entail that the ways they can be used are never neutral. They can only be used in homogenizing ways.[9]

Whether or not Grant's specific argument of the computer's homogenizing effect on society is completely accurate, his point is a good one: the computer is a unique entity with specific capabilities that restrict the ways in which it is to be used. And these restrictions are anything but value-free.

Technological Objects Are Intertwined with Their Environments. Technological objects are not only unique in themselves, but the particular sets of properties and capabilities inherent in them interact in unique ways with the rest of reality. This interaction is very complex and is not completely determined by the technological object itself: different patterns of use also enter in. But each technological object, given its properties and capabilities, opens up certain possibilities for interac-

9. George Grant, "The Computer Does Not Impose on Us the Ways It Should Be Used," in *Beyond Industrial Growth,* ed. A. Rotstein (Toronto: University of Toronto Press, 1976), pp. 117–31.

tion with both its cultural and its natural environment, and correspondingly closes down other possibilities.

We can take the effects of modern technological processes as an example. When these processes release waste heat and carbon dioxide into the atmosphere, the apparent result is the heating up of the earth's surface and the consequent alteration in the entire ecology of the planet—the so-called "greenhouse effect." The valuing underlying the properties and capabilities embedded in such technologies as electrical generation, industrialization, and deforestation affects the way these technologies interact with the natural environment. In this case, it leads to the apparent increase in the earth's average temperature. But the effect—in this instance and others like it—is much more far-reaching than this.

Technological tools and products—given their very nature—are also intertwined with their environments: they require certain supports that are, in turn, not neutral. Television is a marvelous thing. It brings the world directly into one's living room. Sights and sounds most persons could never before experience are now available at the turn of a dial. But in order to function as a medium of information and entertainment, television needs a large, complex network of supports—a steady electrical supply, broadcasting stations, relay satellites, production and repair facilities, government regulation of airwave allocation, and more. The systems that have emerged to support private television viewing are truly staggering in size and complexity.

Lewis Mumford has argued that modern technological societies have lost "their independence and their self-sufficiency"; consequently, "they must either organize and safeguard and conserve a worldwide basis of supply or run the risk of going destitute and relapse into a lower and cruder technology."[10] This is the case because technological objects themselves have embedded within them the results of valuing. These results demand certain types of support systems if the technological objects are to be used at all.

The various support structures themselves are anything but neutral. They carry within them particular decisions, decisions that affect their impact on society as a whole and on a given society's relationships with other societies. These embedded decisions also necessarily affect those persons who play a role in them.

As they interact with their environments, technological objects both affect those environments in certain ways and impose certain conse-

---

10. Lewis Mumford, *Technics and Civilization* (New York: Harcourt, Brace & World, 1934), p. 232.

quences on societies and the natural creation. And those consequences are not neutral. This can be seen in a detailed study by Pertti Pelto of the adoption of snowmobiles by the Skolt Lapp people of Finland.[11] In the 1960s the Skolts decided to change their method of herding reindeer by replacing their dogsleds and skis with snowmobiles. But the very nature of the snowmobile—the valuing reflected in it—and the way it had to be used resulted in the breakdown of the traditional Skolt society. Langdon Winner summarizes the consequences:

> From one point of view the Skolts knew exactly what they were doing. They adopted the Bombardier "Ski-Doo" to make herding faster and more efficient. From another point of view, however, they never knew what hit them. The changes they saw taking place in long-established patterns of life just "happened" as the community made a place for this new instrument of production.[12]

The crucial point is that the process of designing and fabricating the snowmobile was not neutral. Valuing led to certain decisions being embedded in it. Once the Skolts decided to use the snowmobile to herd reindeer, certain consequences necessarily followed from the nature of those decisions embedded in the snowmobile.

CONCLUSIONS

It should be clear by now that the reality of the value-ladenness of technology is independent of the acceptance or rejection of arguments about the propriety of this value-ladenness. It is simply a fact that technology has carried and will continue to carry, with it and within it, the valuing decisions that people have inevitably—even if unconsciously— made in doing technology. Obscuring this fact with the approach of declared neutrality has been very costly. It is one of the chief contributors to the extent to which technology seems to be out of control. In presuming that technology has its own inner logic, its own wisdom independent of the hearts of human beings, society has neglected to deal with the value-ladenness of technology, and has thus granted technology a kind of autonomy.

11. See Pertti J. Pelto, *The Snowmobile Revolution: Technology and Social Change in the Arctic* (Menlo Park, Calif.: Cummings, 1973). Summaries of Pelto's findings are given in N. Bruce Hannay and Robert E. McGinn's "The Anatomy of Modern Technology: Prolegomenon to an Improved Public Policy for the Social Management of Technology," *Daedalus* 109 (Winter 1980): 28–29; and Langdon Winner, *Autonomous Technology* (Cambridge: MIT Press, 1977), pp. 86–88.

12. Winner, *Autonomous Technology*, p. 87.

In the meantime, technological actions have taken on a distorted inner wisdom, one that leads to an exaggerated, unbalanced emphasis on scale, control, uniformity, and integration. Technology has assumed a prominent place in people's lives, and consequently an emphasis on results and the working rule "If it can be done, it should be done" have conspired to push other aspects out of their lives. More and more people may feel that the emphasis placed on technological knowledge squeezes out the need for, and the time to pursue, spiritual knowledge. If so, then it is emphatically not the case that the direction of modern science and technology increases knowledge, but rather that it increases some *kinds* of knowledge at the expense of others.

Exactly the same point must be made about the assertion that we should pursue all sorts of technology because technology broadens our range of choices. The truth is that technology increases the range of some kinds of choices at the same time that it precludes others. The use of computers opens up some choices and closes down others, such as processing the sort of information that its system can't handle. Air travel may open up the options of ease and rapid transit, but it limits schedule and destination flexibility, and precludes the simple pleasure of stopping to enjoy the scenery. For the most part, the alteration in the pattern of available choice is not random but is determined by the value-loading of technology. This makes it all the more important that we explore value-loading further.

If the value-loading of technology is a part of responsible human action, it is, within limits, subject to alteration by human beings. It has not yet moved beyond the possibility of human control. But society may abrogate this possibility of control by failing to have the courage or the insight to oppose the present trends.

Hans Jonas thinks the key attribute missing in present-day society is the insight to evaluate and judge technology. He is pessimistic, describing the search for an adequate ethical theory for our age as looking "suspiciously . . . like a fool's errand." He gets stuck—we all get stuck, he argues—in attempting this errand: "For the very same movement which puts us in possession of the powers that have now to be regulated by norms—the movement of modern knowledge called science—has by a necessary complementarity eroded the foundations from which norms could be derived; it has destroyed the very idea of norm as such."[13]

All that remains, according to Jonas, is a "feeling for norm," some

13. Hans Jonas, "Technology and Responsibility: Reflections on the New Tasks of Ethics," *Social Research* 40 (Spring 1973): 31–54.

inner, nonrational recognition that such a thing exists. What is necessary is to fan this smoldering spark into flame. Yet Jonas despairs, for only religion could do this, and religion, he concludes, is no longer there to be summoned to humanity's aid.

This chapter—indeed, this entire book—rests on the commitment that Jonas is correct in his belief that religion is needed, that norms from outside humankind's experience are necessary—and that he is profoundly wrong in his belief that religion is no longer there. God is still there. His truth is still there. But humankind needs to acknowledge his presence and truth.

CHAPTER FOUR

The Cultural Mandate and Modern Technology

DOING TECHNOLOGY IS A CULTURAL ACTIVITY. THEREFORE, IF WE ARE to analyze and understand technology and our responsibilities in regard to it, we must understand the nature of the broader culture within which technological culture formation is done and our technological responsibilities are fulfilled. We must understand something of the whole before we can understand the part. Thus this chapter begins by considering human beings as formers of culture. It then traces the major historical lines that have shaped Western culture, and ends by considering how the responsible Christian should react to the dominant trends present in our technologically oriented Western culture.

HUMANKIND AS FORMERS OF CULTURE

Humankind in the Image of God. In simple, eloquent words Genesis sketches the story of humankind's creation: "So God created man in his own image, in the image of God he created him; male and female he created them" (Gen. 1:27). Thus human beings—those wonderfully complex, not fully comprehensible creatures—came to be. Naturalists, ancient and modern, may see humans as nothing more than sophisticated animals, and we can in fact learn about human anatomy and physiology by studying animals. Yet the Bible forever separates the two, seeing human beings alone as divine image bearers: "In the image of God he created him." Only human beings were made by God's special act of breathing into their nostrils.

And yet, for all their dignity and value, men and women are not divine, but created; their being is of a different order from God's, and thus they depend on him while bearing his own "image and likeness" (Gen. 1:26; 5:3). The nature and destiny of humankind can be grasped only from this standpoint. The Bible interprets men and women, therefore, as essentially religious. They have been made to know God as well as to obey him. G. C. Berkouwer observes, "It is clear enough from Scripture that its concern is with the whole man, the full man, the actual man as he stands in God's sight," and lives out his servanthood before God.[1]

As divine image-bearers, human beings are creative in the sense that they have the capacity to form something, whether that something be a sculpture, a novel, a tool, an agricultural procedure, a philosophy, or their own lives. Many animals are very clever. Beavers dam up streams to create ponds and then build safe, secure lodges on those ponds. Birds use their instinct to build intricate nests. Bees build hives and organize their work by a clear division of labor. But none of these animals possesses human creativity; none possesses the self-consciousness needed to be creative. Only human beings can review their activities and reflect self-consciously on them. No beaver experiments with a different type of lodge in order to improve its efficiency or appearance—or for the sheer joy of doing things differently. Only human beings do that; only human beings possess creativity.

As image bearers of God, human beings are responsible before God for their activities. They are accountable for the way they exercise their creativity: what they do with their lives, what and how they shape, mold, and form. God has established a law by which men and women are expected to live. The God-given command to love him above all and our neighbor as ourselves sums up a host of moral imperatives, or normative principles, that God has established and has revealed to humankind in various ways. This makes men and women religious beings in a way no plants, animals, or physical objects ever can be. Human beings alone have the ability to grasp God's law and then, through their creative efforts, respond to it in either loving obedience or selfish disobedience. Thus, as knowing, self-consciously creative, and responsible beings, men and women are unique in the universe.

The Cultural Mandate. After God created human beings in his image, he issued what has come to be called the cultural mandate: "God blessed them and said to them, 'Be fruitful and increase in number; fill the earth and subdue it. Rule over the fish of the sea and the birds of the air and over every living creature that moves on the ground' " (Gen. 1:28). We are also told that God "put [man] in the Garden of Eden to work it and take care of it" (Gen. 2:15). There are many other instances in the Bible where it is made clear in one way or another that human beings have the God-given opportunity and duty to be workers, doers, actors in God's

---

1. G. C. Berkouwer, *Man: The Image of God,* trans. Dirk W. Jellema, Studies in Dogmatics (Grand Rapids: Eerdmans, 1962), p. 31.

creation. (See Psalm 8, Isaiah 45:18, and Colossians 1:15–20.) Human beings—even in the ideal state of Eden, before sin had entered the world—were not to live in passivity and ease, simply enjoying God's creation as it was presented to them without contributing anything of their own intelligence or efforts. God gave men and women the gift and the duty to be developers of culture; he called them to work, fill, subdue, and rule his rich creation. These are the terms Genesis uses. Philosopher Richard Mouw ably explains the nature of the filling and subduing to which Genesis 1 refers:

> The command to "fill" the earth here is not merely a divine request that Adam and Even have a lot of babies. The earth was also to be "filled" by the broader patterns of their interactions with nature and with each other. They would bring order to the Garden. They would introduce schemes for managing its affairs. To "subdue" the Garden would be to transform untamed nature into a social environment. In these ways human beings would be "adding" to that which God created.[2]

Because human beings are created in God's image—because they possess self-consciousness, creativity, and responsibility—they are to exercise their creative capacities as agents responsible to God. At the dawn of this world's existence, the whole creation—the physical world, plants, animals, and humankind—was both good and pregnant with unimaginable riches and possibilities. As Adam and Eve worked together in the garden in which God had placed them, they no doubt marveled in joy and thankfulness at the riches they day by day discovered; but they could have realized little about all that their newly born world contained.

The cultural mandate means that men and women as cultural agents have been placed in creation in order to bring the creation to its full development. They are to open up the creation, to bring to light the treasures that the Lord God has stored up in it. In that opening-up process all things are designed to come into their own and to be assigned their own place. There is a continuity to this development, with succeeding generations being able to bring out more complex, more intricate aspects of creation by building on the achievements of prior generations.[3] The original paradise before sin was a rural garden; the future paradise that will mark the culmination of human history is a city, the new Jerusalem of Revelation 21.

Doing technology—the forming and transforming of natural creation

2. Richard J. Mouw, *When the Kings Come Marching In* (Grand Rapids: Eerdmans, 1983), p. 16.
3. See Erich Sauer, *The King of the Earth* (Exeter, England: Paternoster Press, 1962), pp. 80–83.

with the aid of tools and procedures—is a part of human beings' activity as formers of culture. Doing technology is one way humankind fulfills the cultural mandate. But it is important to note that the cultural mandate is not simply a call for humankind to build culture—any culture—or to construct bigger and more sophisticated technological tools and products no matter what their nature or effects. Human beings are to act as cultural agents in keeping with God's normative will, in keeping with his love command, and thereby to act as responsible agents.

This means that human cultural activity—the developing of God's creation—is not to be done arrogantly or thoughtlessly. Men and women are to use their God-given creative powers and their moral sense to fill, subdue, and rule the creation. But this must be done in the proper context, in which God is the creator and upholder of the creation. As God's cultural agents on earth, human beings are to interact with the creation with the same gentle love and concern God showed in creating the world, in giving "water to all the beasts of the field," in making "grass grow for the cattle," in planting and watering "the cedars of Lebanon," and in giving the lions their prey (Ps. 104:11, 14, 16, 21). Human beings are to subdue and rule God's creation, but in such a way that they bring out the beauty and excellence God has placed in his creation; they are to allow creation's potential to flower. In the process they become—paradoxically—ruling servants. They rule the creation in such a way that they also serve it.

Since the Fall, humankind fulfills the cultural mandate in an imperfect, fractured manner. Yet the cultural mandate as given in the Bible still stands as an expression of God's will for his image bearers on earth.

Is Christianity to Blame?   Some observers have pointed to Christianity in general and its conception of the cultural mandate in particular as a chief cause of the dislocations, destruction, and impending catastrophes that have resulted from modern technological developments. Carl Amery has argued that the development of technology and what he sees as its menace are the direct, necessary consequences of Christianity.[4] Theodore Roszak also blames Christianity for clearing the way for all-devouring, exploitive scientific-technological developments.[5] Probably the best-known and most frequently cited articulation of the thesis that Christianity is to blame for the technological evils present in Western

4. Amery's views were discussed in the symposium on religion and the rise of technology in which Daniel Cerezuelle, Katharine Temple, and Mark Swetlitz took part. See *Research in Philosophy and Technology,* vol. 6, ed. Paul T. Durbin (Greenwich, Conn.: Jai Press, 1983), pp. 175–205.

5. Theodore Roszak, *The Making of a Counter-Culture* (Garden City, N.Y.: Doubleday, 1969).

society is "The Historical Roots of Our Ecological Crisis," the article by Lynn White, Jr., published in 1967 in *Science* magazine.[6] Exploring White's argument in detail will help reveal if the charge against Christianity is in fact fair.

White argues—correctly—that modern technology arose when science and technology were wedded in the mid-nineteenth century. But this is only the beginning of his argument. He insists further that both Western science and Western technology found their roots in Christian, medieval Europe.

More specifically, White claims that four characteristics of Christianity were instrumental in making possible and encouraging the rise of modern scientific technology. The first is Christianity's view that history is linear, not circular, as the Greeks and Romans had thought. Christians believe that history has a beginning and an end, and that progression marks the unfolding of history. Second, White sees Christianity as the destroyer of animism, a belief system that posits that spirits exist in natural objects such as rivers, trees, and hills. Because Christianity desacralized nature, it cleared the way for an exploitive approach to nature. Third, White contends, Christianity "is the most anthropocentric religion the world has seen."[7] It views the world and all of nature as created by God to meet humankind's needs. "Christianity . . . not only established a dualism of man and nature but also insisted that it is God's will that man exploit nature for his proper ends."[8] Finally, White argues that Christianity, at least in the West, emphasized coming to know God and his mind through a growing understanding of nature, his creation. Christianity thereby gave impetus to an empirically based science.

White is correct on several counts. He is correct, first of all, in attributing the linear view of history to Christianity. As a result of the growing influence of Christianity, the pre-Christian view of history—the so-called cyclical or circular view—disappeared from the scene. That view of history was oriented to the rhythms of nature, the circular course of the seasons, the cycle of day and night; it was oriented to the rhythmic progression of rising, shining, and perishing. According to this view, there could be no such thing as cultural development, because history continually returned to where it had been before. In contrast, the Bible speaks clearly of a beginning—the act of creation—and an end of history: the consummation of the creation in the kingdom of God. It is particularly as a result of this view of history that Christianity—especially since

6. Lynn White, Jr., "The Historical Roots of our Ecological Crisis," *Science* 155 (March 10, 1967): 1203–7.

7. White, "The Historical Roots," p. 1205.

8. White, "The Historical Roots," p. 1205.

Augustine—has placed a heavy emphasis on cultural development and, within that framework, has at times spoken of progress. That progress is then linked with the fulfillment of the cultural mandate.

White is also correct when he argues that Christianity destroyed animism by making a clear distinction between the Creator and the creation. But here White takes too simple a position and misses important insights of historic Christianity. To say, as White does, that "To a Christian a tree can be no more than a physical fact"[9] is to miss totally the Christian concept of this earth as created by God and thereby imbued with meaning that goes much beyond its mere physical existence. (See Colossians 1:16–17.) Wesley Granberg-Michaelson is correct when he writes, "White and others are right in underscoring Christianity's rejection of animism. The tree is not a god. But modern thinking, rather than biblical faith, concludes from this that the tree is only a physical fact."[10]

White's assertion that Christianity views created reality as a means of coming to know the Creator is also correct; this idea was especially prominent in the teachings of a number of the Protestant Reformers and their followers.[11] Christianity thereby did function as a stimulus to early science. Isaac Newton and Blaise Pascal stand as examples of Christians whose faith in God led them both to acknowledge God as Creator and to explore the nature and coherence of his creation.

The discussion thus far might appear to suggest that White's analysis is essentially correct and that Christianity is indeed to blame for the technological evils humankind has loosed on this planet—and, we might add, to be praised for the good that technology has done. The conclusion would then be that moving away from Christianity would be a partial answer to today's technological predicament. But White's fourth contention—that Christianity is profoundly anthropocentric—needs to be examined. Here White's argument exhibits major deficiencies, deficiencies that significantly affect his overall conclusions.

Christianity does indeed teach that under the cultural mandate humankind has the duty to fill and subdue the earth, to develop its natural resources, to give form to the riches God has placed in it. This point is closely related to the linear view of history, since history moves forward via humankind's cultural activities. But—and this is a crucial point—the linear view of history and the fulfillment of the cultural mandate associated with it may not be represented simply by a straight line. For beginning and end, and everything in between, are dependent on and oriented

9. White, "The Historical Roots," p. 1206.

10. Wesley Granberg-Michaelson, *A Worldly Spirituality: The Call to Take Care of the Earth* (New York: Harper & Row, 1984), p. 45.

11. See R. Hooykaas, *Religion and the Rise of Modern Science* (Edinburgh: Scottish Academic Press, 1972).

toward God as the Creator of all things. In a sense God is related vertically to the present and to history. The movement of history and the fulfillment of the cultural mandate has not only a horizontal dimension but also a vertical, transcendent one.[12] God's normative standards for humankind's cultural activities constitute a transcendent orientation. It is this orientation that makes responsible, appropriate, measured cultural development possible. God calls humankind to act in harmony with his normative will, and humankind has the obligation to respond positively, in freedom and responsibility.

This transcendent orientation qualifies the perspective of the natural creation as something over which human beings are to rule. Humankind has been given dominion over creation—which is what White recognizes—but it is a peculiar, servant-like dominion—which is what White misses. Humankind's rule over the creation must be done in keeping with God's normative standards, and therefore it is to be a gentle rule in which humankind cares for and brings out the riches and true nature of creation. This is a far cry from the exploitive, abusive, ruthless conquering of creation that White sees Christianity blessing. Properly understood and consistently lived, Christianity does not support the argument of White and others that it has led to the present predicament in which modern technology has placed modern societies. But this is not the whole story.

When the transcendent dimension is lost, when persons deny the existence of God's normative standards and instead follow their own self-oriented standards, the Christian linear view of history and the cultural mandate are debased and secularized. There is movement in history, there is still cultural development and change, but it is secularized, no longer Christian. Humankind's constant tendency is to substitute love of self and love of one's own class, state, or society for the love of God and neighbor that lies at the heart of God's normative standards.

History has shown Christians are no more immune to this sin than to any other. They have frequently—perhaps more often than not—conducted themselves as lords and masters of the natural environment, and in so doing they have increasingly lost sight of the peculiar value and place of the created ecosphere. More than one scholar has correctly pointed out that in Christian theology one can hardly find a study on the natural creation, on the plant and animal kingdoms.[13] In addition, as a result of an uncritical acceptance of a one-sided view of the cultural mandate, few

---

12. There is a tradition that distinguishes between the word *transcendent* and the word *transcendental*, using *transcendent* to refer to God's relationship to his creatures, and *transcendental* to refer to human beings' relationship to God and his normative standards. Here, however, *transcendent* is used to refer to something transcending human existence.

13. See, for example, Gerhard Liedke, *Im Bauch des Fisches* (Stuttgart: Okologische Theologie, Dreuz Verlag, 1979).

systematic reflections on modern technology have been initiated by Christian theologians. Indeed, Christians have often not seriously concerned themselves with either the negative or the positive consequences of modern scientific-technological development. They have viewed technology either as something that is naturally good or as a development that is neutral in relation to the Christian faith. The point is that even Christians—who in theory accept the cultural mandate as a duty to be carried out in subjection to God's normative will—have in practice often emphasized the theme of progress and cultural development for its own sake, without reference to the divine constraints within which proper and responsible cultural development is to be sought.

These tendencies—all too present within Christendom itself—have been strengthened and reinforced by a secularization movement that has its roots in the Renaissance, the Enlightenment, and modern philosophy, and has come to play a powerful role in modern society in the past two centuries. It is to this movement that we now turn.

FOUR LINES IN HUMAN HISTORY

To understand the forces that have shaped the broad trends in human cultural activity in general and in technological activity in particular, it is helpful to examine four basic lines running through human history. It is easier to understand these four lines if we first recall what the great Christian apologist C. S. Lewis once wrote about "a civil war, a rebellion" raging in the universe, with our earth being "enemy-occupied territory." According to Lewis, this war is between the fallen angel Satan, an evil power who "has made himself for the present the Prince of this World," and God, who created this world good and beautiful. "Christianity," says Lewis, "is the story of how the rightful king has landed . . . and is calling us all to take part in a great campaign of sabotage."[14]

It goes against the modern, scientifically oriented, empirically committed mind to speak of demons and forces of evil abroad on this earth. But Paul makes clear in his letter to the early church in the city of Ephesus that a deadly struggle is indeed taking place on this earth: "For our struggle is not against flesh and blood, but against the rulers, against the authorities, against the powers of this dark world and against the spiritual forces of evil in the heavenly realms" (Eph. 6:12). There is a monumental war going on in which God and his angels of light are pitted against the dark forces of evil. Through the power of Christ's redemp-

14. C. S. Lewis, *Mere Christianity* (New York: Macmillan, 1952), pp. 36–37.

tion, God is in ultimate control, and his victory is assured. Nevertheless, human history is being lived out in the midst of a war. Human beings develop culture, do technology, and mold human history in—to use a term Lewis uses—no-man's-land. We do so in the midst of a continuing struggle between the hosts of heaven and the dark powers of hell.

Creation. Genesis 1:31 tells us, "God saw all that he had made, and it was very good." From this beginning human beings have been called to work the creation and to take care of it (Gen. 1:28; 2:15). They are to act as God's cultural agents in such a way that the cultural products created will, together with heaven and earth, always praise the Creator (see Pss. 104 and 148). This is the meaning of the cultural mandate. Human beings were and are under an obligation to care for the earth in keeping with God's will, to work as servants of the creation by bringing out and caring for the riches, blessings, and potential God has placed in his good creation.

Shalom—right relationships among human beings, between God and human beings, and between human beings and the natural creation—marked God's original creation. There was work to be done, but it was done in joy, delight, and humble acknowledgment of God's will and rule.

The Fall. This first line of history was followed by a second line: the fall of humankind into sin. Prompted by the fallen angel Satan, humankind rebelled against God and his rule, refusing to work and act within the bounds set by God's will and declaring independence from God in order to "be like God" (Gen. 3:5). Human beings refused to fulfill their original cultural task as God's servants; they allowed themselves to aspire to the role of creator. They declared their autonomy from God and his normative will. They joined Satan and his dark forces of evil and God's good creation became—to use C. S. Lewis's apt phrase—enemy-occupied territory.

History is thus no longer a wholesome unity; it is continually being disrupted and destroyed because humankind no longer lives to satisfy the will of God. The additional elements of a curse and of destruction have entered in. The way of life and human culture has become the way of death. Thorns and thistles have sprung up, marking humankind's work in creation with an arduousness and a drudgery unknown before the Fall (see Gen. 3:17–19).

The cultural mandate has not ended, however. It remains valid, but human beings have not been able to fulfill it well. Thus agriculture and animal husbandry were developed, musical instruments were invented, and tools of bronze and iron were made (see Genesis 4)—but these cultural developments were accompanied by jealousy, pride, and murder. In fact, it was Lamech, whose family played key roles in these developments, who bragged, "I have killed a man for wounding me, a young man for injuring me" (Gen. 4:23b).

Human beings sought to build their own kingdoms and to make names for themselves through their achievements. With the earth "full of violence" (Gen. 6:11), God sent the Deluge and put a devastating end to humankind's machinations. But afterwards—with the cultural mandate renewed (Gen. 9:1–7)—human beings sought to "make a name" for themselves by building the Tower of Babel (Gen. 11:1–9). This kind of arrogance and hubris has repeatedly marred human history. Humankind has repeatedly attempted to build a kingdom of man minus God. This is the line of the Fall, which runs through all of human history.

Redemption. But there is a third basic line in human history. God did not leave humankind alone to wallow in the mire of death and destruction brought on by their rebellion against him. God broke into human history to bring redemption in the form of his Son, Jesus Christ. Men and women had proven too weak to withstand the temptations of Satan; they had quickly capitulated and joined the rebellion. Therefore God himself came to do battle with the dark powers of this world and to set human history back on its proper course again.

In the Old Testament one already finds many examples of God coming to redeem through the agency of various leaders: judges, kings, prophets, and others. But these redemptive initiatives—while giving glimpses of light, hope, and life—time and again failed to prevent apostasy. In Jesus Christ, however, humanity encounters the second Adam. He does what the first Adam should have done; what is more, he does his work in a creation ravaged by suffering and death. That is his victory. And through the Holy Spirit his redeemed children are also enabled to live lives of power and victory.

This means that human beings are again empowered to be formers of culture in service to God, not in service to their own selfish ends. Jesus came to proclaim "the good news of the kingdom of God" (Luke 8:1). He came to break the power of the rule of the dark forces of evil and to reestablish the gentle rule of God the Father. The kingdom of God is thereby the kingdom of shalom. This means that those who have been redeemed by Christ and share in his power through the Holy Spirit are, among other things, empowered to shape culture (which includes the doing of technology) in service to God and within his normative standards.

But all this is not to say that the struggle between God and Satan does not still rage on. It does. Satan and his dark forces of evil have been mortally wounded by Christ's life, death, and triumphal resurrection. Their doom is sealed. But their ability to spread hate and death about this earth is still strong; their power to work their evil is all too real. Thus we are not to look for an evolutionary development toward the kingdom of God, the kingdom of shalom, here on earth. We have no reason to expect that human history will be marked by uninterrupted improvement. We are traveling from a garden, by way of a wilderness and sometimes monstrous cultural achievements, to a new and holy city. But the created universe will be completed only in a new heaven and a new earth. Then all forms of alienation—between God and humanity, among human beings, and between human beings and animals and the rest of creation—will be overcome (Isa. 11 and Rev. 21). Shalom in all its fullness will be ushered in.

It is this perspective of history that gives courage and hope. In union with Christ, human beings can begin to fulfill their cultural mandate. Not spotlessly, to be sure. In the midst of a reality that is infected with sin and evil, they are underway to God's kingdom of shalom, a kingdom that, because of the fallenness of this world, cannot be of this world. Only some precursors of that kingdom can be expected in this world. Human work, therefore, only provisionally and partially shows something of this kingdom of shalom. Humankind is able to recapture some—but only some—of the glorious tasks given at creation by which men and women care for, work, subdue, and rule God's creation in keeping with God's normative will. Although sin and its effects have not been banished, some of what was lost has been given back to humankind.

Secularization. The first line of history as we presented it (creation) is continued in the third (redemption), however powerfully the effects of the second (the Fall) are still present. But the second line—the Fall—is also continued and even strengthened in the fourth line, the one that is governed by opposition to the redemption of Christ. Having been set free by the redemption in Christ, human beings in their cultural goals and drives all too often deny God and allow themselves to be guided by self-centered motives instead of de-emphasizing themselves and concentrating on God and neighbor. Time and again human beings seek their own kingdoms of pride and hubris. That is the process of secularization.

In modern society the forces of secularization are indeed very powerful. In some profoundly significant ways, we live in a post-Christian era. It is important to note how we have come to this secularized position.

During the Middle Ages society was permeated by Christian presuppositions concerning humankind, earthly life, and the hereafter. Often, of course, Christian principles were violated in practice, and people's understanding of them was always partial and imperfect. But society's basic understanding of the world was deeply rooted in Christian presuppositions.

The Renaissance, the Enlightenment, and modern philosophy played crucial roles in the victory of secularism over Christianity in the modern age. Peter Gay has rightly located the heart of the spirit of the Renaissance in its view of human freedom, with freedom simplistically defined as the absence of restraints: "Man is free, the master of his fortune, not chained to his place in a universal hierarchy but capable of all things."[15] The spirit of the Renaissance was to declare humankind's freedom to set its own course unencumbered by a world structured by Christian beliefs. The Renaissance had a very strong impact in Europe in terms of secularizing Western society, because it lavished attention on classical Greek civilization, ignored the church, and emphasized human observation and human achievement.

Modern philosphy, which began in the seventeenth century, carried further the Renaissance spirit of human mastery and autonomy. Francis Bacon argued that humankind should use its powers and skills to conquer and harness nature to meet human needs. Isaac Newton—although he himself worked within a clearly Christian framework—established theories that convinced many that God was unnecessary for the day-to-day upholding of the universe. René Descartes saw the human mind as autonomous and free to construct its own frameworks, and John Locke and Adam Smith freed the political and economic spheres from the need for divine intervention and guidance. One after another, the pillars that had upheld a Christian world and life view—one which saw God as a moving, controlling, law-establishing being—were destroyed.

What was started by the Renaissance and carried forward by modern philosophy was completed by the Enlightenment in the eighteenth century. Humankind sought to declare its autonomy from God's normative will. It was thought that human beings—by the power of their own reason and by observation of themselves and nature—could fully understand the world and chart a sure path to endless human progress. The hubris of such a view is overpowering, but its appeal is strong. And a series of scientific and technological discoveries, beginning in the seventeenth century and continuing into the twentieth, have given it great credence. This is the point of view that now appears to be culturally dominant in modern Western culture.

It is extremely difficult to grasp in a single picture the mutual rela-

---

15. Peter Gay, *The Rise of Modern Paganism,* vol. 1 of *Enlightenment* (New York: Knopf, 1967), p. 266.

tionships between the four main lines of history, particularly the relationship between the line of creation and redemption on the one hand, and that of the Fall and secularization on the other. But one thing is certain: the power of secularization cannot be the last word on humanity's situation. The line of creation and redemption remains firm, sure, and, in an ultimate sense, inviolable. This is the reason why societies—including the realms of science and technology—can always seek and return to the kingdom of God. The lines of creation and redemption will ultimately triumph, for Christ has won the struggle against the dark forces of evil. Secularization remains a powerful force in our world; its demonic works are all around us. It is wrong to believe that humanity can usher in the kingdom of God by its own efforts. Nevertheless, we must also recognize that God, not Satan, is in charge. The darkness of secularization cannot overcome the light of redemption. There is hope.

TECHNICISM

The powerful line of secularization present in modern Western culture has as its reigning characteristic the belief in human autonomy and power. Humankind has put itself at the center of all things and declares that it will find progress and life—its own salvation—by taking its destiny into its hands and bending history to its will. Hans Jonas has accurately described the spirit of this view: "To become ever more masters of the world, to advance from power to power, even if only collectively and perhaps no longer by choice, can now be seen to be the chief vocation of mankind."[16] According to the secular view, God is dead, and his normative principles are a forgotten vestige of the past. We now must make our own way in this world, guided by reason and empowered by science and technology.

This drive for human autonomy and mastery apart from God and his will manifests itself in technology in what we will call *technicism*.[17] Technicism reduces all things to the technological; it sees technology as the solution to all human problems and needs. Technology is a savior, the means to make progress and gain mastery over modern, secularized cultural desires. Technology thus becomes its own reason for existing. This "technology for technology's sake" is the ultimate form of tech-

16. Hans Jonas, "Toward a Philosophy of Technology," *Hastings Center Report* (Feb. 1979): 38.

17. One of the authors of this book, Egbert Schuurman, would like to point out that we are here using the term *technicism* in a narrower, more specific sense than he has used it in some of his other writings. Elsewhere he has used *technicism* to refer to the general will to power and spirit of autonomy that marks modern secularized culture.

nicism. More specifically, technicism is marked by three key characteristics or beliefs: (1) technological change—the development of ever more complex, ever more sophisticated technological objects—is inevitable; (2) such change represents progress, leads to improved conditions for humankind; and (3) there are technological solutions to the problems engendered by technological change. Technicism says that humankind can use its hands and minds—its technology—to build a kingdom of plenty, ease, and peace. Thus if something can be done, it should be done—no questions asked. "You can't stop progress!"

Time and again technicism reveals itself in statements of the scholars, businesspersons, and politicians of our society. Emmanuel Mesthene of Harvard University, for example, has written "Can we . . . control our biology and our personality, order the weather that suits us, travel to Mars or to Venus? Of course we can, if not now or in five or ten years, then certainly in twenty-five or in fifty or a hundred."[18] Simon Ramo, chairman of the board of the TRW-Fujitsu Company, has written,

> There is already a gross imbalance between technological and sociological process. Will the transition to the new society be orderly or chaotic? Civilization must adapt, the impact of technology must be absorbed. We have no take-it-or-leave-it choice. The expanding, increasingly fast-paced, complex, and interacting world urgently requires solutions to the problems of its physical operation of production, communication, transportation and resources control and distribution. Because technological creativity is able to do so, it is furnishing the answers. . . . [19]

And President Ronald Reagan, while touring a space flight center, declared that people who don't support space exploration "do not see that as we acquire more and more knowledge from new technologies, we no longer move forward in inches or feet, we begin to leap forward. There's nothing that the United States of America cannot accomplish if the doubting Thomases would just stand aside and get out of our way."[20]

Technicism constitutes a faith, a new religion. It is something beyond themselves that men and women who have denied God can believe in. It may not be fully understood, but they know it is good and that it will bring the salvation of material prosperity. In response, Senator Mark Hatfield has sounded an appropriate note of caution:

18. Emmanuel G. Mesthene, "Technology and Wisdom," in *Philosophy and Technology: Readings in the Philosophical Problems of Technology,* ed. Carl Mitcham and Robert Mackey (New York: Free Press, 1983), p. 115.

19. Quoted by Carl F. Stover in *The Government of Science* (Santa Barbara, Calif.: Center for the Study of Democratic Institutions, 1962), pp. 9-10.

20. Quoted by David Hoffman in "President Uses Launch to Attack 'Pessimists,' " *The Washington Post,* August 31, 1984, p. A3.

In a collective sense, we are threatening to become the emotional by-products of society's one-dimensional exaltation of scientific and technological achievement. Dazzled by material success, we have developed a new religion: the worship of progress itself. Whereas people once looked toward God for salvation, they now direct their daily lives toward the domination of nature and fellow human beings in a ceaseless quest for economic prosperity.[21]

This religion of technicism—emerging out of the secularization of culture—has modern, technologically oriented society in its grip.

EXILES IN BABYLON

We live in a secularized society; more particularly, we live in a secularized scientific-technological society. Men and women worship at the feet of their own technical prowess, believing that they can achieve their own salvation by building more and better technological objects, that they can find peace and contentment in a self-indulgent plethora of material goods. The resulting culture can be considered a culture of Babylon.

This assertion is challenged by some. Various forms of this culture of Babylon have been around as long as human history, they point out, and our era is no exception. It is true that the motivating spirit of Babylon, the spirit of autonomous self-will, is as old as the Fall, and that it has manifested itself in various degrees and forms throughout history. The present age, however, is marked by the fact that this motivating spirit— following a long spiritual-historical development and fortified by the possibilities of modern technology—has produced an unprecedented effect that embraces the entire world. Previously unimaginable scientific-technological possibilities run parallel with the secularization of culture. It is precisely this reciprocal reinforcing link between secularization and major, unquestioned technological developments that in some profound ways marks modern culture as a culture of Babylon.

A massive power complex has arisen as a consequence of this link, increasingly intertwining the domains of technology, science, economics, and politics. This power complex fits the description of Babylon given in Revelation, a description that stresses the decadence of Babylon—its luxurious wealth, arrogance, power, and godlessness— and the great admiration it inspired:

21. Mark O. Hatfield, *Between a Rock and a Hard Place* (Waco, Tex.: Word, 1976), p. 157.

"Fallen! Fallen is Babylon the Great!
  She has become a home for demons
and a haunt for every evil spirit,
  a haunt for every unclean and detestable bird.
For all the nations have drunk
  the maddening wine of her adulteries.
The kings of the earth committed adultery with her,
    and the merchants of the earth grew rich from her excessive
    luxuries."

. . . .

" 'Woe! Woe, O great city,
  O Babylon, city of power!
In one hour your doom has come!'

"The merchants of the earth will weep and mourn over her because no one
buys their cargoes any more—cargoes of gold, silver, precious stones and
pearls; fine linen, purple, silk and scarlet cloth; every sort of citron wood,
and articles of every kind made of ivory, costly wood, bronze, iron and
marble; cargoes of cinnamon and spice, of incense, myrrh and frankin-
cense, of wine and olive oil, of fine flour and wheat; cattle and sheep;
horses and carriages; and bodies and souls of men."

. . . .

" 'Woe! Woe, O great city,
  dressed in fine linen, purple and scarlet,
  and glittering with gold, precious stones and pearls!
In one hour such great wealth has been brought to ruin!' "

(Rev. 18:2–3, 10–13, 16–17)

So too in our time—under the line of the Fall and secularization—
many have forsaken God as the source of meaning, hope, and direction;
in his place they see material prosperity and earthly power as bringing
salvation. They seek to escape the consequences of the Fall and of sin
itself by their own efforts. The kingdom of God is then replaced by a
human kingdom rooted in this earth. In that process the normative principles God has given humankind are cast aside.

Babylon. Five dominant impulses or driving motives in Western
culture mark it as a Babylonian culture. The first is the *will to power*
independent of God's will and direction. Already at the time of the Fall,
the basic motive was a will to power, to "be like God." Adam and Eve
wanted to live outside the bounds set by God's order for them, to exert
their own wills independent of any restraint. They sought autonomy and
power.

Today more than ever humankind seeks power—riches, luxury, and domination over nature, animals, and other societies—apart from any recognition of God's sovereignty over all human activities. Whales are hunted down and slaughtered, and so threatened with extinction; farm animals meant to enjoy the natural world God made for them are confined in cages and pens and pumped full of chemicals that stimulate growth; highly toxic chemicals are carelessly discarded in the earth; sulfur dioxides released into the atmosphere are killing whole forests; peoples are held in fear and subjugation by helicopter-borne troops armed with the latest automatic weapons; and political hegemony is maintained by storehouses of nuclear weapons, the use of which would end civilization. The natural creation and fellow human beings alike are trampled and scorned in modern society's relentless drive for power and domination.

A second mark of the culture of Babylon is *rationalism* or *scientism*. Rationalism in technology is responsible for the characteristics of science also becoming the characteristics of technology. This entails much more than simply the use of scientific knowledge in technology; it entails the unlimited application of the dynamics of science to technology. Because science is abstract and limited, technology is also channeled within limited, narrow boundaries. The controlling influence of science in technology is partly responsible for the relentlessness and rigidity with which technology is pursued.

A third mark of Babylonian culture is *technicism*. Everything is reduced to the technical. Many technologists are so charmed by the spell of this faith that they make what can be made and perfect what can be perfected, regardless of the consequences. This faith says that the way to a better tomorrow is through technology, through bigger, more sophisticated, more complex technological objects. We do not need God for salvation; we can save ourselves through the efforts of our own minds and our own ingenuity.

The faith of technicism leads to the growth of technological power, a power that technologists claim to be able to control but to which they easily succumb. They have fallen under the powerful spell of their own work: their own technology. Viewpoints and standards outside of the technical receive little if any attention. Technologists' creativity and sense of responsibility as whole human beings are thus repressed, and they become a menace to both nature and culture.

A fourth mark of Babylonian culture is its *absolutizing of the profit motive*. A sense of stewardship is excluded at the outset. The great overruling goal becomes the maximization of profit and the growth of material prosperity. Over-production of certain kinds of goods results.

This overproduction often occurs at the expense of the natural environment, which is exploited and polluted, and at the expense of the laborer, who is viewed as a technical link in the production process rather than as a responsible, whole person. In addition, so-called "developed" countries often take an exploitive, dominating position relative to less powerful, less technologically sophisticated countries.

Under the influence of this absolutizing of the profit motive, technological development has a disturbing, destructive effect. The result is wasteful, predatory exploitation. Weak societies are held down by more powerful societies; the environment is polluted and destroyed; workers are dehumanized. Unnecessary technological objects are produced and are available at far too low a price. For neither all the human costs nor all the costs to nature and to the reserves of basic natural resources have had price tags attached to them.

The fifth mark of today's Babylonian culture is the *political power* used to support and reinforce the other four marks. The all-too-real tendency is to use political power to support and give substance to the will to power, to the rationalization of technology, to technicism, and to an absolutized profit motive. As a result, political power is not used to bring about social justice, to right the wrongs of a Babylonian culture and set society on the right paths; it is used to support and abet the gigantic technological complexes of Western society.

Although modern technological society does exhibit the characteristics of a culture of Babylon, it cannot be said that modern Western culture and all Western societies are purely and totally Babylonian. There are exceptions—islands of hope and pockets of resistance—and there are important currents running counter to the cultural impulses of Babylon just described. There are the civil freedoms, for example, found in the Western liberal democracies of Western Europe and North America, and there is the strong religious faith—which is all too frequently privatized—found in some Western societies, especially the United States. Nevertheless, the basic cultural impulses that are shaping the direction of Western society in the late twentieth century are those of Babylon, not of God's Word.

Exiles. The pessimism of the current discussion is almost overwhelming. It cannot be denied that the line of the Fall and secularization is exceedingly powerful in modern society, that our culture is a culture of Babylon marked by arrogance, pride, and a love of power. What are Christians who live in such a culture to do? What is their responsibility?

Three possibilities present themselves. One is a culture-negating position that says that the way to redemption in a fallen culture is through redemption from culture itself and the cultural task within creation.[22] Christians who take this position withdraw from culture and recognize no responsibility to perform cultural tasks. The world is to be rejected. But this position runs directly contrary to a biblical understanding of the cultural mandate. Christians are to be workers in this world—*Christian* workers, but workers nonetheless.

A second possible position is the one according to which Christians accommodate secularized culture. In his book *Christ and Culture,* H. Richard Niebuhr says that those taking this position ''feel no great tension between church and world, the social laws and the Gospel, the workings of divine grace and human effort, the ethics of salvation and the ethics of social conservation or progress.''[23] In short, ''they harmonize Christ and culture''[24] by seeing key elements of current modern culture as congruent with biblical principles. One might think, for example, of the progress made in medicine, the emphasis placed on personal freedoms, and the presence of commendable virtues in certain societal leaders and many citizens. But this position is not an appropriate one, either. True, a survey of Western, technologically oriented culture does not present a picture of total, unrelieved depravity, but the course that Western culture is taking is fundamentally wrong. We are going down the wrong road. It is a road of secularization—of human denial of God and his will—and of human pride.

Neither washing one's hands of present-day culture nor accommodating it is appropriate. Another choice must be made. In this choice we must continue to honor the fact that there is a cultural mandate. As Christians we are to be doers of technology seeking to fulfill their God-given mandate to shape and mold culture in keeping with God's normative will. But in fulfilling the cultural mandate, we take part in the line of creation and redemption, while the prevailing line of our culture is that of the Fall and secularization. Thus we are exiles in our own culture—exiles in Babylon.

To be an exile is to be caught in the tension of being redeemed from sin, yet still being sinful and still living in a world of sin. Christians must accept and affirm the cultural mandate by thinking of themselves as citizens of the heavenly kingdom, by not loving the world, by not looking for an enduring city here on earth but ''looking for the city that is to come'' (Heb. 13:14). Exiles are not the builders of the prevailing culture,

22. This position is the one that H. Richard Niebuhr has labeled ''Christ against culture'' in his famous study of differing Christian orientations towards culture entitled *Christ and Culture* (New York: Harper & Row, 1951).

23. Niebuhr, *Christ and Culture,* p. 83.

24. Niebuhr, *Christ and Culture,* p. 83.

but neither are they slaves. They live and exist in a state of tension with that culture. They live in it but they are also separate from it.

Love for God demands this status of exile, but the same love demands involvement: the act of turning toward and addressing that culture in love. The proper cultural stance, then, is neither one of avoidance and negation nor one of accommodation. It means living by the inspiration of another cultural dynamic and following other normative principles than those prevailing in modern secular culture. The Christian's animating motive—namely, the desire to live and work by the power of the love and grace of God—is diametrically opposed to the will-to-power motive of Babylon. It entails the absolute rejection of the pretentious aim, by means of science and technology, to establish a counter-creation in which human beings themselves establish life's meaning. It means living and working in obedience to God and his normative standards.

Finally, exiles realize that it is unlikely that they will completely remake the society in which they live. They are faithful; they are obedient. But they realize their faithfulness and obedience will meet with strong resistance from the dominant culture. Similarly, Christians in a secularized, technological culture are faithful and obedient. The kingdom of God is within them. And they will sometimes be able to see cultural fruits flowing from their obedience and faithfulness. The Bible offers examples of this: Joseph in Egypt and Daniel and Esther in Babylon. Nevertheless, our expectations rest on the provisionality and relativity of our work despite all its worth and meaning. The kingdom of God is not of this world. It originates with God, and as it comes down from heaven it takes shape and form on earth. For that reason we should be weaned away from the idea that the kingdom of God is the point of culmination of human history or of our cultural efforts. Evil is too deeply rooted in our corrupted hearts and in the structures of this world that we could, out of ourselves, build a sinless society or even a markedly improved one.

True, with God all things are possible, and through the faithfulness of men and women he has indeed "conquered kingdoms, administered justice, . . . shut the mouths of lions, quenched the fury of the flames, . . . and routed foreign armies" (Heb. 11:33–34). But this does not mean that we can expect God's kingdom of shalom to be ushered in by our cultural efforts. Christians are likely to remain in a state of tension with modern culture, and thus to feel like exiles in some important ways. God's kingdom of shalom—whether in its current fragmentary form or in its glorious fullness in the culmination of human history—is God's gift to us, not something we wrench out of a fallen culture by our own efforts.

Culture-forming Christians in today's secularized culture are in much the same position as were the people of Israel in exile in Babylon, when the prophet gave them this word from God:

This is what the Lord Almighty, the God of Israel, says to all those I carried into exile from Jerusalem to Babylon: "Build houses and settle down; plant gardens and eat what they produce. Marry and have sons and daughters; find wives for your sons and give your daughters in marriage, so that they too may have sons and daughters. Increase in number there; do not decrease. Also, seek the peace and prosperity of the city to which I have carried you into exile. Pray to the Lord for it, because if it prospers, you too will prosper."

. . . .

"For I know the plans I have for you," declares the Lord, "plans to prosper you and not to harm you, plans to give you hope and a future." (Jer. 29:4–7, 11)

CHAPTER FIVE

A Guide to Responsible Technology

IF WE ARE TO FIND OUR WAY AS EXILES IN A SECULARIZED CULTURE, foreign to the Christian's beliefs and commitments, we need a guide. We cannot go by our own lights. The spirit of the age is too strong and the way back home too long for us to find our way without assistance.

Technicism says our guide is to be found in technology itself. Technology is the solution to all human needs and problems. It calls men and women to take their fate into their own hands, to control the natural world and themselves with greater and more sophisticated technology.

But the only true guide is God's will and his norms for our lives. That guide calls us to love God above all and our neighbor as ourselves. If we follow that guide, we are able to be in the world but not of the world. "Do not conform any longer to the pattern of this world, but be transformed by the renewing of your mind. Then you will be able to test and approve what God's will is—his good, pleasing and perfect will" (Rom. 12:2). The starting point for valuing in technology is not human thinking and speculation but the will of God.

To follow this guide, we must begin by seeking God with obedient hearts, prepared to first hear and then do his will. The first step in seeking technological wisdom, therefore, is not thinking or doing, but listening. This is an important point to emphasize at the outset, because the tendency of the times is to associate technological activity with busyness: defining practical problems, seeking practical solutions, getting on with it. But this presumed strength of human technological activity can all too easily become its fatal weakness, for it is because of this orientation toward practical mastery that humankind is tempted to declare itself master and to forget the living God. Thus we begin with the requirement of humble, obedient listening. If we stand in awe of the majesty of the one true God, we are less likely to stand in awe of technological powers, less likely to allow them to control our lives.

This starting point applies as much to finding a normative structure for doing technology as to any other human activity. We must be careful not to overintellectualize our understanding of God's address to us. One listens and responds not only—or even primarily—with the mind, but with the heart. At the same time, it is not enough to maintain that good technology follows straightforwardly from a right heart, because technology also involves the intellect and rational problem-solving. If we are open to God's will in both heart and mind, we can follow the dictum of Martin Bucer: "The whole of human life, individual and social, must be ordered according to the will of God as revealed in the Bible."[1]

But in undertaking this task we must continually recall that the line of the Fall and secularization is a strong, active force in society and in our own lives. Thus we must be aware that even as we strive to know and understand God's will, the distortion of technicism, the love of power, and the arrogance of the drive for autonomy can all affect us. The lines of history are in tension with each other, not only in society but also in individual lives. But, though we need to recognize our own finitude, it is important that we press ahead in our effort to know and follow God's will.

If this guide is to give the modern age the direction it so desperately needs, we must first try to understand the nature of what we are seeking. Thus far we have referred to God's will and his normative standards and principles, which stand in sharp contrast to humankind's own standards founded on a belief in its own autonomy, in its ability to chart its own course independent of God. But now greater clarity is called for. This chapter first considers the nature of God's will as it is reflected in normative standards for human beings' technological activities, and then it suggests the specific normative principles that apply to activities related to technology.

A THEORY OF NORMATIVITY

Knowledge of Norms. We can presume that Christians agree that unity characterizes the person of God, and therefore characterizes his creation. In addition, we will presume that Christians agree that God's will is normative for humanity, and that human beings can know something of the principles that conform to God's revealed will. But there still remains a question concerning the unity of knowledge about the world. Is there a system of knowledge that leads to a grand scheme for a Christian society? Does it give a detailed blueprint for human institutions by which to organize our lives? What claims can be made for this humanly structured knowledge as compared to God's revelation itself?

1. Quoted by I. John Hesselink in *On Being Reformed: Distinctive Characteristics and Common Misunderstandings* (Ann Arbor, Mich.: Servant Books, 1983), p. 109.

There are those who warn against trying to deduce a system of social knowledge from Christian principles. D. L. Munby, for example, who has written several books on a Christian approach to economics and society, holds that any attempt to synthesize divine and social truth is doomed. Particularly wrongheaded is the attempt to deduce a Christian social pattern from Christian theology in some sort of Platonic way. Any such attempts are doomed to fail, according to Munby, because the facts are too diverse, society is too complex, and the human mind is too limited. But, although he does not believe in a grand intellectual framework for Christian social thinking, Munby is quick to add that this does not mean that there are no Christian principles of social action and social order. Such Christian principles are, in his view, not the result of close theological reasoning based on impeccable theological axioms, "but rather the judgments that naturally arise when Christians (of varied backgrounds) look at the twentieth century world. They do not form a system, nor do they enable us to act in any particular situation with any sort of certainty of general Christian approval. They are maps on a very small scale."[2]

But if Munby rejects the notion of a system of knowledge deduced from general Christian axioms, he nevertheless avoids the opposite idea that tempts Christians: that all judgments regarding cultural matters are private, subjective, and individual. Munby maintains that there are Christian principles and standards that will, up to a point, help us judge the institutions and arrangements of social and economic order.[3]

Munby's tentativeness is appropriate if it is meant to reflect humility about human knowledge. One must not expect to find a complete system of normative standards for cultural activities through simple deduction from basic biblical principles. One must avoid the kind of pride that emerges from a self-confident assurance that he or she has worked out a tidy, comprehensive system for living according to God's will. All human doing—including theorizing—is done by beings whose knowledge is incomplete, whose insights are imperfect, and whose understanding is often blinded by their own sinful natures.

Based on the unity of the creation and on the unity of God's will, however, human beings can strive for agreement between their actions and their articulation of the normative principles for those actions. This struggle involves the intellect, but it is not first and foremost a rational or deductive activity. It is an activity that seeks obedience to God's will through faithfulness to his revelation and guiding Spirit.

2. D. L. Munby, *God and the Rich Society: A Study of Christians in a World of Abundance* (London: Oxford University Press, 1961), p. 7.

3. Munby, *God and the Rich Society*, p. 8.

An approach based on Christian normative principles looks outside of human existence and experience for its authority. Because God's revelation is dynamic—that is, ongoing through the work of the Holy Spirit and in the creation around us—we can gain insight into Christian principles that is not solely the work of human powers. This means two things: first, any claim to Christian principles must be shown to comport well with the Bible and with the creation; and second, any insight gained into these principles must be communally tested.

Any claims made for biblically based normative principles must be made with care.[4] There must be no confusion between the constructs of the human intellect and the message and authority of the Gospel itself. Furthermore, we Christians must remember that knowledge of ultimate truth does not itself guarantee that we possess the knowledge needed to make specific daily decisions. We are aware of the power and preciousness of the truth entrusted to us—the truth of Jesus Christ as Lord and Savior. Armed with this truth, we may be tempted to believe that we know all truth, and that our pronunciations regarding the things of this world are always right. Likewise, there is an ever-present danger to try to read too much into the Bible. Not every phrase, sentence, verse, and chapter is to be literally read and applied to our own situation. Although we must be alert to these potential dangers, we must not lose God's Word as our anchor.

Christian principles for cultural activities must comport well with biblical revelation. "Comport well" carries with it a creative ambiguity. On the one hand, it asks for a strong relationship, one rooted in the source of God's Word. On the other hand, it does not detail this relationship. Thus this claim does not suggest that all the principles for culture formation are detailed in the Bible nor that they can be deduced directly from the Bible. Nor does it specify a purely intellectual relationship; it recognizes that what is required by God's law is inscribed on our hearts, even the hearts of unbelievers (see Rom. 2:14-15). What is true of biblical revelation is also true of general revelation.

The task of testing principles against the Bible and God's revelation in his creation is a task given not only to individuals but to the church as a whole, Christ's body. Thus every Christian is to test his or her conclusions with other members in the church. Every Christian should stand

4. Here and elsewhere in this book the phrase "biblically based normative principles" is used to refer to normative principles rooted in and emerging out of Christian perspectives. As such they are based on the Bible in a broad sense. But this phrase is not intended to imply that these normative principles are based on the Bible in a narrow, exclusive way. As the context of the discussion in this chapter makes clear, these normative principles are molded by our understanding of both God's Word and his creation, and our understanding of them is accomplished not by a simple, mechanical process but by the struggles of mind and heart.

ready, in humility, to be corrected and guided by the brothers and sisters in Christ. This means that a division of labor may sometimes be needed, with some called to undertake different aspects of the task depending on their gifts and abilities.

Clearly, the task of discerning biblically based normative principles to guide the doing of technology is not an easy one. One must carefully, prayerfully, and humbly seek to discover which normative principles comport well with God's will revealed in both his Word and his creation.

A question remains, however, concerning knowledge of God's normative standards. It is clear that the key reference point for establishing Christian normative principles is the command to love: " 'Love the Lord your God with all your heart and with all your soul and with all your strength and with all your mind'; and, 'Love your neighbor as yourself' " (Luke 10:27). The question which then emerges is how concrete one can be or even attempt to be in articulating the demands of this command. Perhaps it is so rich and all-encompassing that no attempts should be made to particularize it. But if this is so, why did God give humankind the Decalogue, of which the command to love is the summary? Why has he addressed us in so many ways with his revelation?

It is both possible and advisable to articulate more precisely what the command to love means in relation to the various facets of humankind's life on earth—in relation to marriage, parenting, business and economic life, worship, political life, and technological activities. Of course, the command to love does not make specific pronouncements about these various spheres of human doing, but our Lord has not left us alone. By using our hearts and minds, by heeding God's revelation of himself and his will in his Word and his creation, we can say much about which specific normative principles comport well with his revelation.

Characteristics of Christian Normative Principles for Technological Activities. Before going on to specify certain key normative principles that should guide technological activities, it will be helpful to consider three characteristics that should mark them: they should be adequate in scope, make necessary distinctions, and integrate the diversity found in society. We will consider each of these characteristics in turn.

First, a Christian normative approach to technology must be *adequate in scope*. It is improper to treat technology in isolation; its own internal character and its place in human society forbid this. Indeed, opposing the idea that technology is neutral implies that technology neither begins nor proceeds in a value-free manner, nor are its effects on society neutral. In addition, the reality that God created is clearly multiform in character. An incredible richness and diversity—which ought to be preserved— characterize both the human and the nonhuman creation that technology touches. Human beings must, to the best of their limited powers, seek to reflect this diversity in their approach to the principles that ought to guide technology. This means that reference points—the points of contact between understanding technology and understanding other aspects of life—must be numerous. These reference points are themselves complex, reflecting the complexity of created entities. A proper normative approach must, therefore, be broad in scope.

A broad approach to forming normative guides for technological activities stands in clear contrast to overly narrow ways of valuing technology. Technicism is narrow: it reduces technology to a naive vision of progress or simply to technology for technology's sake. Technicism views the world with blinders on: all it can see is technology, and so it plunges ahead without truly seeing where it is going. As a result, resources are wasted, ecosystems are damaged, the workplace is dehumanized, and the needs of future generations are discounted.

Closely related to technicism are approaches that solely emphasize efficiency or economic growth. In these approaches, one or both of two views are held: (1) economic growth is the measure of social progress, perhaps in terms of the standard of living, and (2) all growth is good—that is, indiscriminate growth is valued.[5] Both of these approaches take much too narrow a viewpoint, one that fails to see all of human life and thus fails to see that some growth is unhealthy, obstructive, or pathological.

In reaction to such approaches, certain critics are seeking a new way to relate technology to the "quality of life"—a set of social indicators responsive to the many dimensions of human well-being.[6] They want progress to mean more than merely economic growth or increased efficiency. Certainly their recognition of the need for a richer, more comprehensive concept of progress and human life is laudable. But their promising intentions usually founder because they lack a starting point for an alternative system of valuation. They usually know what such a system should *not* be: it should not value greater technical sophistication for its own sake, it should not be limited to monetary measures alone, it should not attempt to derive a single measure of welfare, it should not value efficiency above all else, and so forth. But they face a formidable barrier to setting forth a new set of values because most of their approaches are limited to human values, and human beings express their values in a bewildering variety of ways.

What is desperately needed is an approach that has both a broad

5. See Fritjof Capra, *The Turning Point: Science, Society and the Rising Culture* (New York: Simon & Schuster, 1982), p. 214.

6. See, for example, E. F. Schumacher, *Small Is Beautiful: Economics as if People Mattered* (New York: Harper & Row, 1973).

scope—one that recognizes the richness and variety of human life and social and natural reality—and a firm anchorage, a reference point. Christians can achieve exactly such an approach by rooting their normative principles in God and his revelation. They believe that the coherence of human life comes from something—from Someone— entirely outside of human existence. Their view is a radical departure from the human-centered views so pervasive today. These views claim that human beings are autonomous and thus never need to look outside of themselves or their own existence in order to determine what is right. But this is an arrogant and idolatrous claim. That human beings take thought and give form to culture is indeed true; these are gifts and tasks given to them by God. But the standards and principles for culture transcend human thought and form-giving: they are based on God's will. Thus a Christian view of the scope of a theory of normativity comes not only from a reaction to the reductionism of other approaches but also from an appreciation of the scope of God's dominion.

Essential to a Christian approach, therefore, is the confession that there is only one true God and that all things are from him, unto him, and through him. Nothing in his creation escapes his power; nothing means anything outside of his will. Accordingly, there is a wholeness that marks his creation and the service that his creatures are to render to him. And although this wholeness was broken by sin, the possibility for wholeness has been restored through the redemptive work of Jesus Christ. Earlier we observed that although technology is only one means of culture- forming, it is a means that has a remarkable power to affect virtually all aspects of culture. Retention or restoration of wholeness is thus crucial to our perspective on technology. It is all the more crucial because human beings have too often forgotten to take the demands of wholeness into account in their technological activities, and consequently they have concentrated their attention and powers on one part of their existence to the exclusion of others.

A second requirement of Christian normative principles for technological activities is that they *make necessary distinctions*. This follows from the diversity referred to above. The overarching normative principle is love: love of God above all and love of one's neighbor as oneself. But knowing and following this principle of love requires that one give it its due in all areas of human existence. Loving one's neighbor is different from loving one's wife, which in turn is different from loving one's children. Love is exercised one way in the classroom, another way in the courtroom, and another way in the bedroom. Human lives have a variety of facets, and each of them must be granted a place; each has its own meaning and significance in the context of the whole. These facets reflect an appropriate, created diversity, and thus the normative principles for technology will likewise have to be diverse, since technology affects all of these facets of human existence.

These facets must be taken into consideration in determining the scope of normative principles. This means that the effort to restore wholeness and proper scope is not first of all directed toward perceiving life in its entirety but toward making distinctions about aspects of the whole. Restoration of the whole thus takes the form of restoring all parts to their proper place. To do so successfully, we must know something about proper place; we must be able to distinguish facets of life such as the economic, the social, and the political. On what basis can we make these distinctions? To answer this question we need to consider carefully the nature of differentiation in the world.

Up until now, the argument has been that the universe is characterized by both unity and diversity. The unity reflects the fact that all creatures are God-related and are held in being by his sovereign will. There are several kinds of diversity: the diversity of creation, the diversity brought about in history by responsible human action, and the perverse diversity brought about by sin and human finitude. If one grants that reality is created, the diversity of that reality follows from simple observation. For example, all persons are created in God's image, a unifying fact of enormous importance; yet all are different. It is not that sin has made persons different, but that God intended them to be different. The created diversity of nature is likewise abundantly clear both from the Genesis account and from all human observation.

The natural sciences treat this diversity as a matter of fact. Many academic observers, not only Christians, would strenuously object to any attempt to collapse the distinctions between, say, chemistry and biology. Such systematic distinctions are helpful and appropriate for two reasons. First, they are helpful because they allow specialization of analytical tools and human energies. The field of science is too complex to grasp without division of knowledge and labor, so specialization is in order. Second, systematic distinctions are appropriate because they reflect the natural order. The claim the Christian scientist would want to make is that the distinctions refer, to some extent, to the kinds of diversity God created. The natural sciences may be shaped by certain traditional elements, but more than mere tradition or accident accounts for the distinctions they make.

Before looking for a parallel in human culture and the academic disciplines by which it is studied, one needs to understand the relationship between the distinctions made by the natural sciences and the differentiation created by God. That there is created diversity in the natural world is readily conceded. But what can we know of this diversity? How do we perceive it? Not in a presuppositionless way, generally speaking. In some sense, our investigations of God's creation and hence our knowledge of it are constrained by the general limits of our ability and means for knowing. The creation has its own integrity, diverse facets of God's making, but our possibilities for knowing them are limited by our finitude and sin. All of us therefore see through a glass darkly. To put it another way, diversity of the created natural reality has ontological status. It is "real"; it flows from the very nature of the creation. But our appreciation of this fact is hampered by epistemological difficulties. We are limited in our knowing. Thus human claims for created diversity should always be somewhat tentative.

The issue of created natural diversity is relevant to our consideration of technology, but the issue of formulating normative principles for technology comes into its own in a different realm—that of culture. Therefore, a question emerges: Is there created cultural diversity in the same sense that there is created natural diversity? The answer is, quite simply, no, because the diversity of the cultural world is much more complex than that of the natural realm. In the natural realm, normative principles can rest on the diversity that God created and placed in the creation. But in the cultural world, some differences are inherent in creation, some are the result of appropriate, God-approved culture formation, and some are the result of sinful, self-centered culture formation. Consequently, biblically based normative principles for technology must relate to cultural diversities according to the sources that have produced them.

The third requirement of Christian normative principles for technology is that they *integrate the diversity found in society* so that there is no conflict among its facets. Each facet or aspect deserves its place—must receive its due—but all must also cohere so as to form a whole. This means that the normative principles for technology must mesh with those for the other areas of human activity. Dutch economist Bob Goudzwaard has expressed it well: "The norms of economic development and those of ethics, the norms of justice and the unfolding of technique, ought never to be played off against each other. Because God's command is undivided, the norms set by him must be seen and observed in their mutual coherence."[7]

There are those who would agree with the prior point regarding the need to recognize differentiation in culture. They hold, for example, that life has a number of dimensions, including the technical and the ethical,

7. Bob Goudzwaard, *Capitalism and Progress: A Diagnosis of Western Society,* trans. and ed. by Josina Van Nuis Zylstra (Grand Rapids: Eerdmans, 1979), p. 65.

and they argue for rigid domains for each: there is a sphere where the technical is all that counts, the sphere of technology proper; there is a sphere where the ethical counts, most likely the realm of personal deportment or human interactions. Of course the areas might intersect, or at least become tangentially related, as when ethical choices depend on technological possibilities. The modern technology of nuclear weapons and artificial life-support systems, for example, necessarily produces new ethical issues. But essentially, the proponents of this view claim, these spheres are independent of each other. Although there is an element of truth in this position, in and of itself it is too narrow. The realization that ethical choices rest to some extent on technological mechanisms is appropriate, but so is the recognition that one's technological choices rest upon implicit or explicit ethical criteria. And technological choices must be made not only in using technology but in doing technology as well.

Another viewpoint is that of John Naisbitt, author of the popular work *Megatrends*. Naisbitt realizes that a high-tech society, although it has accomplished much in some areas, has left something undone, some need unfulfilled. To compensate for this lack of fulfillment, people have turned to "a counterbalancing human response—that is *high touch*. . . . The more high tech, the more high touch."[8] To Naisbitt, the issue is balance: "We must learn to balance the material wonders of technology with the spiritual demands of our human nature."[9] But this balance is an external, after-the-fact kind: "Our response to the high tech all around us was the evolution of a highly personal value system to compensate for the impersonal nature of technology."[10] And how do we know that this personal-spiritual longing is real, that people value it? Because, says Naisbitt, we can observe the self-realization movement, a movement that has economic reality. "Value," says Naisbitt, "is whatever people are willing to pay for."[11]

A basic problem with Naisbitt's approach is that he sees technology as a given in the material domain, a given that people can only react to and compensate for by attempting to restore balance in their lives by emphasizing the personal and the spiritual. To grant the technological as a given to which there can be only a personal reaction is to cede most of the ground for a proper technological response. This kind of balancing prefigures quite a grim future for human life and the rest of creation, and in addition, its starting point is wrong.

8. John Naisbitt, *Megatrends: Ten New Directions Transforming Our Lives* (New York: Warner Books, 1982), p. 35.

9. Naisbitt, *Megatrends*, p. 36.

10. Naisbitt, *Megatrends*, p. 36.

11. Naisbitt, *Megatrends*, p. 31.

What is needed is a different view of the structure of technological normativity and the normative principles that emerge from it. This view recognizes the broad scope of technology, gives due respect to the appropriate, God-willed diversities present in society and the natural creation, and yet seeks to guide technology so that the various facets of society and creation cohere even as each is given its due. The task is formidable, our knowledge and insight are limited, and—it is hoped—our humility and tentativeness are clear. Despite our limitations, we must press on to outline specific normative principles that, if pursued simultaneously, will lead to a truly responsible technology.

A STRUCTURE OF NORMATIVE PRINCIPLES

The Basis of Normative Principles. As stated previously, the basis of the normative principles for technological activity is God's will, especially as expressed in the Great Commandment to love God above all and one's neighbor as oneself. The challenge is to take this general command and determine more specifically what it means in terms of humankind's technological activities. In doing so, it is helpful to begin by recalling the cultural mandate discussed in the previous chapter. Technological activity is a form of cultural activity. It is thereby a way of fulfilling the cultural mandate, which is itself one way of living out the Great Commandment. Thus what was said in the previous chapter applies here. Technology is to be done as a form of service to our fellow human beings and to the natural creation. This means that we are to develop technology in such a way that the blessings, riches, and potentials God has put in creation are allowed to flower. We are called to do technology in such a way that the creativity and joy for which God created men and women can exist in abundance, the riches of the physical world can be uncovered and utilized, and the plant and animal worlds can be perceived and used for what they are and for what God intends them to be.

Two specific concepts are involved here. First, humankind in its technological activity is to show respect for the various entities in God's creation by developing and using them as he intends. We should seek to understand the differing natures of a wild deer and a domesticated dog, of a young fruit tree and a two-thousand-year-old redwood. The nature of these entities should influence humankind's development and use of them. These uses and developments should first of all honor the natural entity itself and bring out the riches God has imbued it with; uses should not primarily serve humankind's immediate, self-centered needs or desires. To wrench out of something by human efforts what God never placed there is to do violence to creation and the Creator alike. To use a rare, two-thousand-year-old redwood to build patio decks is to do violence to the nature of what God created. The appropriate "use" of such a tree is to allow it to continue as a living psalm of praise to its Creator.

Second, our technological activity should reflect love for God and neighbor by expanding, not constricting, the opportunities for men and women to be the loving, joyful beings God intends them to be. Our technological activity should increase opportunities for us to freely choose and act, and thereby contribute to society.

Thus a starting point is to ask—whether as a researcher, designer, fabricator, distributor, purchaser, or user of a technological object—if that object uses entities from God's creation in a manner that respects their God-given nature and purposes, and if it increases human beings' opportunities to be the joyful, loving, creative beings God intends them to be. Technological activities that are in keeping with the command to love and attempt to meet these two criteria help make possible humanity's search for God's kingdom of shalom, a kingdom of activity, dynamism, and vibrancy, but also a kingdom of peace, harmony, and joy.

A Structure for Normativity. The discussion thus far sets forth a view, a goal, but it does not say enough about how we are to faithfully seek that vision of shalom. What we need is a structure for recognizing and organizing normative principles for valuing with respect to technological activities. According to our earlier discussion of the characteristics that should mark the normative principles guiding technological activities, such a structure should be adequate in scope, make necessary distinctions, and integrate the diversity found in society.

A helpful, compelling scheme for developing such a structure can be found in the thought and writings of the Dutch philosopher Herman Dooyeweerd.[12] He has posited the existence of fifteen "modalities," or aspects of reality, within which all human activity—including technological activity—takes place. The fifteen are as follows: (1) the arithmetic, that aspect of reality which relates to discrete, individually separate quantities or entities; (2) the spatial, that which relates to continuous extension; (3) the kinematic, that which relates to motion or movement; (4) the physical, that which relates to possession or exchange of energy; (5) the biotic, that which relates to life, the living aspects of reality; (6) the sensitive, that which relates to feelings; (7) the logical, that which relates to the making of distinctions; (8) the historical, that which relates to forming and developing human culture; (9) the lingual,

---

12. See Herman Dooyeweerd, *Roots of Western Culture: Pagan, Secular and Christian Opinions* (Toronto: Wedge, 1979). A good summary of Dooyeweerd's thought can be found in L. Kalsbeek, *Contours of a Christian Philosophy* (Toronto: Wedge, 1975).

that which relates to the development and use of symbols to convey meaning—for example, the use of language and numbers as means of communication; (10) the social, that which relates to the interactions of human beings among themselves; (11) the economic, that which relates to the stewardship of economic resources; (12) the aesthetic, that which relates to the development of, sensitivity to, and use of harmony and beauty; (13) the juridical, that which relates to the meting out of what is due entities in creation; (14) the moral, that which relates to love and the claims of love; (15) the pistic, that which relates to faith, trust, or belief.

Dooyeweerd would argue that all fifteen aspects of reality are involved in technological activities—and, for that matter, in all other human activities. But normative principles arise only from the last eight aspects, since the first seven by their very nature involve "laws" or principles that cannot be broken. They are automatically obeyed by all persons. The kinematic law of gravity and the biotic process of metabolism, for example, are necessarily followed. But the last eight of these aspects of reality all involve human choice, and all thereby involve valuing and human responsibility.

It follows that to do technology responsibly and appropriately, each of these last eight aspects must be given its due. Each one involves normative principles that must be followed if one is to fully obey the command to love in technological activities. To slight any one aspect of reality—not to give it its due—is to practice a technology that is incomplete, and to fail to live up to one's full responsibility. In being sensitive to all eight of these aspects, one will recognize and respect the natures and potentialities God has placed in his creation, behavior that will lead to the opening up of opportunities for one's fellow human beings to fulfill their God-given callings. But this will be done only if these normative principles are pursued simultaneously: all must be followed at the same time, not some to the exclusion of others.

Seeking appropriate normative principles for these eight aspects of reality leads to a normative structure that meets the three critical requirements outlined earlier. Because this approach emphasizes the multifacetedness of reality, it helps insure adequate scope and the recognition of diversity. And because this approach emphasizes the simultaneous pursuit of the resulting normative principles, it also serves to integrate the diversity found in creation.

The next part of this section suggests certain normative principles that apply to each of the eight aspects of reality. These are the normative principles for activities related to the doing of technology. As such, they represent an attempt to link basic biblical principles to valuing in technology, and serve as a guide to responsible technology.

The Normative Principles. Cultural appropriateness is the normative principle for the aspect of technological activity known as culture formation. Cultural appropriateness is achieved by making appropriate decisions regarding five sets of opposites: continuity and discontinuity, differentiation and integration, centralization and decentralization, uniformity and pluriformity, and large scale and small scale. Technicism generally assumes that only discontinuity, integration, centralization, uniformity, and large scale are good, that they represent cultural progress. But more and more examples are proving this assumption wrong. E. F. Schumacher, for instance, has shown that if we develop only large-scale technologies, we will reach a critical point beyond which control of these technologies is no longer possible.[13] That is why he has pleaded for small-scale or intermediate-sized technologies wherever appropriate.

But how is one to decide what is culturally appropriate? Of course there is no neat, magic answer to this question. One should be guided by the other normative principles, by the command to love, and by one's understanding of and respect for the God-intended diversity found within creation and humankind. Using these guides, people may sometimes conclude that a break with past practices (discontinuity) is needed, but they may make it more gradually—in a series of small steps—than they would if they were not taking cultural appropriateness into consideration.

Perhaps an example of the proper application of this principle will help. Victor Papanek, author of *Design for Human Scale,* gives an example of what he calls "minimal design intervention."[14] It concerns all five opposites mentioned, but it is especially relevant to the continuity-discontinuity facet. In Tanzania, women and young boys thresh maize, corn, and other grains to separate flour and vegetable oils from the chaff and husks. They do this backbreaking labor for eight to nine hours a day. A group of Taiwanese consultants proposed the introduction of electric grain grinders to help with this difficult and arduous task. If this idea had been implemented—assuming the availability of electricity—the entire harvest could have been ground in minutes. But concomitant with this increased productivity and efficiency would have been the destruction of social groupings and interactions that were of crucial importance in that culture. The solution to the problem was to introduce the Tanzanians to a variety of hand grinders that would reduce the stren-

13. Schumacher, *Small Is Beautiful.*
14. Victor Papanek, *Design for Human Scale* (New York: Van Nostrand Reinhold, 1983), p. 9.

uousness of the grinding activity while maintaining the social groups that had been established by this activity. In this instance we see both continuity and progress (discontinuity) being given their due. The solution chosen showed proper respect to the Tanzanian culture—its nature and peculiar strengths were recognized and taken into account.

Another example can be found in the development of nuclear power. If the principle of cultural appropriateness had been followed, the move to nuclear energy would have been more cautious. But initially it was thought that nuclear energy was *the* solution to modern energy problems, and it was developed without proper vigilance. Recently we have begun to see that this very development creates some serious difficulties. Nuclear energy is dangerous in the wrong hands, safety problems have not been fully eliminated (the safe operation of nuclear power plants and the safe disposal of nuclear wastes are still unanswered challenges), and costs are skyrocketing. In view of these problematics, there is a great danger that people will simply assume a reactionary stance. Certainly we need to develop alternative, renewable energy sources and increased conservation efforts, but it is possible that we can also find ways to responsibly develop nuclear power. To do so—to develop it in keeping with biblically based normative principles—means that development will have to be slowed down and more attention will have to be paid to the questions of radioactive wastes and safety. If it is decided that nuclear reactors are required on a limited scale, it may be necessary to build them underground for safety reasons. The need is to proceed slowly, carefully, thoughtfully.

The normative principle of cultural appropriateness was ignored in the United States' thoughtless rush to develop nuclear power. Because a technicistic mind-set was dominant, it was all too easy to assume that nuclear power—representing discontinuity, integration, centralization, uniformity, and large scale—was the way to go. Too few questions were asked; society simply plunged ahead. The ghosts of uncompleted, abandoned nuclear power plants stand today as silent testimonies against those politicians, bureaucrats, corporate executives, and technical designers who ignored the cultural normative principle.

The normative principle that emerges out of the symbolic aspect of technological activity is *information or openness*. Technological activities involve using linguistic and numerical symbols (language and numbers). In using these symbols it is important that one be open about the information to which he or she has access. For technological activities to proceed properly and for those using technological products and tools to do so responsibly and safely, there must be a constant, accurate flow of information. Closely related to this normative principle is that for the social aspect of technological activity—namely, the normative principle of *communication*. Social interaction marks technological activities; they are seldom engaged in by individuals acting alone. And clear communication is necessary if this social activity is to proceed properly and responsibly.

These two principles taken together establish the need for open communication. Open communication is essential if persons are to fulfill their responsibility as planners, doers, and users of technology. Without open communication there can be no knowledge; without knowledge there can be no fulfilling of responsibility. If a nuclear engineer is holding back vital information concerning the safe operation of a proposed nuclear power plant, how can a power company executive make a responsible decision? If a purchaser of an electrical appliance does not know the electrical use levels of competing brands, how can he or she make a responsible purchase aimed at reducing the electricity used and thereby reducing pollution and saving fossil fuel resources for future generations? Clearly, information and therefore communication are essential for loving, respectful, responsible technological activities.

The normative principle that should be followed in the economic aspect of technological activity is *stewardship*. Many economic resources—both material resources and human resources—are involved in technology. The principle of stewardship says that all of these resources are to be respected and given their due. The created nature of material resources is to be respected by being brought out and developed, not recklessly exploited. Stewardship thus condemns environmental pollution, the killing off of whole species of plants and animals, and the profligate use of precious, nonrenewable resources. But it also speaks to the use of human resources. Human work is an economic resource, but human workers are much more than economic resources. They are to be respected, treated as image bearers of God.

The aesthetic aspect of technological activity relates to harmony. Technology involves making material objects which then stand in relationship to human beings and the rest of creation. These objects should be characterized by *a delightful harmony*. They should be a joy and a delight because they work properly and are satisfying to use, and because they have a beauty of line and form.

There are three ideas inherent in the term "delightful harmony" that need to be sorted out. In *Art in Action,* Nicholas Wolterstorff distinguishes two of these ideas by defining what constitutes excellence in a spade: "A good spade is one that serves its purpose well. And that in turn consists of two things: being effective for digging holes, and proving generally good and satisfying to use for this purpose."[15] Wolterstorff first points out that a harmonious technological object must do the job it was created to do; he then points out that it should be pleasing to use. This can involve several things: that it is satisfying, both psychologically and physically, to use; that it is a delight to look at; and that it is marked by a certain grace and simplicity that is both functional and beautiful. The melding of function and beauty is at the heart of the meaning of delightful harmony.

The third facet of delightful harmony is its promotion of right relationships—a delightful harmony—between humankind and God, between differing cultures and societies, between persons within a culture or society, and between persons and the natural creation of plants, animals, and physical features. These right relationships come close to being the defining characteristics of shalom—that is, they come close to representing the vision of the creation as it would be if all the normative principles were faithfully followed.

Technology also involves the juridical, the meting out of what is due societies and cultures, human beings, and the natural creation. Here the normative principle is *justice*—all persons are to be given what is rightfully due them as God's image bearers, and the rest of creation is to be shown the respect that it is due. Injustice is to be opposed. Thus, in pursuing technological activities one is always to ask what his or her activities and decisions mean for other cultures and societies, for workers, for consumers, for future generations, for the plant and animal world, and for material resources. Technology should do justice to the material things it uses by bringing out and developing the potential God has placed in them. Will a certain technology dehumanize the workplace, displace workers, tear traditional cultures apart, violate family stability, destroy a beautiful, free-flowing river, wipe out certain plant and animal species, or waste physical resources? Or, alternatively, will this technology give due respect to fellow human beings, other cultures, and the natural creation? The normative principle of justice asks what is due every creature and object, and then seeks to safeguard it.

The moral aspect of technological activity involves love and the demands of love. The normative principle here is *caring*. Caring goes beyond justice and asks not only if technology embodies what is due persons and other entities, but if it reflects a loving care for them. In doing technology we are to act as servants, to love and care for—to

---

15. Nicholas Wolterstorff, *Art in Action: Toward a Christian Aesthetic* (Grand Rapids: Eerdmans, 1980), p. 156.

safeguard the well-being of—our neighbors, near and far, and the natural creation.

The eighth and final aspect of technological activity is the pistic aspect—that which is related to faith. The normative principle involved here is *trust*. This principle has two distinct aspects. One relates to the technological objects being produced and suggests that they must be dependable: their users must be able to count on them to meet the claims of form and function made about them. A vehicle that is marketed for rugged, off-road use must have the kind of suspension, engine, transmission, and braking power that make it suitable for such use. In addition, the appearance of an object should match its intended use. To build a vehicle that looks like an off-road vehicle but has qualities that make it suitable only for use on paved highways is to violate the normative principle of trust. A second facet of dependability is safety. One should be able to trust that a technological tool or product will be safe if put to its intended use.

The second aspect of trust is faith in Almighty God. This aspect suggests that ultimately our technological activities spring from a faith commitment. We do not relate to technology as free, autonomous scientists, public-policy makers, corporate executives, consumers, or technical designers. Instead, we do our valuing in technology in response to a faith commitment. For the Christian this faith commitment can be made only to Almighty God, the Creator of all.

Too often, however, technology is dominated by a faith commitment to technicism, a belief in a narrow, human-centered, technologically oriented vision of progress as the means to human salvation. Link technicism to an insatiable greed for material wealth, and what emerges is the picture of how technology is normally perceived and used in the Babylonian culture of modern society. Less "advanced" societies are dominated and exploited. Workers are valued when needed for production purposes, but they are discarded and forgotten as soon as "progress" terminates their economic usefulness—or they are forced into mind-numbing, routine work that violates their dignity and shows them no respect as image bearers of God. The material environment is polluted to the point that it becomes dangerous to humankind and animals, species of plants and animals are snuffed out, precious resources are wantonly wasted, and whole ecosystems are destroyed by dams, drainage projects, and deforestation programs.

The normative principles presented here—and the love and respect underlying them—point in a very different direction. It is a direction of cultural development and growth that occurs in the context of right relationships, justice, caring, harmony, and open communication. These principles point us toward God's kingdom of shalom, a kingdom only he can bring to fruition, but a kingdom that, by his grace, we can presage in the work of our hearts and hands.

But to do so we must pursue all of the normative principles suggested here simultaneously. It is not a matter of picking and choosing among them, nor a matter of pursuing all of them in isolation from each other. They are all aspects of a single norm: love. That is why they overlap, build upon each other, and reflect each other. They are not separate, discrete principles; to obey one, we must obey them all. Only then will we point toward the kingdom of shalom, that kingdom of harmony, joy, justice, love, and peace.

CHAPTER SIX

Technology and Science

IN PREVIOUS CHAPTERS TECHNOLOGY WAS DEFINED AND VIEWED AS A particular type of human cultural activity. As such, technological activities are to be engaged in responsibly—as a form of service to God, humankind, and the rest of creation—and in obedience to biblically rooted normative principles. But it has also been pointed out that our age is in the grip of a technicistic mind-set that sees men and women as autonomous beings, responsible to no one but themselves, and technology as the path to human salvation. Service and obedience have become forgotten terms.

The next five chapters take this basic perspective and flesh it out more fully and trace some of its crucial implications by examining the relationships between technology and such things as science, economics, politics, and the technological design process. This examination will contrast technology done in response to technicism with technology done in response to biblically based normative principles. Such scrutiny will help provide additional insight into how modern society has come to have its present shape.

This chapter begins this effort by exploring the relationships among science, technology, and society. One's perspective on these relationships significantly molds one's entire view of technology. For many, science and technology are the bearers of progress, the means by which we gain the understanding necessary for proper societal development. For others, an overestimation of the role of science and technology in our practical lives and an inability to disentangle the two represent the most disturbing trend in contemporary society. Scholars are also increasingly concerned with the historical interactions of science, technology, and society. Their concerns are marked by analyses of the origins and development of postindustrial society, and by explanations of the modernization of the West and of the possible extension of modernization to developing nations.

The basic purpose of this chapter is to highlight the historical development of technology, particularly its relationship to science, in order to show how science has come to decisively shape technology. To truly understand contemporary technology we need to examine and understand the link between science and technology and the historical development of that link. In so doing we will come to see how science's shaping of technology has helped lead to technicism and a technology that violates biblically based normative principles.

The first section of this chapter looks at the conventional view of the science-technology relationship and argues that a new view is needed. The following section offers a historical sketch of the connection between science and technology and its changing character in Western culture. Next the chapter examines some characteristics of modern technology that reveal the decisive influence of science. The last section analyzes how the decisive shaping of modern technology by science erects barriers that hinder the development of responsible technology.

THE SCIENCE-TECHNOLOGY RELATIONSHIP: THE CONVENTIONAL VIEW

Focusing on the science-technology relationship may strike some as strange, because conventional wisdom views this relationship as an unproblematic given. The conventional view sees science as concerned with basic, systematized knowledge and theories of the natural world. Science operates on a high level of abstraction; it deals with reality generally, seeking to develop theories of the broadest scope. Specific, concrete manifestations of reality are then explained in terms of these theories. Thus the knowledge of science is basic, fundamental, general. Technology is seen as being, at best, applied science. Technology takes the general, abstract theories and acquired knowledge of science and applies them to specific, concrete, practical situations. The physical sciences, for example, develop abstract theories and knowledge concerning gravity, motion, and the properties of physical materials; technology uses these theories and this knowledge to design and build a bridge. Clearly, the conventional view perceives science as clearly preceding and founding technology. Technology exists as an intellectual parasite living by the grace and imaginative creativity of a beneficent scientific enterprise. Technology is not seen as a possessor of fundamental knowledge in the way that science is.

Vannevar Bush, former director of the United States Office of Scientific Research and Development, expressed this standard position almost forty years ago:

Basic research leads to new knowledge. It provides scientific capital. It creates the fund from which the practical applications of knowledge must be drawn. New products and new processes do not appear full-grown. They are founded on new principles and new conceptions, which in turn are painstakingly developed by research in the purest realms of science.

Today, it is truer than ever that basic research is the pacemaker of technological progress. In the nineteenth century Yankee mechanical ingenuity, building largely upon the basic discoveries of European scientists, could greatly advance the technical arts. Now the situation is different.

A nation which depends upon others for its new basic scientific knowledge will be slow in its industrial progress and weak in its competitive position in world trade, regardless of its mechanical skill.[1]

A more recent publication by the British government supports an identical view of the interaction between science and technology. It maintains that "the justification for [basic research] is that this constitutes the fount of all new knowledge, without which the opportunities for further technical progress must eventually become exhausted."[2] If basic science is the source of all new knowledge, then technology itself is, by implication, merely a derivative enterprise. The person engaged in technology is simply applying scientific knowledge to the task at hand.

This view of technology has been held not only by modern apologists for scientific research but also by many historians of science. In the main, the history of science has been interpreted as the development and elaboration of theoretical concepts—an intellectual, internally rarified history of scientific ideas. According to this view, scientific concepts, once developed, necessarily find embodiment in technology, and technology in turn affects society.

Recent studies in the history of technology have begun to challenge this assumed dependency of technology on science. These studies strongly suggest that although science does influence technology, this influence is frequently indirect and does not provide an adequate explanation for much technological change.[3] But the conventional view of science is persistent.

1. Vannevar Bush, quoted by Edwin T. Layton, Jr., in "American Ideologies of Science and Engineering," *Technology and Culture* 17 (1976): 689.

2. Quoted by M. Gibbons and C. Johnson in "Relationship between Science and Technology," *Nature,* July 11, 1970, p. 125.

3. Among the many recent studies calling into question the accepted view of the relationship between science and technology, see Thomas Parke Hughes, "The Science-Technology Interaction: The Case of High-Voltage Power Transmission Systems," *Technology and Culture* 17 (1976): 646–62.

The close identification of technology with science and the perceived consequences of this alliance also find more popular forms of expression. The most optimistic form is the lingering belief—an aspect of technicism—that advances in science and technology are virtually synonymous with the progress of humanity. Knowledge—especially scientific knowledge—so expands human powers that humankind's fondest dreams are finally realizable. The breadth of humankind's vision for a better life is nearly matched by its actual grasp and understanding of nature. Roy MacLeod has argued that "historically, science has promoted an image of scientific rationality as the norm of truth, making that which is possible, necessary; that which is necessary, unavoidable; and that which is unavoidable, 'efficient.' "[4] Technology, when viewed as following in the wake of science, participates in this process of liberation.

The pessimistic alternative is expressed by those who harbor a profound fear that science and technology have failed us.[5] In this view, humanity's great hope that emancipation from the constraints of nature effected by science and technology would culminate in humanity's self-determination and freedom has been dashed by history. Technology appears to be slipping more and more out of human control, becoming, along with science, an independent power that holds sway over our lives and the world. Those who hold this view see technology's threat to humankind's existence and its inherent power resting firmly on the assumption that science is the basis of modern technology. For many, the haunting metaphor of Ralph Lapp is all too real: "No one, not even the most brilliant scientist alive today—really knows where science is taking us. We are aboard a train which is gathering speed, racing down a track on which there are an unknown number of switches leading to unknown destinations. No single scientist is in the engine cab and there may be demons at the switch. Most of society is in the caboose looking backward."[6]

If we are to gain a better insight into modern technology, we will need to reassess the conventional view of the science-technology relationship and in fact disabuse ourselves of the prevalent ideas that science is preeminent and that technology is simply applied science.

4. Roy MacLeod, "The 'Bankruptcy of Science' Debate: The Creed of Science and Its Critics, 1885–1900," *Science, Technology, and Human Values* 7 (Fall 1982): 2.

5. Note the title of the recent book by Colin Norman: *The God That Limps: Science and Technology in the Eighties* (New York: Norton, 1981).

6. Lapp, quoted by Alvin Toffler in *Future Shock* (New York: Bantam Books, 1971), p. 431.

A HISTORICAL PERSPECTIVE

Science and Technology: The Development of a Tentative Unity.
From antiquity until about 1600 the liberal arts were clearly separated
from the mechanical arts. The liberal arts were considered the domain
of scholars, who were able to utilize rhetorical skill and logical and
mathematical methods in establishing a science. The mechanical arts
represented the domain of "vulgar mechanics," who needed to use
their hands in such pursuits as farming, mining, and navigation, and in
such crafts as pottery. The prejudice against manual labor was deeply
ingrained in the university's structure. The contemplative life, the life
of the mind, was the ideal. Experimentation—the dissection of a ca-
daver, for example—was not considered germane to the formation of a
science and was deemed beneath the dignity of a university professor.
Logical skills in argumentation and the ability to read classical Greek
and Roman literature were the trademarks of correct knowledge and
proper academic taste.

This is not to suggest that the ancients lacked interest or ability where
mechanical or technical projects were concerned. The first complex machines produced by human beings were automatons, attempts to model
or simulate nature and to domesticate or control natural forces. Heron's
hydraulic singing birds and automaton theater, the water clock of Ath-
ens' Tower of Winds, and the elaborate planetary and calendrical display of the Antikythera Mechanism of the first century B.C. all derived
from the same tradition. This tradition sought to understand the world
through tangible technical devices or models (*theoriks*). But these technical achievements of the Greeks were usually seen as being distinct
from theoretical science, from the domain of philosophy and rhetoric.

This radical separation of the liberal arts and the mechanical arts began
to be undermined during the Italian Renaissance. It spawned a trend
toward civic aggrandizement, which brought together humanistic intel-
lectuals and groups of artisans in northern Italian city-states. Out of this
contact there developed a strong tradition of art and engineering with a
new mathematical or scientific orientation. This tradition in turn convinced some humanists of the practical value of mathematical and natural
knowledge—not as it was embedded in the systems of the Schoolmen
based on Aristotle and Aristotelian commentaries, but rather as it was
embodied in the experience and practices of those who worked with
physical materials and artifacts. In the subsequent flowering of the northern Italian city-states, one can discern how the writings and attitudes of
painters, sculptors, architects, and military engineers were used to whet
the public's appetite for security, splendor, and spectacle, and thus

forged a major link between humanistic, scientific, and technological attitudes and activities.

Leonardo da Vinci (1452–1519) was one of the first of many late fifteenth- and sixteenth-century figures who sought to forge a link between the technical construction of a desired object and the discovery of the basic structures of nature. His investigations in hydrophysics, for example, entailed not only the observation of such natural hydrological processes as cloud formation but also the solving of problems in such technical projects as artificial irrigation and the construction of canals. As an engineer, Leonardo was concerned with making practical applications of knowledge rather than searching for the rational foundation of this knowledge in a theoretical way. Knowledge of nature was equivalent to its construction, which was revealed by experimentation and deductive reasoning. For da Vinci, experimentation was an activity—involving work, invention, and labor. As Eugenio Garin has commented, "In this sense all experimentation, since it is a mediation between nature as it actually is and the realization of all the possibilities, is on the one hand an understanding of real and necessary processes, and on the other a constructive labour."[7] In the area of mechanics, Leonardo considered mathematics to be an indispensable practical aid: "Mechanics is the paradise of the mathematical sciences, because by means of it one comes to the fruits of mathematics."[8]

This initial intellectualizing or "scientizing" of technical activities—which actually began with painting and architecture in the sixteenth century—had a major, twofold impact. First, it emphasized the elements of scientific knowledge present in the practical or mechanical arts. This emphasis found a ready audience just at the time when printing came into existence and made it possible to disseminate such knowledge beyond the confines of the universities. The publication and subsequent reprinting of numerous books on anatomy, painting, architecture, military engineering, machine construction, and navigation, as well as such classic texts as Euclid's *Elements,* attest to this enthusiasm for knowledge.

This interest in the elements of scientific knowledge present in the practical arts went hand in hand with a second, reciprocal effect: the influence of the practical arts on science. As the applicability of science to practice became an increasingly widespread assumption, it was ar-

7. Eugenio Garin, *Science and Civil Life in the Italian Renaissance,* trans. Peter Munz (Garden City, NY.: Doubleday, 1969), pp. 65–66.
8. Da Vinci, quoted by E. J. Dijksterhuis in *The Mechanization of the World Picture,* trans. C. Dikshoorn (New York: Oxford University Press, 1969), p. 256.

gued that scientific knowledge not only could but should be enriched by the kind of direct experience of nature that artisans alone had embraced during the Middle Ages. There was an insistence that knowledge must be sought directly from nature and from the results of experiments on natural objects. This insistence shaped treatises on painting, like those of Leon Battista Alberti and Leonardo da Vinci, works on mining and military engineering, like those of Georgius Agricola and Guido Ubaldo, and books on anatomy, like that of Andreas Vesalius.[9]

To be sure, the speculative tradition of natural philosophy associated with Aristotle did not immediately wither under the attacks waged by disaffected humanists and rising artisan-engineers. Instead, the two traditions developed in an atmosphere of tension throughout the Renaissance and the early modern era, and the Aristotelian tradition remained dominant within the major universities well into the seventeenth century. But over time the development of new practical concerns became increasingly important.

A century after Leonardo da Vinci, Francis Bacon took a decidedly strong position against the idea of a division between the mechanical arts (technology) and both science and the liberal arts more generally, and between manual labor and intellectual work. Bacon formulated a concept of human mastery over nature that was much clearer and more forceful than any previous articulations of it, and assigned this mastery a prominent place among human concerns. There is in Bacon's thought an emphasis on the unity of truth and utility. The unity of the mechanical arts and the sciences is guaranteed by the adoption of a new method: the empirical, experimental, and systematic study of phenomena. Only then do the twin human intentions of knowledge and power coincide in a single intention because "that which is considered a cause in the theoretical sphere is considered a rule in the operational sphere."[10] In the third aphorism of *The New Organon* (or *True Directions Concerning the Interpretations of Nature*), Bacon expressed this idea with style: "Human knowledge and human power meet in one; for where the cause is not known the effect cannot be produced. Nature to be commanded must be obeyed; and that which in contemplation is as the cause is in

9. For a general discussion, see Paolo Rossi, *Philosophy, Technology and the Arts in the Early Modern Era: 1400–1700*, ed. Benjamin Nelson, trans. Salvator Attanasio (New York: Harper & Row, 1970), pp. 1–17. More specific texts include Leon B. Alberti's *On Painting*, trans. John R. Spencer, rev. ed. (New Haven: Yale University Press, 1966); Georgius Agricola, *De Re Metallica* (New York: Dover Publishing, 1950); and, on the Italian engineers, Stillman Drake and I. E. Drabkin, trans., *Mechanics in Sixteenth-Century Italy: Selections from Tartaglia, Benedetti, Guido Ubaldo, and Galileo* (Madison: University of Wisconsin Press, 1967).

10. Rossi, *Philosophy, Technology and the Arts in the Early Modern Era*, p. 161.

operation as the rule."[11] Bacon proposed a path to understanding that
proceeded directly from the senses by induction and by a course of
methodically conducted experiments: "In order to penetrate into the
inner and further recesses of nature, it is necessary that both notions and
axioms be derived from things by a more sure and guarded way, and that
a method of intellectual operation be introduced altogether better and
more certain."[12]

Bacon's aim was to make science and the mechanical arts useful. His
goal was humanitarian: to improve humanity's lot and to "cultivate
truth in charity." This task required human beings to master nature, the
highest and most excellent level of power. Bacon believed that obtain-
ing power over one's fellow human beings was a clearly inferior action
because it lacked charity. A crucial aspect of Bacon's argument—and
one that he and many of his readers assumed—is that it is only through
the progress of the arts and sciences that mastery of nature is achieved.

Bacon believed in the utilitarian value of mastering nature, but he
also had a deeper reason for arguing for the preeminence of such mastery among human concerns. He believed that religion was engaged
with science and the arts in a mutual effort to overcome the damage
incurred by humankind's expulsion from Paradise: "For man by the fall
fell at the same time from his state of innocency and from his dominion
over creation. Both of these losses, however, can even in this life be in
some part repaired; the former by religion and faith, the latter by arts
and sciences."[13] This argument depends first of all upon the idea that
the Fall had two consequences: loss of moral innocence and loss of
dominion over creation. It also depends upon the claim that two separate agencies—religion on the one hand and the arts and sciences on the
other—can mitigate the evil effects of the Fall. The beneficent double
progress of religion and of the arts and sciences was assumed to be
divinely ordained and innocent of evil. Bacon did not suspect that scientific and technological advance could be anything but ethical and profit-
able to humanity.

The unity of knowledge and its utility was later echoed by René Descartes (1596–1650) in his *Discourse on Method* (1637):

> But as soon as I had acquired some general notions concerning Phys-
> ics . . . I believed that I could not keep them concealed without greatly
> sinning against the law which obliges us to procure, as much as in us lies,
> the general good of all mankind. For they caused me to see that it is

11. Francis Bacon, *The New Organon* (Indianapolis: Bobbs-Merrill, 1960), p. 39.
12. Bacon, *The New Organon*, p. 42.
13. Bacon, *The New Organon*, p. 267.

possible to attain knowledge which is very useful in life, and that, instead of that speculative philosophy which is taught in the Schools, we may find a practical philosophy by means of which, knowing the forces and the actions of fire, water, air, the stars, heavens and all other bodies that environ us, as distinctly as we know the different crafts of our artisans, we can in the same way employ them in all those uses to which they are adapted, and thus render ourselves the masters and possessors of nature. This is not merely to be desired with a view to the invention of an infinity of arts and crafts which enable us to enjoy without any trouble the fruits of the earth and all the good things which are to be found there, but also principally because it brings about the preservation of health, which is without doubt the chief blessing and the foundation of all other blessings in this life.[14]

Although Descartes' method took a more mathematical and mechanical turn than did Bacon's, the goal was the same: to discover "the principles, or first causes of all that is or can be in the world,"[15] and, having done so, to construct and recast nature in a technical way. The construction of nature—that is, technical realization—was perceived as going hand in hand with the scientific knowledge of nature. Clearly, Western thought no longer supported the strict separation of the scholar's realm of theoretical science from the artisan's or mechanic's realm of practical invention and building.

This declared unity of the knowledge generated by the arts and sciences and its utility in practical affairs was a dominant concept well into the eighteenth century. Indeed, in Diderot and d'Alembert's *Encyclopédie,* the massive work (published between 1751 and 1772 in twenty-eight volumes) that was a major influence during the Enlightenment, science and technology were discussed without any indication that they were separate categories of human cultural activity. Present-day distinctions between "pure" science and "applied" science (technology) were actually not introduced until the nineteenth century, when the utility of "pure" science became important.[16]

Despite Francis Bacon's announcement of the marriage of science and the mechanical arts at the beginning of the seventeenth century, it was almost three centuries before the marriage was fully consummated. In practice, both continued to be essentially separate enterprises. This

14. Cited in *The Philosophical Works of Descartes,* ed. Elizabeth S. Haldane and G. R. T. Ross, 2 vols. (Cambridge: Cambridge University Press, 1969), 1: 119–20.

15. Descartes, *Philosophical Works,* 1: 121.

16. See I. B. Cohen, "Fear and Distrust of Science in Historical Perspective," *Science, Technology, and Human Values* 6 (Summer 1981): 23.

separation did not necessarily imply a lack of contact, however, or even a loss of vision or desire to fulfill Bacon's dream. The next two subsections sketch—in broad historical strokes—the interdependence of science and technology during this long period of time. Following this sketch is a consideration of the emergence, in the late nineteenth century, of a scientific technology in which science and technology engaged in intense interaction.

The Reliance of Science on Technology. Up until the nineteenth century, the reliance of science on technology was characterized by three things: a tendency to introduce metaphors drawn from the realm of technology into the study of nature; the use of technologically developed objects in scientific work, which often played a role in encouraging scientific thought and knowledge; and the development of technological instruments and apparatuses that influenced experimental science.

The diversity and intricacy of European technology during the Middle Ages and throughout the Renaissance and early modern period were—contrary to popular opinion—extremely impressive. The construction of large cathedrals, the invention of the weight-driven clock, the changes in methods of farming and mining, and the harnessing of water and wind as energy sources mark this as an extremely inventive era. But all these advances were not rooted in scientific theories and knowledge. The work of cathedral builders, miners, navigators, and other innovators ran far ahead of the limited scientific knowledge of the time. In fact, there was little contact or dialogue between the camps of science and technology—between, for instance, those involved in mechanical inventions and those interested in developing a science of mechanics.

As we saw earlier, it was not until the Renaissance and the appearance of the artist-engineer—embodied by Leonardo da Vinci—that there was much interaction between technology (the mechanical and practical arts) and theoretical science, particularly mathematics. The Renaissance conviction that mathematics should be applicable to the mechanical arts had been illustrated largely by the role that mathematical proportions played in architectural structures, machine design, and human anatomy, and by the Pythagorean number theory of harmony in music. The advancements of the seventeenth century, especially the work of Galileo (1564–1642) and Descartes, offered a reinterpretation of that relationship, a reinterpretation presuming a "mechanization of the world-picture." The machine and its scientific conception in a quantitative theory of mechanics—or, better, the machine as embodied mathematics—were seen as providing a key to the interpretation of nature and its proper mastery. The machine came to be seen as the dominant metaphor for nature and deeply influenced the study of it.

Galileo believed in this relationship of machine and nature and in the use of technological objects in scientific thought and knowledge. He had seen machines such as water pumps and hoists being used in the Venetian shipyards and had seen them described and illustrated in Ramelli's *Le Diverse e Artificiose Machine* (1588). These beliefs and influences shaped his scientific work. Galileo's approach to nature rested on the firm conviction that the structure of reality was essentially mathematical. He believed that the mathematical forms of thought corresponded to a mathematical order underlying the world of sense perception:

> Philosophy is written in this grand book, the universe, which stands continually open to our gaze. But the book cannot be understood unless one first learns to comprehend the language and read the letters in which it is composed. It is written in the language of mathematics, and its characters are triangles, circles and other geometric figures, without which it is humanly impossible to understand a single word of it; without these, one wanders about in a dark labyrinth.[17]

But, Galileo noted, the essential simplicity of the mathematical laws of nature was frequently obscured by things like friction and air resistance. If one imagined the removal of these impediments, he claimed, the true simplicity of the laws became apparent. This process of idealization was also applicable in experimental procedures in which one used devices that approximated the ideal as closely as possible, such as friction-free planes and pulleys and weightless strings. Out of such thought emerged the scientific theories of the vacuum, atmospheric pressure, and mechanics. But it was technical, practical machines that preceded and stimulated such scientific theories.

After positing this theory of nature, Galileo turned his attention to developing a quantitative analysis of machines. No longer would a machine be judged solely by such qualitative criteria as whether or not it was aesthetically satisfying, well-built, and able to function without failing in emergencies. Now quantitative criteria would be applied: How much power did the machine produce? How efficient was it? Did it obey or illustrate mathematical theories of structure?

While Galileo brought mathematical analysis to bear on machines and other artifacts, Descartes took a further and historically more de-

---

17. From Galileo's "The Assayer," found in *Discoveries and Opinions of Galileo*, ed. Stillman Drake (Garden City, N.Y.: Doubleday-Anchor Books, 1957), pp. 237–38.

cisive step. He claimed that nature itself was mechanistic in character. The world was cast in the image of an artifact, contrived by a geometer-God. Natural bodies and artifacts produced by skillful artisans differed only in size. In fact, Descartes believed, those most adept at constructing automatons were best suited to describe the true processes of natural phenomena—the mechanisms hidden in them. For Descartes, a growing tree and running clockwork were, for all intents and purposes, the same. He saw the natural creation as a machine whose construction—and therefore, in principle, also its reconstruction—was subject to deductive understanding. Technological activity not only involved the use of the hands in traditional arts and crafts, but included the mind's capacity to utilize mechanical concepts such as shape, size, quantity, and motion, and to construct (or reconstruct) the world machine. All notions of animation, internal spontaneity, and purpose were rigorously excluded in this view of nature. Change was nothing but the result of the mechanical collisions of minute particles, called corpuscles or atoms, the mechanical motions of which could thoroughly explain the world. Either one sought mechanical explanations or else one had to "renounce all hope of ever comprehending anything in Physics."[18]

The dependence of science on technical devices for a view of and approach to nature dramatically altered the human-nature relationship itself. This mechanical world became an *object* to be mastered and commanded by means of humankind's scientific knowledge and technical know-how. Nature became increasingly viewed as a plaything, a treasure chest whose sole purpose and meaning was to satisfy humankind's wants and desires. Nature stood in the shadow of humankind's technical capacity to alter it to serve its own ends.

The work of Galileo and Descartes illustrates that technological devices and machines (in our terminology, "technological objects") served both to stimulate the development of scientific theories and knowledge and, as Descartes in particular illustrated, to provide metaphors that led to the development of models of a broad understanding of nature.

A third and perhaps more intimate connection between science and technology lies in the area of scientific instrumentation and apparatuses that enhance experimental approaches in science. For a scientist the fascination of experiments is many-sided. The equipment itself has a special charm: it is an irresistible combination of gadgetry and artistry. There is equipment for making measurements such as clocks, meters, and graduated cylinders. There are also apparatuses for extending the

18. Christian Huygens, *Treatise on Light,* trans. S. P. Thompson (London: Macmillan, 1912), p. 3.

human senses, such as microscopes, telescopes, and amplifiers. At the heart of the experiment is the equipment that enables experimenters to isolate the effect they wish to study and to separate the possible causes of it.

During the seventeenth and eighteenth centuries, this particular relationship of science and technology led to the development of ever more sophisticated instruments and procedures. The role of measurement was given increasing importance in scientific disciplines. When increasing demands spurred by the Industrial Revolution were made for new synthetic materials, more precise machine parts, and more uniform standards of weights and measures, these technological achievements internal to science were exploited in ever larger arenas.

In summary, technology provided a stimulus for the development of science by doing three things: (1) introducing technical metaphors that were used in developing scientific theories or models such as the mechanical view of nature; (2) providing firsthand experience with technological objects, which encouraged the development of scientific thought and knowledge; and (3) influencing experimental methods of science through the development of apparatuses and instruments. It is important to note that in all three of these ways technology was leading science, not following science, as conventional wisdom would have it.

The Reliance of Technology on Science. The discussion thus far has made it clear that science relied on technology during the centuries prior to the emergence of modern technology in the nineteenth century. But there was also a countercurrent during this time period that involved the reliance of technology on science. This countercurrent was marked by technological developments, particularly those in the productive sector, which placed increasing demands on science for appropriate techniques, methods, and discoveries. This current became particularly strong as the Industrial Revolution gathered strength in the eighteenth and nineteenth centuries.

Although it is generally agreed that the dependence of technological progress upon science has increased substantially during the course of industrialization, there are widely varying opinions about the degree of that dependence. Some have argued that technological progress was already heavily dependent upon science in the early stages of the British Industrial Revolution—that in fact numerous intimate networks linked scientists and the business community.[19] Others have stressed the trial-and-error nature of technological developments. It has also been sug-

19. See "The Historiography of Technical Progress," in Nathan Rosenberg's *Inside the Black Box: Technology and Economics* (New York: Cambridge University Press, 1983), p. 13.

gested that in the pre-industrial period, science and technology were isolated from one another. In 1963 A. R. Hall, a historian of science, said of pre-industrial technology, "We have not much reason to believe that, in the early stages, at any rate, learning or literacy had anything to do with it; on the contrary, it seems likely that virtually all the techniques of civilization up to a couple of hundred years ago were the work of men as uneducated as they were anonymous."[20] But this is certainly an overstatement. The Renaissance tradition of the artist-engineers and their use of mathematics in public-works technology simply cannot be downplayed in a historical consideration. Nor can we dismiss the experience of Galileo and his contemporaries in the seventeenth century.

One's view of science significantly affects one's perception of the relationship between science and technology. If one defines science as highly systematized knowledge placed within the framework of a well-formulated theory, one can claim that this type of knowledge probably had minimal influence before the late nineteenth and twentieth centuries. The impact of technology on science thus defined was much greater than the impact of science on technology. If, on the other hand, one stresses or selects scientific procedures—particularly experimental and testing procedures—then one can detect an earlier and more intimate dependence of technology on science. Although *scientific knowledge* was not required for technological innovation in a wide range of industrial activities, there were a number of areas in which the use of *scientific methods* became pronounced. Indeed, a conscious attempt to employ scientific methods in the crafts and industrial arts is apparent from the mid-eighteenth century onward.

A classic example is the work of James Watt (1736–1819). He performed many experiments with steam in order to improve the steam engine. His eventual partnership with Matthew Boulton created a firm that was responsible for the building of many steam engines for British factories and mines. A second example is provided by the English engineer John Smeaton (1724–1792). Before designing and building waterwheels, he frequently made extensive experimental tests on model waterwheels in order to improve their efficiency. Smeaton undertook similar systematic studies, including model building, in his efforts to improve the efficiency of the Newcomen steam engine. Because it required huge amounts of coal to function, it could be used only in mining areas. By replacing the old intuitive methods of craftsmen-designers with more exact and systematic testing methods, Smeaton discovered a way to double the efficiency of the engine without radically altering its design.

20. A. R. Hall, quoted by Rosenberg in "The Historiography of Technical Progress," p. 13.

This use of scientific methods to advance technology can also be documented in a number of other fields. In the nineteenth century, shortages of materials such as saltpeter, soda, and steel began to limit industrial output in the chemical and engineering industries. Extensive efforts were made to develop systematic methods by which these materials could be produced and their quality ensured. There are numerous examples: the efforts to improve the quality of steel, to improve the construction of locomotives, to guarantee the purity of yeasts in the brewing industry, and to produce artificial fertilizers.

The persons who introduced these scientific methods into technology were seldom contributors to the scientific field—in most cases they knew little about science. When they succeeded, it was not so much by applying contemporary scientific theories or knowledge as by launching a frontal attack on a recognized technical problem. The search for new and improved sources of power and the economic drive to cut costs and produce raw materials and manufactured goods more efficiently represent two major themes in this relationship of technology to science.

Scientific Technology. We have noted that before the nineteenth century there were few technical inventions that were directly based on scientific discoveries. Rather, inventions were based almost solely on empirical insights with no discernible direct scientific input. Many of those working in technology employed certain scientific methods—that is, utilized controlled studies with various parameters and variables—but there was no direct translation of a scientific principle or discovery into a technical object. The paths from science to technology and from technology to science were generally circuitous.

But by the nineteenth century the search had begun for a more direct path between science and technology. The intense interaction that occurred resulted in a scientific technology. It seemed that the vision of Leonardo da Vinci and Francis Bacon would at last be realized. The proposed marriage between science and technology was at last to be consummated.

The results were far-reaching and decisive. Not only were technology and science changed in the process, but so were other institutions. The industrial research laboratory was established, engineering and technical schools were created, craftsmen were gradually displaced by engineers and scientists, and new bodies of systematic knowledge—engineering sciences—were developed within technology proper. The relationship between scientific developments and technological innovations—up until this time poorly structured and basically unsystematic—was placed on a firmer foundation. Technological growth, actuated by political-economic interests and the requirements of wartime research, led to increased industrial research and development, to independent institutions of applied research, and to a shift of technical education from the shops to academic settings. In short, technology was increasingly viewed as a science with its own methods, knowledge, and engineering theories; science in turn found its general theories concretized in specific technical situations.

It would take us too far afield to highlight all these developments. But the formation of the engineering sciences gets at a fundamental issue in the interaction of science and technology and therefore requires further consideration. The issue is how science, with its characteristics of analysis, abstractness, and idealization, interacts with technology, with its expressed intent to solve concrete problems.

The rise of scientific technology was a movement in which engineers in particular borrowed methods from physics and chemistry in order to develop a science tailored to the needs of engineering practice. An example from nineteenth-century American history illustrates the beginning phase of this process. As early as the 1830s an enthusiastic group of scientists, technologists, and reformers wished to foster a connection between Newtonian mechanics—a part of classical physics—and the "golden age" of mechanical invention. James Renwick, a professor at Columbia College, wrote two books in an attempt to bridge the gap. The first, *The Elements of Mechanics* (1832), was a straightforward exposition of the science of mechanics. The second book, *Applications of the Science of Mechanics to Practical Purposes* (1842), gave an overview of the mechanical technology of the day. The first book would not have been very helpful to a practicing engineer designing, say, waterwheels. But the principles of the first book were not embodied in the second to any great extent. The second book articulated some maxims or rules that could guide the technologist, such as "In a given undershot wheel, if the quantity of water expended be given, the useful effect is as the square of the velocity"; and, "In a given undershot wheel, if the aperture whence the water flows be given, the effect is as the cube of the velocity."[21] Both of these rules express a quantitative relationship between science and humanmade devices. The rules are certainly not derivable from the principles of mechanics—that is, from abstract scientific theories and knowledge—but they are the result of borrowing and utilizing the *methods* of science to found new technological sciences.

By 1900 the engineering sciences represented a fairly complex system of knowledge. It ranged from how-to rules in handbooks to highly systematic sciences dealing with such issues as the strength of materials, the theory of elasticity, and the theory of structures. To the outsider the latter are hardly distinguishable from the theories of a basic science like physics.

The similarities and differences between the two, however, help explain why technologists began to develop the engineering sciences. First, there are the similarities: both engineering science and basic science conform to the same physical laws, although one deals with humanmade devices and the other with natural entities and events. They are also similar in that their tenets are built up and disseminated through similar cultural means such as textbooks, articles, and classroom and research teaching. And they are both cumulative in the sense that they build on previous knowledge.

But there are also important differences between basic science and the engineering sciences. The major purpose of basic science is the acquisition of knowledge about physical structures and their interactions, while the long-range goal of the engineering sciences is the creation of objects, although knowledge-producing activities are embedded in this larger problem-solving activity.

Because of these differing goals, the two bodies of knowledge differ in both style and substance. This is apparent in the way the knowledge is formulated, the problems to which the knowledge is adapted, and the depth of detail the knowledge is designed to provide. Although there are elements of idealization in the engineering sciences—for example, its macroscopic model of a beam as a bundle of fibers—it hardly ever involves idealization at the microscopic atomic-molecular level. The engineering sciences prefer to exclude structural explanations that incorporate nonobservable entities such as atoms and molecules, but instead focus on empirical quantitative relationships which relate observable entities and their properties. The engineering sciences by their very nature are less abstract and idealized than the basic sciences; they are much closer to the ''real'' world.

The nineteenth-century movement to recast and develop engineering knowledge into a form analogous to the theoretical knowledge of basic science was fueled by a variety of motives. For some it represented the final step in a long process toward a thoroughly ''scientized'' technology. Technology, too, would finally be able to claim the certainty, glamour, and mantle of immunity long attributed to science. Many engineers were in fact willing to be called applied scientists, to downplay the role that creative design plays in technological activity. Others viewed the engineering sciences as producing data that enabled them to bypass the absence of a useful quantitative theory. They could get on with technological projects when no useful theoretical knowledge was available. For both of these groups the engineering sciences provided increased control over recalcitrant nature, and increasingly they began to view basic, theoretical science and its methods and results as instrumental in a larger technological context. This complex and reciprocal interaction of science and technology that developed in the nineteenth century has culminated in the twentieth century in the modern industrial and governmental research laboratories. Collaborative interdisciplinary research is carried out by teams of scientists and technologists in these laboratories.

The precursor of the modern industrial research laboratory was the German dye industry of the late nineteenth century. Here chemical research was used in the development of new products. Later this type of interdisciplinary research found a home in the electrical industry—for example, in the General Electric Research Laboratory founded in 1906. The growth of this type of research and development laboratory in the United States is impressive: from one thousand in 1927 to well over five thousand forty years later.

The concentrated work undertaken on a specific problem or a mission-oriented project in these laboratories blurs the line between science and technology. As part of a large research complex, those trained in one discipline often switch roles and participate in and contribute to work in other areas. Scientists sometimes do technology, and technologists sometimes do science. The contemporary interaction between basic science and technology has therefore resulted in a diversity of activities. The activities of the modern research establishment may (1) incorporate scientific work so long established that it has become part of the common understanding of the technological community, (2) rely specifically upon recent scientific work and do the additional scientific work needed to fill certain gaps before the technological project can be considered feasible, and (3) enlist scientists for the applied scientific work necessary for a particular technological task.

This modern diversity of activities cautions one not to overstate the dependence of technology on science. Even in the twentieth century, science cannot be viewed as the father of technology. Technology is not reducible to the application of prior scientific knowledge. The doing of technology builds up its own repository of knowledge—knowledge of skills, methods, techniques, and designs that do or do not work. This knowledge often precedes and transcends scientific knowledge and explanation. In addition, the technological needs and desires of society often set the agenda for scientific research. Nevertheless, the dominant trend in modern technology increasingly considers science—its methods, knowledge, characteristics, and discoveries—as the standard for technological activity.

CHARACTERISTICS OF MODERN TECHNOLOGY

In order to assess the culmination of the ways in which scientific methods and outlooks have come to decisively shape technology, it may be beneficial to briefly compare modern technology to earlier or classical technology. Although there are both similarities and differences between modern and classical technology, for our purposes we will highlight four distinctive features of modern technology.

Material Resources. The material resources used in early technology typically consisted of basic raw materials readily found in nature. Humanity's environment was to a great extent natural, and the required materials, if not readily at hand, were usually obtained from nearby sites. Modern technology has dramatically altered that situation. It often demands highly refined and processed materials specifically developed to have certain desirable properties—for example, plastics, alloys, and synthetic semiconductor crystals. These materials already incorporate and reflect a prior scientific-technological activity. They are caught up in technology's drive toward ever-greater artificiality and scientific abstraction.

Tools, Machines, and Energy Sources. It is evident that there has been a dramatic change in the tools, machines, and energy sources utilized in technological processes. Early technology relied almost exclusively on hand tools and power generated by human and animal effort and by the use of materials such as wood and moving water. In modern technology, human skills, both technical and mental, have become increasingly embodied in machines, automated production processes, procedural systems, and robots. Their use necessarily requires that a great deal of analysis, planning, and research be done before the production process can begin. Similarly, energy sources such as electrical and nuclear power require extensive scientific and technological sophistication before they can be harnessed.

Knowledge and Methods. Modern technology can also be distinguished from classical by the knowledge and methods it uses. Classical technology was largely guided by tacit knowledge of the materials to be technically formed. The crafting methods to be used were learned in a family or a guild and handed down from generation to generation. The craftsmen or artisans worked with particular objects and had to know all their specific properties. Such knowledge could not be specified in a formal deductive account. In fact, no description of artisans' techniques nor of the materials and objects on which they worked could consist of anything more than the simplest elements of the subject. Occasionally this knowledge was expressed in the form of rules. Today we tend to depreciate them by referring to them as "rules of thumb" or by describing them as "crude" or "empirical,"[22] but these rules harbor genuine knowledge, however incomplete they may seem to the unversed. Of necessity craftsmen had to develop a personal, tacit knowledge of their materials and techniques and what they could do with them if they were to produce finely crafted artifacts. There was a subtle interaction between worker and material.

In modern technology this tacit knowledge has been supplemented— or, all too often, supplanted—by other forms of knowledge: the knowledge acquired by the systematic application of experimental and testing methods, and the knowledge that is rooted in a scientific understanding of physical entities and their patterned interactions. Sometimes there are scientific theories and knowledge concerning reality that the technologist can readily adapt and use in solving a technical problem. But more often new knowledge and findings are needed; what science has discovered and theorized about is too abstract or too general to be of much help with the immediate, concrete problem at hand.

In the latter case, modern technology has increasingly replaced the so-called trial-and-error methods of the past with a vast array of systematic and scientific methods. These range in scope from testing methods such as towing tanks and wind tunnels, experimental parameters variation, similitude techniques, and mathematical and physical modeling, to scientific or quantitative design techniques and systems engineering. Modern technology's dependence on these methods is increasing. Although these methods and approaches can be used to address a particular technological need, they are also frequently employed in research efforts to create a general fund of scientific knowledge, which is then tapped in future situations.

It is clear that craftsmen's intimate sense of their materials and their resolve to solve an immediate particular problem have slowly been replaced by more scientific, disinterested approaches. These methods require a great deal of abstraction, generalization, and idealization if they

22. See Edwin T. Layton, Jr., "Technology and Science, or 'Vive La Petite Difference,'" in *Philosophy of Science Association, 1976*, vol. 2, ed. F. Suppe and P. D. Asquith (East Lansing, Mich.: Philosophy of Science Association, 1977), p. 174.

are to meet with any success. In this endeavor, however, many constitutive elements are lost, neglected, or, more often than not, deemed irrelevant.

Today it is impossible to regard modern technology, with its dynamic effects and highly sophisticated methods, as a mere craft supplemented by ingenious inspirations. The scientific influence on technology is fully evident and, as we have seen, consists in the utilization of both methods and findings of scientific research. Because the knowledge component of modern technology has become more detailed and explicitly quantitative, this knowledge is being embodied and objectified in computer programs and systems engineering approaches as procedural systems. These procedural or control systems are then used as schemes for the production, management, and use of technological objects. If the worldview of the past saw nature as a machine—as mechanical in structure and function—then the shift today, as Marx Wartofsky has indicated, is to "an information and control system, with memory, feedback, decision procedures, orientation, even teleology. The calculating device becomes a control device."[23] The control of technological processes has passed from the hands and minds of craftsmen and artisans to quantitative, often computerized systems and those who have created them.

The Tools and Products of Technology. The complexity of modern technological objects represents one of the most striking differences between classical and modern technology. Not only do many of the technological tools and products of today have a large number of component parts, but each of these parts is also highly differentiated in nature and function. This differentiation in turn requires elaborate patterns of integration, which adds to the complexity. The internal integration required for the proper functioning of a car's engine is an example. By contrast, classical technological objects were relatively simple. To be fair, they were sometimes composed of numerous parts—witness Gothic cathedrals, Roman aqueducts, Egyptian pyramids, and seventeenth-century windmills. Some, such as the intricate mechanisms of early Greek mechanical automatons, even possessed a measure of complexity. But this complexity was due to the repeated use of a few basic mechanisms. Nowhere in classical technology does one find an intricate web of internally dependent, highly differentiated parts as one does today in modern technological objects.

23. Marx Wartofsky, "Philosophy of Technology," in *Current Research in Philosophy of Science*, ed. P. D. Asquith and H. E. Kyburg, Jr. (East Lansing, Mich.: Philosophy of Science Association, 1979), p. 174.

THE HEGEMONY OF SCIENCE IN TECHNOLOGY

This chapter's recital of the development of modern technology has allowed us to follow the historical movement from a technology centered on crafts toward a technology heavily influenced by and dependent on scientific methods and knowledge. The result has been the "scientizing" of technology. This development of an intimate interaction between science and technology raises a barrier to the pursuit of a responsible technology done in keeping with biblically based normative principles. In this last section of the chapter we first consider the exact nature and results of the hegemony of science in technology, and then consider the consequences of this hegemony for following normative principles.

The Nature of Science's Hegemony. In the previous sections of this chapter we have seen how, over a long period of time, science and technology have evolved from activities that were largely separate and distinct in nature into activities with many interactions and cross-fertilizations. In this evolution technology has gradually appropriated many of the methodologies, approaches, and findings of science.

Crucial to understanding the nature of the impact of science on technology is recognizing that science, as it is practiced and viewed in modern society, often slides into scientism. The essence of scientism is to regard science not merely as a very active and efficacious force but as the standard to which reality should conform and by which various cultural manifestations are to be judged. One of the most deep-seated tendencies of our modern times is to exaggerate the role of science in human affairs and thereby to treat science as the dominant actor or force in culture. In scientism there is an overriding proclivity toward substituting the analytical results, models, and abstractions of science for reality itself. Two characteristics of science have had a particularly strong impact on how modern technology is done, and when the practice of science degenerates into scientism, their negative impact on technology is hard to exaggerate. These characteristics are science's method of analysis and synthesis, and its abstract, theoretical, explanatory nature.

The first of these—science's method of analysis and synthesis—emerged from the scientific revolution of the seventeenth century. A hundred years ago John Stuart Mill described it "as the method of detail; of treating wholes by separating them into parts . . . and breaking every question into pieces before attempting to solve it."[24] This method

---

24. John Stuart Mill, cited by Arnold Pacey in *The Maze of Ingenuity: Ideas and Idealism in the Development of Technology* (New York: Holmes & Meier Publishers, 1975), p. 138.

of analysis created the possibility of breaking down the complexities of physical phenomena—for example, the gravitational attraction between terrestrial and celestial bodies—into several distinct areas: such as earth-apple, earth-moon, and earth-sun relationships. In addition, each isolated phenomenon was reduced to what were considered its primary and secondary qualities. Primary qualities—such as those of space, time, mass, motion, and quantity—were considered to be objectively real. Secondary qualities—such as taste, color, and smell—were considered to be subjective, qualities observers attributed to entities; they were not "real." Galileo, a strong proponent of this way of thinking, explained the distinction between primary and secondary qualities in this memorable passage:

> As soon as I form a conception of a material or corporeal substance, I simultaneously feel the necessity of conceiving that it has boundaries of some shape or other; that relatively to others it is great or small; that it is in this or that place, in this or that time; that it is in motion or at rest; that it touches, or does not touch, another body; that it is unique, rare, or common; nor can I, by any act of imagination, disjoin it from these qualities. But I do not find myself absolutely compelled to apprehend it as necessarily accompanied by such conditions as that it must be white or red, bitter or sweet, sonorous or silent, smelling sweetly or disagreeably; and if the senses had not pointed out these qualities language and imagination alone could never have arrived at them. Therefore I think that these tastes, smells, colors, etc., with regard to the object in which they appear to reside, are nothing more than mere names. They exist only in the sensitive body, for when the living creature is removed all these qualities are carried off and annihilated, although we have imposed particular names upon them, and would fain persuade ourselves that they truly and in fact exist. I do not believe that there exists anything in external bodies for exciting tastes, smells, and sounds, etc., except size, shape, quantity, and motion.[25]

In the hands of many seventeenth-century scientists, this "method of detail" with its quantitative emphasis became far more than an operational method to be applied in various situations. The method largely determined what one took to be real and of primary importance. The method also contained a constructive impulse and no doubt influenced the mechanical view of nature that both Galileo and Descartes adopted. Once the basic elements of reality have been identified and quantified, one can reconstruct reality much like one assembles a machine.

25. Galileo, cited by Lewis Mumford in *Technics and Civilization* (New York: Harcourt, Brace & World, 1963), p. 48. This is a slightly different translation than that found in Drake, *Discoveries and Opinions of Galileo,* pp. 274, 276.

Despite expressing certain reservations about this method of detail, Isaac Newton, the great English polymath, was able to accomplish much with it. In his *Principia* (1687) there is an obvious emphasis on piecemeal and limited inquiry. In examining "the system of the world," Newton deliberately isolated certain factors and neatly side-stepped others about which he was ignorant. Newton actually had little insight into the nature of the operation of gravitation. But he refrained from making hypotheses and restricted his attention to exploiting the mathematical aspects of what he considered to be the relevant factors. He began his mathematical description in a most abstract and limited way, and then later extended it in a process of synthesis to more compli-cated situations.

The application of the method of detail was also extended to practical and technical problems. As early as the 1650s William Petty used this procedure to organize a work force of a thousand "untrained" men whose task it was to make a survey of Ireland. This division of labor was also carried over into the workshop where many surveyors' instru-ments were made. Petty divided "the art of making instruments, as also of using them, into many parts."[26]

Today, this method of detail—of breaking a phenomenon or a situa-tion into its component parts, farming out responsibilities for working on these parts, and then reassembling the whole—is so common in both technical and scientific enterprises that it tends to be taken for granted and its consequences ignored. Although it has a certain practical effi-ciency, it also exacts a price: the loss of a broader, holistic perspective. The danger is that no one sees the entire picture, no one asks how the technological procedures and objects being developed fit into society, how they affect the people who are to use them and the natural environ-ment from which they come and in which they will operate. This danger becomes especially acute when scientism baptizes this method of detail with a certainty and an infallibility it does not deserve. When this hap-pens, tunnel vision all too easily takes over.

A second basic characteristic of science is its abstract, theoretical, explanatory nature. It seeks to know, understand, and explain nature in general terms. It formulates generalizations in a constant drive to for-mulate "laws" or theories with explanatory and predictive power. Sci-ence, therefore, tends to be disinterested, removed from the "real" world of nations, persons, and objects.

Technology, on the other hand, is concrete, specific, and practical. It deals with real-life situations: with living persons and nations, and with

26. See Pacey, *The Maze of Ingenuity*, p. 139.

concrete, material reality. Thus technology, responsibly done, must be holistic. It must ask about its effects on people, cultures, nations, and the natural environment; it must be based on normative principles. Even "disinterested" scientists should be sensitive to the societal consequences of their work; they should approach their work holistically. But it is even more important that technologists do so. The hegemony of science in technology, however, discourages this sort of perspective. The mind-set and approach of modern science tell technologists that they need not concern themselves with the broad picture. "Just do your narrowly defined task well and don't worry about the whole into which it fits; that's not your job" is the prevailing spirit that scientism has helped foster. Again, a kind of tunnel vision comes to dominate.

In Chapter Four it was pointed out that technicism reduces everything to the technological. Technology becomes its own defense; it is believed that humankind through its own efforts can save itself, find solutions to all problems, and build a kingdom of plenty, ease, and peace. In part this faith in technology stems from scientism's blind faith in science and, in turn, the hegemony of science in technology. "Technology will save us" is society's credo because technology is believed to rest on the foundation of science, and science—under the influence of scientism—is seen as being certain, efficacious, and true. It is hard to overestimate the importance of this point.

The Hegemony of Science and Normative Principles. In the previous chapter it was argued that technology should be done in keeping with certain normative principles. The hegemony of science in technology, its discouragement of a holistic technology, and its support for an unbiblical technicism work against a technology done in keeping with these normative principles. (Chapters Nine and Ten, which consider technological design in detail, make this point fully.) The problem is that the hegemony of science has ingrained a bias, a certain direction into the very way in which modern technology is done. A mere alteration of goals, therefore, will not affect it. It is not a matter of steering technology in a different direction; there is something wrong with the internal workings of technology that must be set right. Technology itself must be restructured and reoriented.

In his famous article of 1967, "The Historical Roots of Our Ecological Crisis," medieval historian Lynn White, Jr., roundly condemned what he considered to be arrogant early and medieval Christian views of nature and humanity's relation to it, and the acceptence of the Baconian belief that scientific knowledge means technological power over nature. But he concluded his article with this extremely perceptive remark:

"Since the roots of our trouble are so largely religious, the remedy must also be essentially religious, whether we call it that or not. We must rethink and refeel our nature and destiny."[27] White is indeed correct. If we as a society are to redirect technology in keeping with God's normative will, we must redirect our view of the world—of humanity, the creation, the nature of reality, and our relationship to the Creator of all.

27. Lynn White, Jr., "The Historical Roots of Our Ecological Crisis," *Science* 155 (1967): 1205.

CHAPTER SEVEN

Technology and Economics

TECHNOLOGY AND ECONOMICS ARE CLOSELY RELATED. MOST OB-
viously, both are closely associated with—though not limited to—
material culture. Properly understood, economics has to do with the care
of the creation and the fruitful results of that care. This mandate for care
and fruitfulness was given as part of the creation account: God told the
man whom he had created to till (some versions translate the Hebrew "to
serve") and to keep the Garden of Eden. The fruitfulness of the Garden
was necessary to sustain and develop human possibilities and those of the
rest of creation. This caring for God's garden was rendered as service to
him, as praise for his goodness. As we have noted, God's command to
bring out and develop the rich potentialities he placed in his creation is at
the heart of the cultural mandate. Fullfilling that mandate is thereby a
way of obeying and praising God and, simultaneously, a way of serving
humanity and the rest of creation.

In order to clarify the relationship between technology and economics,
it is helpful to note that economic thought, as it has historically developed, views economics as having to do with the transformation of resources into desired forms for the benefit of consumers, under conditions
of scarcity. Technology is then seen as the means by which this transformation is accomplished. The criterion for evaluating this transformation—and thus the criterion for evaluating technology—is efficiency,
which is made necessary by scarcity. Technological possibilities function as constraints on economic operations, but it is economic valuation
that goes a long way toward determining the desirability of any given
technological transformation. In this view, the economic task consists of
developing and utilizing an evaluative framework for making decisions
about what transformations to make and when and how to make them.[1]

---

1. It is important to note that economics should never be seen as the sole determinant of
the answers to these questions. Political decision-making, the requirements of good design,
and other social and cultural factors all play a legitimate part. Conventional economics has
frequently ignored these components of proper cultural decision-making, sweeping them
under the rug of "as if all other things are equal" forms of economic theory.

Technology, on the other hand, has to do with the specific physical manner in which materials and energy are transformed.

Many aspects of this view can be questioned. For example, what constitutes a legitimate "economic end"? What specific meaning is to be given to economic efficiency, economic resource, economic value, the activity of production, work, and costs? Nevertheless, this view, although limited, does have something to say about the relationship between economics and technology. Technology has to do with opening up possibilities for transforming resources into things that serve God and humankind, while economics has to do with the choices regarding what transformations are good or valuable. On the one hand, potential economic products for which there is no available technology are not feasible; on the other hand, technological objects that are not in some sense valuable (although economic value is not the only relevant kind of value) may be feasible, but are not appropriate. The conclusion is clear: the economic valuing of technology and its products is closely intertwined with technological possibilities.

This intertwinement, however, is not a simple one. This chapter will attempt to correct some of the inadequate views of this relationship and to provide a better basis for understanding how technology and economics are related. We will not only examine the existing relationship between technology and economics, but also explore what their relationship should be. In doing so we will be helped by those who have been influenced by valuable work such as that done by the English economist E. F. Schumacher and have adopted his suggestion that a necessary corrective to the present situation is to develop a technology and an economics "as if people mattered." But while this approach is valuable, it is still too limited. What matters most is loving God above all and one's neighbor as oneself—loving that gives praise to God and service to one's fellow human beings and the natural creation. This praise and service will show itself more specifically in obedience to normative principles. It is as men and women pursue biblically based normative principles such as stewardship, justice, caring, and trust that an appropriate, responsible relationship between economics and technology and between them and the rest of God's world will emerge.

The first section of this chapter compares and contrasts Christian and non-Christian views of economic activity. The next section considers the nature of economic valuing, especially its over-reliance on price valuing and the difficulties this creates. The final section considers the effects technology has on economic activity and the effects that business and consumer decisions have on technology.

TWO VIEWS OF ECONOMIC ACTIVITY

Elsewhere we have explored the nature of technology at some length; here we need to gain some insight into the nature of economic activity. Our common and intimate association with economic activity—we all engage in it every day—is only a partial help and may actually be a hindrance in some ways, because its nature is much misunderstood. True economic activity, rightly understood from a Christian perspective and rightly executed by those who love God, is considerably different from the kind of economic activity that society foists upon us and which many all too readily accept. We must seek a better way.

Conventional Wisdom. Conventional wisdom views economic activity as being imposed by the rigors of scarcity, even if the only conception of such scarcity is that of too little money with which to purchase too many goods. This view implies that if only there were enough of the stuff of this world provided for us, no economic necessity would be imposed on us. There would be no need to make economic choices, and economists would be unemployed. But we are in fact faced with what has been described as the "niggardliness of nature," which at times threatens our very existence and always withholds some of the fruits we want.

The technological-economic path leading from this starting point is the arduous, anxious wrestling with nature to wring out of it its reluctantly granted fruits. The tools in this struggle are something like the implements of warfare, and the result is frequently violent, leaving scars on both sides: the exploitation and the degradation of nature—sometimes described in terms of rape and pillage—and disharmony and angst in the lives of human beings. No one expects economic life to be pretty. In any case, the fundamental underpinning for economic activity in this view— whether Western or Communist—is the need to overcome scarcity. According to John Maynard Keynes, a leading Western economist of the twentieth century, it is a struggle to get out of a tunnel of economic necessity and into the daylight of abundance.[2]

Christian Stewardship. A radically different view of the nature of economic activity begins with God's entrusting the care and use of the earth to humankind. This care began in the Garden of Eden, and although that paradise did not last long, the activity itself continued, though tainted by sin after the Fall. To be entrusted with an endowment of resources and to be given the responsibility to choose how those resources should be

2. See John Maynard Keynes, "Economic Possibilities of Our Grandchildren," in his *Essays in Persuasion* (New York: Harcourt, Brace & Co., 1932).

used is an awesome yet delightful task. Through it the creation is at the same time celebrated and utilized, preserved and brought to fruition.

This task is best described as one of stewardship, one that involves both care and utilization. As the parable of the talents shows us, the steward does not fulfill his responsibility by returning the trust to the master in a pristine, unaltered state. In one of the most frightening passages in the Bible, this sort of steward is condemned to outer darkness (Matt. 25:30). It is apparent that being a good steward involves not only being prudent but also making choices and even taking risks. In carrying out this task of stewardship, it is appropriate to develop technology, to utilize means beyond the limited human motive of power, to develop new and better procedures, and more.

In the process, scarcity will not necessarily be vanquished, although its painful consequences may be reduced. In addition, certain present forms of contrived scarcity—developed through persuasive efforts to increase desire or through monopolistic efforts to restrict supply—may be eliminated. The finiteness of the creation remains a reality under all circumstances, but to the Christian, economics is simply the care for a garden of limited size.

Christian Stewardship and Conventional Wisdom. It would seem that viewing economic activity as an active pursuit of a trust given at the time of creation would come as a breath of fresh air to those who labor under the notion of the niggardliness of nature and economic necessity created by scarcity. Doesn't this alternate view permit the celebration of economic activity, of working and exchanging, producing and consuming in a spirit of cooperation and mutual delight? But this reaction often is not elicited, because this alternate view flies straight in the face of the supposed autonomy of human beings. Embracing Christian stewardship means being servants, not masters; stewards, not lords. To some, sustaining the hope for eventual freedom through material accumulation—though repeatedly shown to be false—is more acceptable than adopting the demeanor and actions of a servant.

The conventional view of economics takes as its most fundamental proposition the assertion that economic behavior is the result of autonomous individuals making choices so as to maximize some subjective quality, such as their psychological satisfaction or pleasure. These individuals are presumed to be cut off not only from any transcendent norms for governing economic activity, but also from human community; they are supposed to make only independent decisions about their own, and no one else's, economic condition. As a result, they never engage in or value the underpinnings of community: cooperation, concern for one's neighbor, or public-spiritedness. Even the place of justice in the good economic life is left in doubt. Economic theory claims that persons compete and struggle for the maximum individual benefit that can be garnered from any given situation. Altruism becomes the antithesis of economic rationality: either it makes no sense at all, or it interferes with achieving economic purposes. This is the economic theory that for more than two hundred years has served to teach those who seek to gain more economic wisdom. According to this view, servanthood is abdication, a surrendering of the battle for supremacy and freedom. Stewardship is for the weak, the losers.

But even those who employ such a view of economics have bridled at its implications. Thus attempts have been made to justify the tenets and consequences of this theory—for example, to show that individualistic pursuit of self-interest really benefits all of society and is therefore justified. A similar argument is that self-interested behavior is inevitable, a part of human nature, and therefore we must make the best of it. Those Christians who employ this argument say such self-interested behavior is the consequence of sin. If self-interest and the desire for self-aggrandizement are inevitable, is it not fortunate (so the argument goes) that they also seem to benefit others by creating wealth? If the banquet table of the rich is filled to overflowing, is it not more likely that crumbs will fall to the floor for the poor? Here is not the place to analyze these attempts to give economic justification for values and behavior that many Christians through the ages have condemned. Suffice it to say that this sow's-ear-to-silk-purse transformation of greed, self-interest, and cavalier exploitation into abundant material riches is entirely too facile.

Another tack often taken is similarly wrongheaded. One way to empty the economic viewpoint of concern for these and other sorts of human evils is to drain it of any real human content. Economic theory then operates from a mechanistic worldview, one in which events are explained not as a result of truly human choices but as the result of impersonal forces. Such phrases as "intersecting supply-and-demand schedules," "too much money chasing too few goods," and "prices as equilibrium values" are used to describe human activity with no apparent reference to human beings. It is very difficult to get at human accountability in such views—and perhaps that is precisely the point. Since individuals are taken to be accountable to no one other than themselves, the very concept of accountability loses all meaning. Economic life, as a result, takes on a kind of autonomy. We are always merely the victims of inflation, unemployment, poor productivity, or pervasive poverty. No one caused these problems, and no one, at least outside of professional policymakers, can cure them. This view—if it is coupled with the view that science and technology are autonomous—establishes a world in which human beings exercise no control. Science, technology, and economics have a direction and inner logic of their own, separate in some sense from their human perpetrators.

The conventional economic view is at odds with the view of stewardship and the responsibility and accountability it implies. As we have already mentioned, stewardship means having been entrusted with a finite but bountiful creation. Even though the creation groans under the burden of sin, it still demonstrates God's handiwork in a marvelous way. But along with bounty, need is also present. This was so from the beginning: Adam and Eve had needs even before the Fall. They needed to eat, to rest, to undertake caring tasks such as naming the animals. In our present world with its created finiteness and its burden of sin—which combine to give us a "scarcity" problem—it is clear that needs also abound. Idleness is not a responsible option. The creation must be both cared for and preserved on the one hand, and utilized to meet needs on the other. In a remarkable test of the hearts of human beings, God has left much of what is necessary to accomplish this task up to human choice. The creation can provide a rich banquet, but it has to be properly husbanded, and choices have to be made concerning how to employ its resources. While the possible transformation of the creation is limited by the laws of that creation, technology allows us remarkable freedom and latitude.

This is not to imply that the actual situation in which we find ourselves does not present scarcity problems. Parts of the world, for example, have agricultural lands that yield very limited harvests, and in many places, population pressures exacerbate this problem. But at the same time, history shows that certain human choices, had they been otherwise, would have alleviated the stringency of the scarcity. Poor agricultural practices, land-grabbing by the powerful, and failure to reckon with natural ecosystems are all cases in point. Thus obedient human choice is still a key.

Given the need to choose and the ability to do so, how then should we choose? Here the economics of stewardship differs sharply from the conventional economic wisdom of the day. The economics of stewardship recognizes that there is seldom a trust bestowed that does not have a set of conditions placed upon it, a set of principles that the owner wishes obeyed. Certainly that is true of God's entrusting his creation to humanity. We are not to look to pleasure principles, personal gain, or limitless growth in production or consumption to answer how we are to choose; we are to choose in keeping with the normative standards God has given us. It is also important to remember that the meaning of obedience in one aspect—the economic—can be understood only in terms of the coherence of the whole. The consequences of economic choices are realized in the context of human life and obedience in other spheres. This means economic choice should be governed by such normative principles as justice and cultural appropriateness, just as any other human choice or action is.

In his *Capitalism and Progress: A Diagnosis of Western Society*, Bob Goudzwaard refers to societies that fail to realize this coherence as "tunnel societies" (playing on Keynes's metaphor mentioned earlier). In these societies, all things—"people, institutions, norms, behavior"—are molded so that they contribute "to the smooth advance toward the light at the end of the tunnel," or in other words are bound by a narrow, closed view of progress. According to Goudzwaard, "Nothing is of essential value in any social relationship unless it is a means to advance in the tunnel." In such a society, norms such as justice and love are bent to serve progress, "while the guides of progress themselves—economic growth, technological innovation, and scientific advances—are raised above normative judgment to the status of 'providers of meaning' for everyone who follows in their footsteps." Goudzwaard's prescription for such a closed society is not to follow blindly through the tunnel, supposing that scientific and technological developments and economic growth will lead to light at the end, but to burst out of the tunnel by following a path "in which the *norms* for human life—like justice, trust, and truth—regain their original validity for our decisions and acts."[3]

Technicism supports a narrow, single-minded notion of progress. Breaking the hold of that outlook would free governments, trade unions, business enterprises, and other social and cultural institutions to regain the possibilities for development along the lines of their own distinct responsibilities. Similarly, says Goudzwaard, individual persons would no longer be required merely to adjust to the pressure of the external demands made by the pursuit of progress, but would gain a new freedom to pursue the meaning of everyday life. In such a society, concern for the creation, the meaning of labor, the dignity of the consumer, the opportunities of poor nations, and the preservation of resources for future generations would take precedence over a narrow concern for economic, scientific, and technological growth.[4]

3. Bob Goudzwaard, *Capitalism and Progress: A Diagnosis of Western Society*, trans. and ed. by Josina Van Nuis Zylstra (Grand Rapids: Eerdmans; Toronto: Wedge, 1979), pp. 183–86.

4. See Goudzwaard, *Capitalism and Progress*, p. 194.

ECONOMIC VALUING

Economic valuing involves placing comparative economic values on economic goods, both resources and products. In the conventional view this implies nothing more than establishing a system of relative prices for goods, prices normally stated in monetary terms. But, although the establishment of prices remains one legitimate aspect of economic valuing in any modern economy, this view is too limited. Monetary prices are inherently limited and limiting, both in the struggle to value things properly within the economic sphere and in the effort to harmonize economic valuing with other ways of valuing.

Although many factors affect technological choices, economic valuing is one of the most important. This is the case because, as we have seen, changing resources into other, desired forms by technological means is central to much of economic production and consumption. It is natural, therefore, that technological choices depend to a large extent on economic valuing. In turn, of course, technological change affects economic valuing in a variety of ways. The issue of technological choice and technological change is discussed later in this chapter. Here we examine some of the issues involved in economic valuing and the closely related and historically powerful concept of economic efficiency.

Optimal Economic Efficiency. We have already considered the underlying presuppositions of the contemporary view of economic valuing. They involve individual, subjective choices made according to some supposed rationally consistent principle such as the maximization of utility or satisfaction. Over the years more effort has probably gone into refining this viewpoint of economic valuation than any other aspect of economic theory. For present purposes, however, we do not need to deal with the details and mathematical refinements of such theory; we need to examine and understand its presuppositions and the resulting conclusions. When we do so, it becomes clear that if the conventional view of economics is accepted as fundamental to economic valuing, it can be shown theoretically that "optimal economic efficiency" can be obtained. This "optimal economic efficiency" is roughly defined as allocating economic resources to their highest valued use—in other words, as maximizing economic efficiency. This conclusion is itself abstract, and numerous questions arise about its relationship to the real world. But these questions are not within our present purview, for by and large they have not detracted significantly from the conceptual content of efficiency nor from the force of the claim for optimal results.

The social force of the optimal efficiency claim comes largely from the notion that it is value-free and incontrovertible. Efficiency, it is supposed, is what we all agree we are after. There is only one rational definition of efficiency and only one rationally obtained optimum path to such efficiency. Thus there can be no disagreement once this path is fully explored; no other way is possible. Only ignorance and bad reasoning can keep us from this optimal result. To know more is to be able to do more and to face new and superior possibilities.

A kind of scientific and technological imperative results from this view. But will this concept of efficiency bear all this weight? Does it incontrovertibly tell us in which direction we should go, and how far?

It is important to note the kind of concept involved here. The notion of efficiency is often bandied about in discussions of technology and economics, but frequently without adequate definition. What is involved is *economic* efficiency, not what is usually called *technical* efficiency. This prevents a most embarrassing possibility. If one were to settle for a simple, intuitive definition of efficiency, one might stress getting the most output for the least input. Oftentimes this is a very important concern, but it is not much help for the issue at hand, which is the optimum efficiency of all possible choices for transformation of resources. For example, being frightfully efficient in making an unneeded and unwanted product is pointless. This is precisely the charge leveled at simplistic planning systems that have been criticized because they do not specify purposes but require only that managers conduct their operations in the most efficient manner. Some ludicrous consequences result: it is alleged that railroad managers, for example, have shipped water back and forth on their rail lines in order to get a very high efficiency rating in terms of ton-miles of goods transported. The result, of course, is valueless.

What is needed is to combine the notion of efficiency in technical terms with a measurement of the value of the inputs and the outputs. This is precisely what the concept of economic efficiency does, its proponents claim. It stresses efficiency directed toward the highest valued use of available resources. Something important is gained in this definition of efficiency. Optimal economic efficiency is indeed a powerful concept. It combines all the positive connotations of efficiency—in today's society at least, few things are more universally condemned than being inefficient—with another immensely powerful concept, that of value. Value contains within itself the potential for philosophical and moral justification of one's actions: one should seek what is valuable and discard what is not. To be able to maximize value efficiently, therefore, makes a powerful claim on people's minds and hearts. In good conscience can we propose doing anything else? Before we give our loyalty to this concept, however, it must be tested further.

The Concept of Value. As might be expected, the critical point in evaluating the concept of economic efficiency is the meaning of the term *value*. When one says that something is economically valuable, what is meant? Defining economic value has been central to the discipline of economics. There are, in modern terms, two main approaches to such a definition, and both reveal something significant about the concept of value. The first, normally associated with the so-called classical school of economics, is that of a labor theory of value. For our purposes, the central feature of this view is that valuable things are those produced by human effort; there is some sort of direct correspondence between human activities and value. The second approach, associated with the later neoclassical school of economics, emphasizes that demand determines value; it is the subjective valuations that consumers place on goods that determine their value. In this definition, as in that of the classical school, the central determinant of economic value is human activity—but in this case people are important as consumers rather than as producers.

Both of these variations on the idea of value emerged out of certain historical and cultural settings. The labor theory of value emerged out of a primarily agricultural perspective. The emphasis on demand emerged at a time when industrialization had proceeded to the point where a certain degree of technological hubris, as well as the problem of the value of machine-produced goods, had developed.

All valuation depends to some extent on historical setting and cultural environment, but it also depends on a normative basis. The normative basis of conventional economic valuing begins with grounding value in human action. This is true for both the labor theory and the demand theory of economic value. The first emphasizes what people do; the second, what people want. But neither attempts to relate value to anything outside of human beings; neither suggests that there is a starting point or reference point outside human choice. Both are grounded in a fundamental error, one that reflects humankind's attempt to create its own reality, to build its own towers of Babel with no constraints—an attempt frequently made in technological endeavors. This is a peculiarly modern problem. These ideas of economic value replace older ones that had to do with notions like intrinsic value—the idea that value could be embodied in the thing itself.

The modern view has abetted the ignoring of the needs of creation. Valuable resources are defined only in terms of humanity's need for them, and in many cases are valued only in terms of the cost of extraction—what must be expended to remove them from the environment—plus the subjective human demand for them. Creation is ascribed no economic value in and of itself. Unless someone can claim a property right or unless a human interest is involved, no economic valuing procedure is usually employed.

This view of value has become embodied in modern culture with two crucial results. First, this valuing, in close association with the idea that human labor imparts value, has led to distinctions between productive and nonproductive labor. Not all classes of human effort are deemed to be equal. Labor is considered productive if marketable goods are produced. Thus the very term *productive*—a term with very strong positive connotations—begins to have a very limited meaning. The second result of economic valuing, closely associated with this market test of productivity, is that productive value comes to be measured in terms of money. This is nothing less than a remarkable narrowing of the possible meaning of economic value. Its implications—as seen throughout the rest of the chapter—are just as remarkable.

The Price Theory of Value. A strong perceived need to gain a common measure of economic value developed because of the requirements of modern rationalism, reflected first of all in the natural sciences, which in turn became the model for the social disciplines.[5] The idea influencing both is that true knowledge is obtained only when measurement is achieved. Economics—strongly affected by a mechanical rationalism borrowed from Cartesian influences and Newtonian mechanics—sought both a precise measuring rod for economic value and, in the spirit of the times, a deterministic view of how economic value comes into being. The result was a price theory of value that today pervades both the halls of academia and everyday consciousness. Price theory holds that economically valuable things are those with prices, that economic value is proportional to price, and that nonpriced entities are economically valueless. In Western views, price is ideally determined by the market, although markets have never functioned without some degree of constraint and influence from private and public nonmarket power.

The implications of the price theory of value are enormous, partly because materialistic economic activity has become a dominant force in society and because economic valuing has a strong effect on another powerful force: technology. The whole notion of progress, in terms broader than just the economic and the technological, is closely related to maximizing the kind of economic value reflected in this narrow view. Individuals and families, for example, often measure their success, and

5. See the earlier discussion of this point in Chapter Six.

sometimes even their worth, in terms of income levels. The question "Are we better off this year?" tends to be answered in terms of the family's income. Nations likewise focus on the growth of a limited monetary measure of output—Gross National Product—as a measure of their success. They refer to it as the measure of their "standard of living," and they vie with one another (particularly East against West) to show that increased output—as measured by price—is proof of superior ideology.

It is not difficult, however, to show that this approach is hopelessly flawed. Its most significant defect is that it fails to recognize the need to simultaneously pursue biblically based normative principles for all of life. It isolates one aspect of life, the economic, and fails to see that right action, progress, or any other term of approbation must refer not only to economic concerns but also to those of justice, love for one's neighbor, cultural appropriateness, and so forth. Such theoretical isolation of aspects of human existence can only do violence to the coherence of life. But this is not the only flaw of the price theory. Even if we focus only on the meaning of the economic aspect, the price theory of value still presents a distorted picture. Its understanding of value and its preoccupation with value have enlarged our concern for some aspects of the economic scene and led us to ignore others.

Economic valuation as reflected in market-determined prices is an inadequate approach to the valuing of technology. The approach is inadequate first of all because market values as represented in prices are the result of individual valuing. Each person decides whether he or she is willing to buy or sell at existing prices. That decision may be influenced by a host of social and cultural factors such as the persuasion of advertising. But the notion of market action presented in price theory is that the total of all the individual actions will bring about a good composite result. This individualistic perspective breaks down in many ways, but for the purposes of this book, it is appropriate to emphasize that much of the task of stewardship is a shared one. No one can do it alone, because the economic and technological systems are far too intertwined for the action of individuals to bear the full responsibility of the task. Persons must make collective decisions about such things as the kind of activities deemed permissible and the bounds within which competitive actions may be taken. Problems with nuclear power, supersonic airplane travel, solid-waste disposal, acid rain, and offroad vehicles illustrate only some of the broad categories in which individual choice, though not unimportant, is inadequate to the task.

Individual choice is inadequate to the task in at least two ways. First, proponents presume that optimal choices are made by the individual.

But optimal choices based on what set of possibilities? Can a consumer decide not to purchase electricity generated by nuclear power or high-sulfur coal? No such choice is presented at the point of purchase. The only way to open up such choice is to take collective action. Second, it is presumed that each individual market transaction is self-contained, that it has no spillover effects. The notion is that goods are received for payments made, and that is the end of the matter. But this is almost never the case.

Acknowledgment of spillover effects has led to a category of "externalities" in economics. An externality is something outside of a market transaction, a result not covered in the price. Such externalities are pervasive: they include a host of benefits and costs, positive or negative, that are not paid for in monetary terms. The beauty of a well-designed building, for example, is appreciated by casual passersby who did not pay for the design. But the best-known externalities are probably those negative ones involved in environmental degradation, oftentimes the result of producing marketable goods. Unless a communal, legal redress is effected, the cost of this degradation is borne in other ways. The cost of a steel mill's pollution of the air and water, for example, is borne not by the purchasers of steel but by those downwind or downstream of the mill. Similarly, the deafening noise of jet airplanes is imposed on those who do not fly. Examples abound.

There are two basic reasons why this category of externalities is so large. First, the more closely intertwined economics and technology become, the more externalities are likely to occur. Because of present intertwinements, all of us are affected by distant political upheavals in oil-producing countries, by electrical power networks that "brown out" because of occurrences hundreds of miles away, by fads that make old standard products unavailable, and by traffic congestion caused by large numbers of motorists trying to get to the same locations. If some people switch to wood stoves to heat their homes, there's no problem, but if too many people in close proximity do it, air pollution threatens the community. When the price of energy drives up the cost of commuting, more people buy houses in or near urban areas, and the poor, through no fault or action of their own, can no longer afford to live there, and have no place to go. As production and consumption activities increase, urban areas grow, and intertwinements of this kind increase. It is a process greatly aided and abetted by the kind of technological change seen in the last few centuries.

Externalities are important and pervasive for a second reason: the internal operations of the market depend for the most part on a single notion of value and exchange—namely, price. Externalities abound because the dimension of price is simply too narrow to contain all that in fact occurs. Spillover is inevitable. This is such an important point that it requires elaboration.

The emergence of monetary prices has established a means by which society can measure economic value on a common scale. This is not merely a theoretical nicety but a fact that allows economic exchanges to take place over the phone and through the mail. Persons need not strike face-to-face bargains each time they exchange goods. Consumers can read catalogs and simply mail checks in exchange for the merchandise they select. Monetary prices have facilitated this kind of interaction so widely that it can now be legitimately argued that there is a single global economy.

But if something is gained, something is also lost. What is lost falls into a number of categories, but the relevant aspect here is that the pervasive pricing of economic goods has led to regarding value and price as synonymous. A concentration on price has meant a corresponding diminishing of the ability to see goods in other than monetary terms or to see a responsibility for their use in other than monetary ways. This is a tragedy, because the responsibilities of stewardship are far broader than those encompassed by price.

The dominance of price valuing has made economic decision-making lopsided. For example, people tend to believe that they know the benefits of technological change because they know the value—the price—of the additional goods it has brought them. Against a gain in Gross National Product or personal income it is extremely difficult to assess the incommensurable changes in the environment, the loss of natural resources, or the disappearance of such things as a pristine countryside. It is tempting to think and argue that one can know the value of priced goods because their value has been measured but that one can have only opinions about or debates over other kinds of value. One feels an obligation to be economical in monetary terms but finds it all too easy to ignore nonpriced economic responsibility. Orio Giarini tried to capture this phenomenon by describing price as analogous to the visible light spectrum of electromagnetic waves.[6] Just as it is wrong to assume that the only waves that exist are those the eye can see, so it is wrong to assume that only priced phenomena have economic value. There is more to a fruitful stewardship of the earth than merely the efficient production of market values. And in the shared responsibility of stewardship, something more must be com-

6. See Orio Giarini, *Dialogue on Wealth and Welfare: An Alternative View of World Capital Formation* (Oxford: Oxford University Press, 1980), p. 102.

municated to each other about economic value than can be contained in price information.

In the area of wealth and welfare, Giarini introduces the concept of "dowry and patrimony" in order to get at the "something more" beyond market values. This concept is meant to "define the stock of natural, biological, and man-made goods available to us from which we derive our welfare in the largest sense."[7] Giarini's "dowry and patrimony" consists of four categories: the natural (physical), the biological, the man-made (cultural), and the monetized (capital). The importance of such a typology is that it ascribes proper importance to the nonmonetized elements of wealth. Without such a concept, Giarini points out, one has a distorted sense of wealth and welfare. For example, wherever natural resources are so abundant that the price of them is low, market wealth is considered to be low. Giarini comments, tongue in cheek, that by our present standards of wealth measurement, heaven is the poorest of worlds because no buying or selling goes on there, whereas hell is wealthy because of its high fuel consumption!

The singular preoccupation with the visible, monetized kind of wealth leads to serious consequences. It leads not only to disregarding the non-monetized portion, but frequently to depleting it in the name of the accumulation of wealth. The result is neither optimum nor responsible and fails to do justice to the multiple sources of human well-being.

The heavy dependence of the market segment of economic activity on factors outside of itself—the nonmonetized portion—is a phenomenon that most economists overlook. One exception is Gerhard Mensch, who estimates that "the 'exchange economy' would collapse within twenty to thirty years if . . . contributions outside of the realm of mammon would cease to flow."[8] What is worse, the market segment of the economy not only takes these contributions for granted, failing in the process to conserve them or build them up, but in many instances actually works against the support and protection of these contributions. It pretends, for example, that self-interest is the only basis for economic motivation. In fact, showing concern for others and living within the social and legal rules of society serve as bases for economic motivation, yet little is done to protect and encourage them. Similarly, the existence of a strong work ethic is crucial for business, yet the person who has succumbed to thoroughly hedonistic business advertising makes a poor worker. This creates tension, because often a business's advertising, though it may

7. Giarini, *Dialogue on Wealth and Welfare*, p. 42.
8. Gerhard Mensch, *Stalemate in Technology: Innovations Overcome the Depression* (Cambridge, Mass.: Ballinger Publishing, 1979), p. 220.

stimulate sales in the short run, is contributing in the long run to the creation of an unsuitable work force. Of course, certain businesses and labor unions have made laudable efforts to be socially responsible. But too often these efforts are after-hours sorts of patchwork; they seldom alter the fundamental set of values by which business and labor operate.

This intertwinement of the priced and nonpriced segments of economic activity creates other problems. The focus on price not only obscures what is happening to the nonpriced portion but also distorts prices: they no longer make any pretense of being a correct measure of value. Clear examples are the widespread instances in which technological methods of production have depleted and spoiled the environment without rendering any economic compensation. In such cases the prices of the resultant goods are inaccurate because they do not reflect the real economic value of the resources used to produce them.[9]

Therefore, the economic valuing of technology must be broadened in two ways. First, the notion of value must include more than priced phenomena, even if this greater inclusion results in the loss of a single, common economic measure such as money. Second, the economic aspect itself—as well as the broader issue of the valuing of technology in all its aspects—must be opened up to the simultaneous pursuit of normative principles. For example, it is not appropriate to reduce the notion of economic normativity to that of efficiency without simultaneously recognizing such normative principles as justice, stewardship, and cultural appropriateness. This demands that society stop encouraging both the restrictive narrowing of the economic sphere and its isolation from the rest of life, as if its logic of efficiency sets it apart, untouched and untouchable by the ordinary concerns of life.

This need for a broader view not only affects private conceptions and decisions regarding economics and technology, but also clearly affects the forming of public policies about technology. Attempts to assess technological impacts or to decide which sorts of technology to subsidize or tax, for example, are dependent on the values that are assigned to the technology and its results. Because there are nonmonetary aspects to these decisions—for example, the effect on the environment or on the natural resources available for future use—an economic encouragement of the wrong sort of technology could result in a decrease in real wealth and welfare at the same time that it results in an increase in monetary values.

---

9. See, for example, the work of Roefie Hueting, *New Scarcity and Economic Growth: More Welfare Through Less Production* (Amsterdam: North-Holland Publishing Co., 1980). Hueting argues that not only have monetary values not been attached to the depletion of the environment, but they cannot be; thus no commensurable measure of value is possible. In other words, prices alone are not an adequate method of valuing.

THE EFFECTS OF TECHNOLOGY ON ECONOMIC RELATIONSHIPS

The historical interaction between technology and the economic realm has been both intense and complicated. There is no need to completely analyze this relationship here, but it is important to highlight some significant aspects of the modern relationship between technology and economics in order to obtain a better idea of where modern technological societies are headed.

Earlier we noted that economics and technology both focus on material culture. Material culture has become immensely important in modern societies because their members usually engage in certain kinds of materialism both as producers and as consumers. As producers they seek to dominate nature and other human beings by the power with which they manipulate material goods. As consumers they have come to suppose that their happiness depends almost solely on the amount of material things they possess and consume. A technology driven by a technicistic mind-set has played a key role, because it has altered the way people function both as producers and as consumers. It has also altered the structure of our economic systems. It has affected the kinds and amounts of material resources societies use as well as the speed at which societies use them. And it has vastly changed the kinds of work that people do. Each of these effects should be further explored.

Effects on Production. The discipline of economics usually defines the relationship between technology and production as the effect of changing technological possibilities on the production of market goods. Such production is usually thought of as occurring within specialized economic institutions such as factories. The literature of economics takes this approach almost exclusively, and the result is a narrowing of the meaning of production similar to the narrowing of the meaning of economic wealth.

Not all productive activities are conducted within specialized economic organizations or solely for monetary compensation. The focus on production in the monetized sector—important as it is in modern market economies—is much too narrow. We will therefore consider productive activities to be work both within and without monetized workplaces. It is clear that society's ability to produce economic goods—which include many goods in addition to priced goods—is deeply intertwined with technological tools and products. This intertwinement is both positive and negative: it can enhance one's ability to be truly productive, but it can also hamper and deplete one's ability to be productive. We will take up the details of this relationship when we consider technology's effects on work and the structure of the economy.

Effects on Consumption. Technology has been responsible for pre-senting society with a vast new array of products and services. In some cases this array has been aimed at meeting basic needs for nutritious food, adequate shelter, and minimum standards of health care. In other cases familiar to those who live in the so-called developed part of the world, technology has been employed to present people with a bewildering array of choices for accomplishing some very incidental tasks and for amusing themselves. Modern consumers have become so used to both the quantity of these sorts of technological objects and the continual parade of new ones that they now have difficulty determining what their true needs are. The mind-set conditioned by technicism naturally assumes that new is better, that the latest model with more buttons, whistles, and gongs will make life easier and more enjoyable. Thus we all too quickly assume that we "need" the latest products: electric toothbrushes, automatic paint-rollers, home video recorders, snowmobiles, home computers, video games—the list is endless.

Technology has clearly made living easier and has enriched us in many legitimate ways. One can thank the Lord for life-giving medical tech-nology, for technology that allows persons to appreciate beautiful music, and for technology that has produced means of communication and trans-portation that enable separated friends and families to stay in touch. But at the same time, there is evidence that this technology-spurred prolifera-tion of goods has increased greed, created unprecedented opportunities to exercise that greed, and, ironically, left most people unsatisfied. The common denominator of both greed and dissatisfaction may be the effect that technological "progress" has had on expectations. People expect technology to provide them with more and more each year, to solve all their problems and soothe their nervous tension, unaware that it is often technology and technologized relationships that have created many of the problems and tensions in the first place.

The high and frequently misplaced expectations that society has of technology may simply be setting technology up for a fall. Attempts to measure whether or not persons are happier now than at an earlier, technologically more simple time are no comfort to the proponents of progress through technological and material aggrandizement. Though these attempts are plagued with conceptual difficulties, they do show that despite all that members of modern, technologically advanced societies have and can do over and above members of earlier societies, they do not feel happier.[10] Why not? Most fundamentally, of course, because people

10. See, for example, Nicholas Rescher, *Unpopular Essays on Technological Progress* (Pittsburgh: University of Pittsburgh Press, 1980).

too often put their trust in things, not God. There is no satisfaction or happiness to be gained that way. Indeed, it is the very stream, pace, and promise of new, technologically produced goods that keeps people dissatisfied with what they have, no matter how good it is. Just around the corner there must be something better, a wonder product to relieve the nagging itch that something is missing, some small inconvenience is not yet subdued.

Compounding this is a very powerful neighboring effect: keeping up with the Joneses. Given sinful human nature, the implications of this effect on the neighborhood level or on the global level—and communication and transportation technology are continually reducing the difference between the two—are great. This so-called demonstration effect has stirred up virtually the whole world in the pursuit of the latest trappings of worldly success. In some ways it is surprising that this demonstration effect works so powerfully in the area of material products, especially those produced by "advanced" technology, and apparently less powerfully in the realms of social, cultural, and religious advances.

The demonstration effect appears to give very great and perhaps unfair advantages to those who possess the technology for producing certain material goods. In the European settlement of North America, the ability to produce colored beads, metal knives and axes, and whiskey gave the white traders tremendous advantages. And certainly such technological objects as weapons helped them win the land they wanted. (One can note that North Americans today have inherited those acquisitions. Their present life-style owes much to the rich resources acquired at very low "prices" at an earlier date.) The demonstration effect is still taking its toll in relationships between rich and poor nations. And the siren song of technicism is constantly telling us that technology is the key to the promised land of power, status, and prestige.

Effects on the Structure of the Economy. Technology has also had an effect on the structure of the economy. Here we consider three kinds of effects: those on economic inputs and outputs, those on spatial arrangements and interactions, and those on the distribution of income and wealth.

Technological change has brought about changes in both *the composition of economic outputs and the composition and allocation of inputs.* In regard to outputs, the changes in consumer products mentioned above have meant an overall shift away from products closely related to agriculture and marked by simple refinements, and towards products with a higher degree of refinement and a greater percentage of "value added" by technological processes. These products tend to be more complex both in their internal structure and in terms of their intertwinement with other products. A car is not only internally more complicated than a bicycle, for example, but depends far more on complementary goods such as fuels and lubricants, roads and parking facilities, and repair and disposal facilities. At the same time, these products affect more and more areas of our lives beyond the simple fulfilling of basic needs. They function in close connection with human capabilities in handling finances, preparing meals, keeping house, and entertaining during leisure hours. And for the most part, these newer products take a heavier toll on the nonrenewable resources of the earth, especially fossil fuels, metals, and minerals.

Likewise, the composition and allocation of inputs has been affected by technology. It is frequently said that resources are created by technology. This is a dangerous view because it seduces us into thinking that unless something is technologically useful, it is not valuable. But it is also true that the ability to make use of many created resources depends on innovations that unlock their potential. It is hardly any wonder that an entirely different mix of resources is used now than was used in earlier times. Moving from an agrarian system to one of heavy industry implies major changes in the inputs of natural resources, capital, and labor. It also introduces competing uses for the same inputs. Land, for example, was once economically important primarily for its agricultural uses. But as towns grew up around agricultural centers, more and more land was put to alternative uses, and now some of the best agricultural land in the world is occupied by homes, factories, and shopping centers.

These sorts of changes apply to other inputs as well—for example, labor. As technological change proceeded, the proportion of the population involved in agricultural production grew smaller and smaller. Those no longer needed in agriculture moved to the cities, primarily to work in factories. That change in turn caused incredible changes in family, social, and cultural life. Now technological change is releasing workers from the factories as robots take over, and where the workers will go and what they will do remain significant questions. This very important problem and other related problems will be considered later, when we discuss technology's effects on work.

One effect of the alteration in the quantity and composition of outputs and inputs has been the creation of new pressure points for nature and human beings, commonly thought of in economics as new scarcities. This is true not only for metals and minerals, but also for such resources as clean air and water, which are now threatened by chemical loading due to herbicide and pesticide use, sulfur-dioxide emissions, and toxic-waste disposal. Even the time available for consumption and production has been effected. It is also true that the technological-economic mode of production has affected family lives, social interaction, and social and cultural values—considerations not strictly appropriate to the conventional framework of scarcity, but important nonetheless. Stresses caused by the pace of modern industrial society reveal themselves in various ''symptoms''—greater use of illicit drugs, increased marital and family tensions, and higher rates of such illnesses as heart disease, hypertension, and cancer. In turn, since people dealing with these problems often have trouble working effectively, the very style of economic production and consumption come back to haunt future economic activity. At present the dominant response to this dilemma seems to be to replace ''unreliable'' workers with new, more technologically sophisticated machines. The question of the fate of these displaced workers—both as producers and as consumers—is yet to be answered.

Need it be this way? Is there something inevitable about the shifts that have occurred and the frantic producing and consuming that have accompanied them? Have modern societies gotten on a treadmill that is exhausting them but getting them nowhere? How can they get off? The answer lies in a change in religion. The trust we put in material things must be replaced with a trust in God and an obedience to his normative will in working out our servant-stewardship. Faithful economic living in a technological age demands following the normative principles of cultural appropriateness, delightful harmony, stewardship, justice, caring, and others. Such an economic life would be far less frantic, would stress the creation less in terms of depletion of resources and degradation of the environment, and would place far more value on the participation of all human beings, even those who are presently economically disenfranchised.

Technology has also affected *spatial arrangements and interactions*. Technology has greatly modified the ability to communicate over long distances and to move materials with speed and power. The effects on spatial arrangements are clear. Early capitalism, for example, grew out of trading ventures that primarily involved seafaring technology. The result was the opening up of commerce on a worldwide basis, the corresponding possibility of settlement of remote areas, and eventual colonization. The effects of industrialization on spatial arrangements are clearly seen in urban developments: urban centers first sprang up near bodies of water—near water power—and later, following the invention and perfection of the steam engine, were liberated from this constraint. These two impacts—colonization and urbanization—may rank among the most important influences of all time on society and culture. It may be too strong to say that they were technologically determined, but they were certainly technologically enabled and driven. The structure of the British Empire, for example, related very strongly to the emerging industrialization of Britain proper and its need for raw materials and product markets.[11]

Urbanization is still very much a hallmark of industrial societies and economies, but technology has now provided a new twist: globally integrated production. Once again communication and transportation play a large role, as do the changing comparative advantages that technology provides. Global corporations now seek out critical resources worldwide, including labor pools that complement their particular technological operations. Once this may have meant seeking primarily large and inexpensive pools of unskilled or craft-skilled labor. Now it is more likely to demand skilled operators and assemblers to work in conjunction with automated assembly operations. Global integration permits the decentralized production of subassemblies in correspondence with the particular comparative advantage of various regimes. The production of a car, for example, may be parceled out: the transmissions may be made in one country, the engines in another, interior parts in a third, the bodies in a fourth, and the final assembly in yet another. Imposed on the technological advantages, of course, are those purely monetary advantages provided by the tax structures of each country and the tariffs and import duties that apply to unfinished versus finished goods. This example illustrates the complexity that results from the long-distance dealing that has come to characterize much of production and commerce. The international financial and brokerage arrangements that allow for all this are truly phenomenal.

What does one say to this globalization? One might argue that it gives certain advantages to the artisans, workers, owners of capital, and managers of the world, because it permits them to locate each other and derive mutual profits from their interactions. In reality it works out somewhat differently, because the powerful and technologically advantaged are frequently able to gain disproportionate profit from these arrangements. This impact on the distribution of income and wealth is important, but more than this is at stake. One of the facts of technological advance and advantage is that being first frequently counts for a great deal. It means claims to extract resources such as oil, copper, bauxite, and chromium in areas inhabited by primitive peoples who do not perceive the value and use of these resources. According to the present laws of the seas, it means that the right to the mineral wealth of a deep sea bed is based on nothing more than the technological power to reach it. It may also mean the

---

11. See Daniel Headrick, *The Tools of Empire: Technology and European Imperialism in the Nineteenth Century* (New York: Oxford University Press, 1981).

development of technological monocultures, in which certain technological directions hold sway merely by virtue of being first.

Under these circumstances, less developed countries do not develop indigenous technologies or indigenous capital-goods industries to produce the capital in which to embody appropriate technology. They remain in the backwater of the technological developments of the more developed countries. In this sense, increased interaction with rich countries may not work to the advantage of the poor countries. In fact, some of the leaders of Third World countries claim that they would be better off if the developed world disappeared into the sea, despite the fabled stores of technological knowledge available to them.

This raises a fundamental point. Do those in the rich part of the world have any responsibility for the effects their technology has, directly or indirectly, on poor nations? Can they—should they—ignore these effects in their calculations of the sort of technology they pursue? The conventional response of the wealthy, technologically more sophisticated societies has been to put self-interest first and to declare that since the poorer, less technologically sophisticated nations have little ability to affect them, these nations can safely be ignored. Yet it is the very powerlessness of the poor that commends them to the special care of God's people. The Bible's message regarding the widow, the fatherless, the poor, and the oppressed needs to be heard in the doing of technology. A technology for the oppressed must be developed.

Simply noting a few of the ways in which technology intertwines all of humanity on a global scale makes it clear that such a technology cannot be bifurcated into one technology for the powerful and another for the weak. Such a division would only perpetuate the imbalance of power and opportunity. True, the poor, underdeveloped regions of the world may at this point require special kinds of technology appropriate to their economic and cultural conditions, but attention must also be given to the dynamics of the relationship between the rich and the poor. Is the technology of the rich and powerful appropriate for the poor? If not, is it not likely to become—perhaps despite our best intentions—an instrument of oppression?

Normative principles such as cultural appropriateness, stewardship, justice, caring, and a delightful harmony need to be followed and applied in light of technology's effect on the poorer, less developed societies of the world. A technology that leads to wealth and leisure for some and sentences others to poverty and arduous efforts to eke out an existence clearly violates God's normative standards. When normative standards are replaced by a self-interested, thoughtless drive for technological change, a wedge is driven between the haves and the have-nots.

It is difficult to summarize the effect of technological change on *the distribution of income and wealth.* It was thought for some time that technological change brought with it greater equality in income because of the increased opportunities for production of marketable goods. Yet it has often been noted that ownership rights to the technology itself and to the resources complementary to that technology result in a tremendous concentration of income and wealth. Technology frequently increases the power of the few by increasing the scale at which they can operate and the extent of the domain which they can coordinate. The advantage of "getting there first" works hand in hand with this phenomenon. Modern technology normally reduces the labor input per unit of output, so in the absence of significant increases in demand for the product, labor inputs—and thus employment opportunities—may be reduced, not increased. Further, dual economies may be created in which the few who are integrated into the technological sector are considerably better off, but many who lose their livelihood to the new technology are disenfranchised. This appears to be the case in so-called showcases of miraculous development such as Brazil, and is increasingly the case in developed countries as well.

It may be that technology, once seen to be the vehicle of new opportunity for the masses, may increasingly share its benefits primarily with the few who are privileged enough to own it or have sufficient education to understand it. What is left for others is a trickle-down effect: the jobs with too little economic significance or too great a need for flexibility to automate. These are frequently dead-end jobs that do not lead to the development of new skills or upward mobility. Typical of the times may be displaced autoworkers who now work at fast-food outlets where a "cook" does not even need to know how to make French fries; he only needs to know that when the light flashes and the buzzer sounds, he has to lift the basket of potatoes out of the fryer.

The implications of this sort of "deskilling" and the wedge that technology appears to drive between the rich and the poor are not limited to a static situation—that some now have more and some have less. An even more dramatic effect is the dynamics it sets in motion, for some people outstrip others in their ability to use their technologically conditioned experience to learn, earn, and progress. This advantage is then perpetuated from generation to generation through the inheritance of both monetary wealth and an entire set of conditions that leads to future wealth, knowledge, and power. This tendency of the rich to get richer and the poor to get poorer is a fundamental distortion of our economic lives, one in which shalom is not present. Market-valued technological power and efficiency only worsen the tendency for some to drive others away from the opportunity to participate. It is precisely this sort of distortion that the

Year of Jubilee in biblical times was designed to rectify. The solution is to redistribute, in one fashion or another, the basis for participation.

Effects on Work. Before understanding the effect of technology on work, it is first necessary to understand the economic view of work. Work is something that most of us react to with some ambivalence. We do not want too much of it, but virtually none of us really wants to be without it either. Our negative view of work may be partly due to the curse of the Fall, which decreed that human labor would thereafter be difficult, but it is also partly due to a failure to clearly understand work and its significance and possibilities. The denigration of work into something of a necessary evil is resulting in a harvest of woes; we are finding that the technological imperative to replace human labor has a nasty side to it.

Properly conceived, work is the formative activity that human beings were put on earth to do. It is not, as some mistakenly believe, the curse of sin, which suggests that the ideal human state in Paradise was idleness. Viewed from the right perspective, work is far more than a means of making a living, of earning claims to material goods necessary for existence, important as this is. Work is the chance to be busy in God's garden—no longer Eden but richly endowed nevertheless. Humanity suffers the unfortunate effects of sin—the toil and drudgery that came with the curse—but we also celebrate new possibilities for work in the redemptive work of Jesus Christ. If in the course of this work we are able to provide for ourselves and our families, we are richly blessed. But the ideal is much more that we live to work than that we work to live (a commonly heard complaint).

Before attempting to analyze work further, we must clearly understand what is meant by work. Can work be subdivided into such categories as economic work, love work, and faith work? What distinguishes work from other activities, and one kind of work from another? We have already alluded to the crude contrast between work and play, with its implication that play is fun and work is not. This view categorizes activities according to subjective human attitudes. All too often we take the approach that if we like an activity, it cannot be work. This is surely a cruel distortion.

The other common way to define work, especially economic work, is by reference to market transactions—that is, generally speaking, whether money changes hands. Thus even prostitutes, for example, are referred to as "working girls" solely because they sell what under proper circumstances would never be called work. But having already considered the limitations of pricing—its inability to embrace everything that constitutes economic activity—we could hardly accept that definition here. Many kinds of economic work do not have prices attached to them. Work done in the home, on weekends, by volunteers painting a widow's house, by children, by retirees, and so on never enters the calculations of the GNP, nor does it readily enter into the standard conception of the purpose of work or where it is done. Yet these kinds of work are frequently economic in character and technologically enabled, conditioned, and modified.

The monetary definition of work has permeated modern society in a way that would be alien to earlier times and people. In the process it has frequently cheapened and sullied our view of work. The standard notion of unemployment, for example, is related only to those seeking but not finding a paying job. Yet being unemployed does not necessarily mean being idle: the unemployed frequently do nonpaying work. Likewise, statistics on the "labor force" count only those who earn pay for work or are seeking paying work; the figures ignore all others. And on the other side of the coin, to be considered "gainfully employed," one merely needs to get paid for something one does, not demonstrate that the activity is worthwhile—productive in any substantive sense—or even morally upright. A parent doing a splendid, conscientious job of raising three small children is not considered "gainfully employed"; a topless dancer in a nightclub is.

The tendency is to reduce the concept of work to paid activity and then to further reduce the concept of what goes on in "workplaces" to a series of rather mechanical acts—even if they are conducted by the human brain—that can be isolated and analyzed. Then if the "economics" (that is, the money) warrants it, the workers so employed are replaced by a machine, computer, or robot. At this point we are a long way from perceiving work as a calling, as a task done to praise God and serve our fellow human beings and the creation. This perspective must be recaptured if we are to be able to understand and weigh technology's effects on work.

Because the literature of economics restricts itself almost exclusively to work for which wages are paid, and because this sort of work is prominent in modern societies, we will turn our attention to it first. Technology and work have always been closely related for the obvious reason that production technology represents the pattern of the nonhuman doing of work. Human skills and strengths are augmented and sometimes superseded by the technological tools used in production. For example, the power to move materials is greatly increased by cranes; the power to process information is greatly expanded by computers. Human work is changed or eliminated by the use of technological tools. Throughout history these changes have been greeted with a variety of responses by the human beings involved. The responses have varied in part because the situations have varied—some technology has improved the workers' situation and some has worsened it—and in part because they have depended on the position and perspective of the particular workers. The Industrial Revolution provides a good example: it degraded the labor of the pieceworkers in the factories of "coketowns" and enhanced the work of the owners and managers of such factories. As this and many other examples show, technological change can significantly affect the quality of work.

It is also important to realize that although the effect of technology on real wages can be important—especially for those living near the subsistence level—this effect does not constitute an adequate perspective on the work-technology relationship. The benefits of working include far more than the wages earned, for work is an important way of realizing human service and potential. Those who decry modern work as dehumanizing have something of this in mind, although they frequently leave their charge too vague to be useful. The goal should be spelled out: work should be seen as the responsibility of God's image bearers to represent him on this earth, to grow as responsible persons, to care for earth and neighbor, to render good fruits—in short, to properly fulfill the cultural mandate. When we compare this conception of human work with the tasks that are done in connection with modern technology, we immediately perceive a large gap. Of course, technology is not entirely to blame. It can certainly be argued that work under primitive, low-level technological conditions can also be very degrading and not at all consonant with the picture of image bearers. Nevertheless, we bear the responsibility for the kinds of technology that have been chosen and the effect that they have had on work. And we could have handled this responsibility better.

Sensitive observers such as E. F. Schumacher and Peter N. Gillingham have reacted sharply not to the use of technology but to the form of technology chosen. Industrialism, say Schumacher and Gillingham, stunts the human personality "mainly by making most forms of work—manual and white-collared—utterly uninteresting and meaningless. Mechanical, artificial, divorced from nature, utilizing only the small part of man's potential capabilities, it sentences the great majority of workers to spending their working lives in a way which contains no worthy challenges, no stimulus to self-perfection, no chance of development, no element of Beauty, Truth, or Goodness."[12] Some have attempted to

12. E. F. Schumacher and Peter N. Gillingham, *Good Work* (New York: Harper & Row, 1979), p. 27.

dismiss Schumacher and Gillingham as opposed to progress, hopelessly idealistic, or utterly romantic. But before doing so we should question our own somewhat conditioned responses to defending the way in which we work. Have we lost sight of what it is really about? Do Beauty, Truth, and Goodness seem completely incongruent with our concept of work? Have we forgotten that work can be the learning, growing experience that Schumacher and Gillingham want it to be? Is it possible, for example, that we have heaped too much blame on television for creating mindless generations, that we should instead investigate what our work has done to us? In answering these questions, it is necessary to adopt not only a self-interested viewpoint—for it may be that God has blessed some of us with good work to do—but also the viewpoint of the least advantaged workers, those most degraded by the industrial system that delivers goods to our doors. Schumacher and Gillingham explain the negative goal of this system: "The basic aim of modern industrialism is not to make work satisfying but to raise productivity; its proudest achievement is labor saving, whereby labor is stamped with the mark of undesirability. But what is undesirable cannot confer dignity."[13]

We will return to the meaning of this emphasis on productivity, but we should note here that modern technology has played a crucial part in altering work in the direction that Schumacher and Gillingham decry. Hendrik van Riessen notes that technology has two parts: preparation or planning, and execution. The tendency is to shift responsibility from execution to preparation in such a way that execution is conducted merely within the pattern of the plan, without any creativity of its own. In fact, creativity at the execution stage frequently disrupts technicized work patterns. Van Riessen refers to this development as the intellectualization of work, and its potential impact is clear.[14] Intellectualizing work enhances the power and perhaps the work satisfaction of the planners and designers. But the intellectualizing of work at this level is frequently accompanied by a de-intellectualizing at other levels, accomplished either directly by reducing the remaining human functions to that of serving the machines or the plans, or indirectly by displacing human workers completely and leaving them to seek unskilled positions.

Technology thus has a qualitative effect on work. It changes the kinds of work that people do, and in the process it changes what they learn from their work, how much control they have over it, how much human volition they exercise, and so forth. It may well be that the same tech-

---

13. Schumacher and Gillingham, *Good Work*, p. 27.

14. Hendrik van Riessen, "The Structure of Technology," trans. Herbert D. Morton, in *Research in Philosophy and Technology*, vol. 2, ed. Paul T. Durbin and Carl Mitcham (Greenwich, Conn.: Jai Press, 1979), p. 303.

nology that enhances these characteristics for some workers simultaneously denigrates them for others. Given the labor-saving character—at the point of application at least—of most of the technology that is currently employed, it seems that there is a disproportionate number of jobs being denigrated compared with those being enhanced.

But what of the quantitative effect of technology on work? The conventional wisdom of our age is that technology creates wealth and employment in the long run. Because of the biased focus on monetary wealth, it is doubtful that this is necessarily true—or will be true in the future—with regard to real wealth. What about employment? Does technology, at the same time that it undeniably forces short-term readjustments, promise long-term employment to all who need work? Because no one knows the future, especially not the future of knowledge and therefore of technology, we cannot be sure. But we can look at some current trends and ask what can reasonably be expected.

One of these trends is unemployment, a plague of our times. There are many causes of unemployment, all of which we cannot elaborate here. But is new technology one of the causes? With regard to employment at least, some have described the present situation as the post-industrial age. The heavy industry that absorbed labor in the transition from agriculture to industry is now experiencing the same sort of shifts in productivity that agriculture experienced previously. As machines—especially robots—take over more and more of the production tasks, workers are displaced. The productivity per worker increases, but unless there are at least proportionate increases in total output, the number of workers required is correspondingly reduced.

As heavy manufacturing industry releases workers, where do they go? The answer seems to be that if they go anywhere in the labor force—and they may not have the needed skills to obtain another job—they are likely to go to the so-called service industry. The problem is that the service industry covers activities as diverse as janitorial services and brain surgery, and thus it is difficult to define the industry exactly. Barry Jones argues that the old three-sector analysis—agriculture, manufacturing, and services—should give way to a five-sector analysis: (1) primary (extractive), which includes agriculture, mining, and similar tasks; (2) secondary, which includes manufacturing and construction; (3) tertiary, which includes tangible economic services (based on the processing or transfer of matter and/or energy); (4) quaternary, which includes information processing (e.g., the work of bankers and real-estate agents); and (5) quinary, which includes domestic and quasi-domestic servicing or making, including unpaid work, home-based work with only incidental remuneration, and professional provision of quasi-domestic services (e.g., those offered by hotels, restaurants, nursing homes, and massage parlors).[15]

The advantage of Jones's division is that it allows analysis of some of the subparts of the service industry, such as information processing. The growth of this sector has been phenomenal; according to one estimate, it accounted for fifty percent of the United States labor force in 1980.[16] But although this growth has been spectacular, it is also being affected by tremendous technological change. Here the power of the computer, in conjunction with new devices for transmitting information such as satellites, is being applied by leaps and bounds. The result is increased productivity, probably accompanied by decreased employment.

Where will the displaced workers go? Jones has suggested they will either join the unemployed or move into new types of employment that are deliberately labor and time absorbing and that are aimed at satisfying individual and communal needs. This kind of work belongs in some ways to his last category, quasi-domestic services, but it is also part of what has been termed the convivial economic sector. The aim of this sector is the provision of services aimed at community well-being. Because communal goods are involved, this sector stands outside the market economy and requires public funding and management. The employment potential in this sector involves a different societal attitude toward the elements of well-being: a fuller recognition that not everything good for humankind comes from private market activity.

Adequate employment possibilities in the future may well depend on society's adopting actions and attitudes toward work that see it as intrinsically providing well-being. This may mean that work should be regarded as an economic output as well as an input. If so, society may decide to make technological and economic decisions that are directed toward preserving labor possibilities. To do so will require something of a change in attitude at all levels. Not only will society need to reconsider public policies directed at subsidizing capital in order to maximize an overall growth rate—thereby displacing labor—but it will also have to exercise economic responsibility with labor possibilities in mind. Here economic theory has not been very helpful. It has continued to regard the decision to work as a labor-leisure trade-off, with wages being the bribe necessary to overcome an inherent preference for leisure. This cannot possibly reflect all the choices involving work, but to the extent that it reflects something of the way we are tempted to choose, we must all change.

15. Barry Jones, *Sleepers, Wake!* (Oxford: Oxford University Press, 1982), pp. 50–52.
16. Marc Porat, *The Information Economy* (Washington, D.C.: U.S. Department of Commerce, 1977), p. 52.

As people regard their own labor possibilities, it may be that real wages as claims upon market goods—such as groceries and other necessities—loom large. But one must not get caught up in the notion that more real wages are always better. Instead, one should see the choice as involving all the aspects of love, service, justice, and moral choice. If work takes on this proper sense of coherence with the rest of people's lives, they are on the way to enriching their lives in a way not measurable by income or monetary levels. To be able to make these choices within the economic system, this larger view of wealth and welfare must be embodied in all levels.

Similarly, society must recognize that work and production take place outside the "workplace"—that is, outside of monetized work arrangements. This kind of work is also affected by technological tools and products. Many of the issues that affect monetized work affect this kind of work as well: the kind of technology that is developed and the way that technological objects are designed and used affect the work one does. Many times this is beneficial—for example, when the drudgery of domestic work is relieved. Few would like to return to the days of chopping kindling to light the stove to heat the water carried from the backyard pump in order to bathe in an iron tub on the kitchen floor. Modern household conveniences save us much time and effort. And while we must be careful not to seek our own convenience at the expense of others' necessities, all of us can rejoice that time released from such work can be put into—into what? Leisure? Not exclusively, it is hoped, but rather into other work: work consisting of loving acts of service and help, of religious study and discipline, and more.

But technologically altered work does not always give only benefits; sometimes it exacts costs as well. These costs consist of more than just those of resource use, which should themselves be weighed carefully. For example, the more we rely on technological objects to accomplish our work—and our play, for that matter—the less we develop our own talents and skills for these tasks; we allow them to atrophy instead. Gerhard Mensch suggests that the more we rely on highly sophisticated stereo equipment to provide us with music, the more we neglect to learn to make music ourselves for our own entertainment and that of our neighbors. Likewise, the more tools we possess to accomplish tasks, the less we need others to help us and the less others need our help. In the process, we no longer celebrate and enjoy the contributions of others.[17] At the same time, technological complexity increases our reliance on experts to repair and maintain the necessary hardware. Thus a change

17. See Mensch, *Stalemate in Technology,* pp. 223–24.

occurs: we may stop sharing with our neighbor, but we may become dependent on the expert.

Thus there is an intertwinement of monetized and non-monetized work. What people accomplish without buying and selling, as well as what they accomplish with it, depends a great deal on the technological tools and products that are available and that have been chosen to be developed. Even the mix of the two kinds of work depends to a significant degree on the technology that is available. Take, for example, weaving on hand looms at home versus the weaving done on massive industrial machines. And there are thousands of similar cases. Have we asked and carefully thought about which kind of work belongs where, who benefits, what the long-term consequences will be, what skills will be developed by technological changes and what skills will atrophy, and who will be able to find adequate work and who will not? In response to questions such as these, have we sought to be led by biblically based normative principles? It seems doubtful that we have tried to grasp the inpact of all these factors; instead we have allowed simple goals such as the pursuit of profit and an aggressive style of technological entrepreneurship to lead the way. Technicism, which pervades modern society, pushes ahead with technological change without pausing to ask questions such as these. But not to ask these questions is to abdicate a broader responsibility for useful work.

If society falters in this broader responsibility and thereby fails to achieve a sense of the importance of meaningful work to people of all aptitude levels, a sizeable portion of the population may face a bleak future. This future may bring an ironic historic twist: the introduction of a new leisure class. Once the social pyramid was capped with a leisure class of idle rich supported by the labor of the masses below them. In the future, it is possible that there will be a social structure that inverts this picture, that a small, hard-working, technologically sophisticated class will be at the top, and a large, involuntarily idle group will be at the bottom.[18] The latter group will be those who lack the skills employable in the technologically sophisticated marketplace, or who simply are not among the lucky few who land the available positions. Even if the productivity of the persons and machines at the top is sufficient to support the consumption of this new leisure class, they may—even if they consume plenty—be deeply impoverished by the lack of satisfying, useful work. And they, along with those who are pushed downward through the deskilling of the workplace, will be substantially disenfranchised, because they will be excluded from the learning experience that leads to future development. At the same time, it must be recognized that some deskill-

18. Barry Jones paints this picture in his *Sleepers, Wake!*, pp. 60–66.

ing could have beneficial aspects if it would make a place available in the work force for some of the inherently less able who would otherwise be excluded.

ECONOMICS, TECHNOLOGICAL CHOICE, AND TECHNOLOGICAL CHANGE

While changes in technology have clearly affected society's economic life, the reciprocal effect—the effect of economics on technological choice and change—is equally important. Indeed, in the long run, economic feasibility is usually the most significant factor affecting technological choice and change. Before exploring the economics of technological choice, it is important to note that economic factors do not stand alone: political decision-making, social mores, and the like are also relevant. However, even they frequently function via the economic valuing process. For example, the political will is frequently expressed in terms of tax penalties or incentives as well as outright subsidies. Likewise, the prevailing social values may well be communicated to inventors and producers through what people will and will not pay for. As in the case of the invention and use of computers, factors such as social acceptance, technical innovation, increased demand, and decreased cost all work in concert to bring about a substantial socioeconomic-technological change.

This history is repeated over and over again: new products and processes must be affordable in the dual sense of being low enough in cost *and* being valued highly enough by those individuals with the money to spend on them. Cars required technical invention and innovation to make them not only attractive means of transportation but also products that could be feasibly manufactured at comparatively low cost. This meant organization of the production process in a specific way, as achieved by Henry Ford's assembly line. But product feasibility also required social acceptance that did not occur overnight. Abandoning horse power for horsepower was difficult for many people. Even when they were convinced that they would enjoy a car, they also had to be convinced that it would provide superior transportation in all weather conditions, that satisfactory and extensive roads were available, and that they should part with perhaps half a year's salary to own one. And before cars could really go anywhere, other people needed to be convinced that cars were enough of a social good to warrant the building of better roads and bridges, and still others had to be convinced of the economic and technical feasibility of supplying gasoline, tires, and other needed automotive services.

In explaining technological change, two factors are almost always closely linked: the economic factors that must hold the promise of cost recovery and profits, and the technological factors that help put such possibilities within reach by finding economically superior objects or ways of introducing them. In turn, both the economic and the technological may be responding simultaneously to other cultural conditions. Thus, if a society suddenly decides to declare war on another people, its technological and economic structures will both move in the direction of enabling this decision. But it is nonsense to say that the resultant technological change—new missiles and bombs, for example—is economically determined. With the warning, therefore, that the economic does not and should not stand alone in any cultural issue, we will go on to address several parts of the economic aspect of technological change.

This section first considers four biases with which people often approach the issue of technological change. Next it considers producers and their role in technological change. Finally, it considers the consumers of technological objects and their responsibility in technological change.

Four Biases. We have already warned against the bias that overemphasizes the economic, as if it were the only thing dictating technological choice and change. This warning is necessary because some tend to focus exclusively on the economic because of its prominence.

Similar warnings against biases are necessary in regard to technological invention and innovation.[19] Many views tend to focus only on the spectacular, major, and frequently atypical examples of invention and innovation. In fact, technological change that affects society is frequently a slow, steady process of improvement and modification, with only infrequent major innovations. Similarly, many views pay excessive attention to the early stages of the process of invention and neglect the later stages. The notion is that technological invention consists of a single large breakthrough, followed by a lag before that invention is utilized. In fact, the period following invention is frequently filled with further modification and innovation to make the process or product suitable for use. Normally the directions chosen for the modifications are strongly influenced by economics, both in terms of the cost of the development process and the potential demand for the result.

A third bias relates to what we discussed in the previous chapter concerning science and technology: too much significance is attached to the development of the scientific knowledge as compared to the tech-

19. This discussion owes much to Nathan Rosenberg's *Perspectives on Technology* (New York: Cambridge University Press, 1976).

nological knowledge necessary for the employment of new technology. The latter is frequently thought of as a lower form of knowledge and therefore as inherently less interesting.

Finally, certain views are biased because they overemphasize continuity or discontinuity. Some study innovation as a hasty, all-out effort to achieve something new, an approach that emphasizes discontinuity. But while the lure of the new is compelling to some, it frequently does not make good sense on the basis of economics and other factors to follow the maxim "Try anything, but do it quickly."[20] Instead, innovation usually involves selective—not general—rejection of past practices. Conversely, other views overemphasize the continuity in technological innovation. These views implicitly assume that no matter how radical the technological change, social, cultural, and environmental discontinuities will not be a problem. For example, it is commonly assumed that the displacement of labor by technological changes in the means of production will not be a problem because other forms and sources of employment will automatically emerge. But this faith in the continuity of employment possibilities may not be warranted.[21]

Producers and Technological Change. Producers' interest in technological change can have a variety of motivations. They may be interested in providing better products, fulfilling a need, or better utilizing existing resources. But their interest may also be nothing more than a strategy for increased market share, profits, growth, or prestige. Earlier we dismissed the attempt to harmonize these two categories, the claim that some sort of "invisible hand" coordinates things in such a way that the pursuit of self-serving goals inevitably or automatically has positive results in the marketplace. It is not impossible that the two categories are in harmony, but it is not inevitable, and in many cases it is unlikely. The "invisible hand" notion has incorrectly dismissed this discussion of a lack of harmony as wrongheaded. The issue of technological change must be evaluated first of all on the basis of how well it serves God and one's neighbor, without the presumption that profits, growth, or power—in short, the trappings of market success—are a sufficient proxy for this service. No producer can be excused from wrestling with the multiple effects of a change in or use of technology simply on the grounds that it clearly increases profits.

Of course, some framework for decision-making is necessary. If a proposed change requires costly inventive and innovative activity, the question of justifying the expense of this activity arises. Within the

20. Mensch, *Stalemate in Technology,* p. 209.
21. See Jones, *Sleepers, Wake!*

narrow framework of market values, the probable costs of research and development are weighed against the probable returns from the sale of the results of the hoped-for technology. If there are no other guidelines, it becomes merely a matter of a complex gamble on whatever seems to promise the highest payoff. In this light, benefits are construed to be whatever money consumers can be convinced to part with. The results of these sorts of strategies are evident in the promotion of new but useless or wasteful products. Nothing sells like the latest fad, and nothing contributes to fads like skillful promotion. It is no accident that many of these fads are directed at children and teenagers, because they frequently offer the least discriminating resistance to clever and powerful promotions.[22]

If maximum profits, growth, and power are not the relevant bases for technological decisions, the way decisions are made must change. Consumers play a role in these decisions, of course, but business—by virtue of its power and opportunities—plays a special stewardship role in the pursuit of responsible technology.

The stewardship role can be exercised in relation to technological change only if it is seen in the context of an interlacing set of moral requirements to which our lives should respond. The economic viability and vitality of a business enterprise are factors that must be considered for the sake of economic continuity, but they must never be absolutized. Care for one's neighbor—especially the poor and powerless neighbor— care for the natural creation, and care for the worker are all part of the decisions of responsible businesses. Technological change must be evaluated in terms of these issues. The attitude that business should concentrate on growth and profits while others take care of environmental protection and cultural development is irresponsible and inadequate. Likewise, the attitude that technological change is dictated by business interests such as competitive advantage or growth in the market share leads to decisions that are in some ways unfair—decisions that slight the needs and rights of workers, for example. The problem is not technology, laments a group of workers recently interviewed by Radio Canada International, but management that regards people as the price of technology.

One issue that stands out clearly in the history of technological change and its effect on the workplace is the drive for increased productivity. In North America, productivity is normally defined in terms of output per unit of labor input. One way to increase productivity accord-

22. See Shirley Roels, ''Responsible Technology and New Product Marketing'' (Calvin College, 1984, unpublished manuscript).

ing to this definition is to increase the amount of capital that augments labor's powers of production. Indeed, this seems to describe much of the technological change embodied in capital goods. But notice that a perverse result is possible. If we continually strive to increase labor productivity, the optimum will occur when all output is produced by machines overseen by a single worker. The output per unit of labor input would thus be maximized, but we would obviously not have achieved a meaningful or appropriate system of production.

We could talk about other meanings of productivity—for example, the productivity of capital or of natural resources. The fact that we usually do not do so but focus instead on labor tells us something about the modern mind-set. Production technology should not exhibit any labor-saving bias, because no factor is cheap or expensive compared to any other if each one is paid in accordance with its output. Entrepreneurs are presumably interested in reducing any cost they can, not only the cost of labor. Yet the new technology definitely exhibits a capital-using, labor-saving bias.

It could be argued that this bias is the consequence of labor unions' pushing the cost of labor above its contribution to production, thereby making it appropriate for entrepreneurs to substitute capital for labor. While this has undoubtedly happened in some instances, it does not seem to be a complete explanation. It may be that costs, at least in terms of direct input costs, are not the only reasons or even the major reasons for replacing people with machines. It may be that certain human weaknesses together with the very things that are so intimately human—creativity, volition, and will—account for the desire to replace workers. Better quality control, greater consistency of output, fewer headaches (especially of an unpredictable kind), the absence of countervailing wills—all these factors may feed the desire to reduce labor input. These factors may indeed have some merit, but it is ironic to have certain human beings working to eliminate the foibles of others from the production process.

Karl Marx noted that modern industrial technology was following the path of liberation of production from the constraints of human limitations. The result, in his view, was the subordination of persons to machines. It is true that machines can do some things better than human beings—and therefore should, in some instances, be substituted for human workers—but this approach must not be taken too far. We must be especially careful of the technicistic mind-set that underlies it. To assume that a machine can do any job better than a human being can is clearly unwarranted. If this approach is taken, the only tasks that will be left for human beings to perform will be those that are, for whatever reason, beyond the peculiar capabilities of machines. Most of them will be tasks of too low a value to warrant valuable machine time or expensive technological development. One example of the mind-set that automatically pursues technological replacement of human-made or natural products is the preference of some for the uniform perfection of artificial turf over the imperfect beauty of natural grass. It is a mind-set that has frightening possible conclusions.

If we are willing—as we should be—to tolerate human individuality in the workplace, we may be missing a good thing by employing a restricted notion of capital formation and productivity increases. Currently the United States government, like almost all Western governments, uses tax incentives to subsidize the capital investments that businesses make in machines. The same changes in tax policy that increased the subsidies of this kind of capital also decreased the amount of funding for labor training. Perhaps this choice reflects the bias against human labor discussed above. Whatever the case, it seems that the superior strategy on the basis of efficiency alone (setting aside for the moment the other immensely important issues related to human development) would be to develop human capacities for work. This grassroots approach holds promise on a variety of fronts but seems beyond the understanding of many policymakers. A better approach would be to analyze the benefits of improving people's capacity for work not merely on the basis of their potential to contribute to market values but on the broader basis of wealth and welfare that we suggested earlier. Such an analysis would call for a substantial increase in concentration on and funding for job training and other labor-oriented programs. It would also result in a pattern of technology development that would differ from the present attempts to replace labor rather than enhance work.

Consumers and Technological Change. Consumers also have an obligation to make responsible decisions regarding technological change. It would be wrong to argue that businesses are not free to pursue profit or power but that consumers may seek whatever bargains they wish in the marketplace and let others worry about the effects. The coherence that should characterize the perspective and activity of businesses should also characterize the viewpoints and actions of consumers.

Too often consumers use a decision-making framework as narrow as that of self-interested businesses. Instead of asking whether the products of new technologies are really needed and what the implications will be for the environment and/or for the jobs of others, they ask only what the products will do for them. The products of the new technology belong to a category of goods that Fred Hirsch calls "positional goods."[23]

23. Fred Hirsch, *Social Limits to Growth* (Cambridge: Harvard University Press, 1976).

Positional goods are valued primarily for their contributions to getting ahead of others in some sense: the newest car, the biggest television screen, and the latest technical gadgetry show one's success and progressiveness, one's ability to outstrip one's fellow consumers.

The problem with the pursuit of positional goods—quite apart from the fact that it may constitute bad stewardship—is that their benefits are so easily eroded. As soon as others begin to copy and catch up, the newest of the positional goods become old hat and useless for their purpose. According to Hirsch, this pursuit is much like standing on tiptoe in a crowd in order to see the parade better: it is a good strategy only until others follow suit. After that point everyone exerts a great deal of effort, but no one is better off. So those who seek positional goods, like the Red Queen of Lewis Carroll's *Through the Looking-Glass,* run as hard as they can just to stay in the same place.

Instead of pursuing materialistic aggrandizement, consumers should willingly be responsible for the fact that they represent, collectively at least, the demand for the benefits of technology. As such, they bear a significant responsibility for technological choice—or at least for its ratification—and for the concomitant costs. The consumer's action is distanced from issues of resource use and care for the environment only because it is usually the sum of consumer choices, not merely the choice of each individual consumer, that creates the effects. This does not excuse individual consumers from responsible action, although it does demand that new attention be paid to the issue of collective responsibility. In either case, the scope of the responsibility for the justice of technological change—its impact on the environment, on natural resources, on workers, on the poor, on Third World countries—lies within the purview of responsible consumer decisions. True, consumers are not solely responsible for these things, but their decisions do belong to the matrix of actions that affect technological change.

Finally, the state has a role to play in making responsible decisions regarding technological choice and technological change. The development and use of technology are not inherently such private activities that they have no public aspects. The presence of externalities alone indicates this. Where issues of public justice are concerned, the state clearly has a role to play, as the following chapter indicates.

* * * * *

In order to correctly view the economics of technology and the technology of economic activity, one needs new understandings of both. In this chapter we have tried to broaden the traditional economic definitions of productivity, work, and consumption. Doing so means perceiving economic activity as a single aspect of our multifaceted lives, limited in scope and yet integrated with all belief and action. There is to be no economics of the marketplace that is isolated from such concerns as care for one's neighbor, justice, community, and care for all the creation, whether priced or not. There is no proper economic justification for a technology that is efficient and nothing else, just as there is no proper economic justification for a technology that enhances corporate profits and nothing else. Developing a proper understanding of economic relationships involves not only recapturing a proper sense of economic stewardship—a giant task in itself, considering where society presently places its loyalties—but also placing the economic aspects of life within God's will for all the other aspects of living. When his normative standards for all of life are simultaneously followed, economics and technology will mesh—not as dual expressions of humanity's hubris and desire for autonomy from God, but as a coherent fulfillment of men and women's call to praise God and to serve their fellow human beings and the natural creation in all their cultural activities.

CHAPTER EIGHT

Technology and the State

MODERN GOVERNMENT IS BIG. OBSERVERS OFFER DIFFERENT EXPLANA-tions of why governments have grown to gigantic proportions in modern Western societies and differ in their evaluations of the positive or negative effects of this growth, but no one denies the fact of big government. And bigness implies power and influence. Indeed, government plays a major role in all modern societies. The size, power, and pervasiveness of government and the major, pervasive role that technology plays in modern society suggest that there must be a profoundly important relationship between the two. If we are to understand technology, we must understand this relationship.

Christians, who see the state as a God-given means "to punish those who do wrong and to commend those who do right" (I Pet. 2:14), have an added reason for examining the relationship between technology and government. In light of the state's position as a means of correcting wrong and rewarding right, what is the God-intended role of the state in relationship to technology? Does the reference in I Peter to "those who do wrong" extend to persons and corporations who commit technological evils? Does God intend the state to play a role in directing and shaping technological development and change?

This chapter explores the relationship between government and technology and what that relationship should be from a Christian perspective of state and society. It first considers the biblical view of the role of the state in society. Then it explores the major role that the American government currently plays in technological activities. Finally, it discusses the possibility of government's playing a guiding role in technology and the factors that work against this possibility.

THE STATE

Down through the millennia many thinkers have written about the nature of the state and the role it plays in society. Their conclusions have differed widely, but almost all of them have perceived the state as the possessor of power, rule, and authority in society. Aristotle, for example, wrote of politics as establishing "rules determining what we should do and what we should leave undone."[1] In the fourteenth century, Marsilio of Padua wrote, "Human law is a command of the whole body of citizens. . . . I mean a command the transgression of which is enforced in this world by a penalty or punishment imposed on the transgressor."[2] In the modern era Max Weber has written that a political relationship exists "if and in so far as the enforcement of its order is carried out continually within a given territorial area by the application and threat of physical force on the part of the administrative staff."[3]

Prominent in all three of these formulations—and in countless others—is the notion of power, rule, and authority. The state rules by making decisions for a society that have the weight of authority: the appropriateness or moral necessity of obedience underlies its decisions, and its power—its ability to compel obedience and to punish those who fail to obey—backs them up.

The Bible also assumes this key characteristic in its many references to government and the state. But it goes deeper in order to answer the questions of the basis of political authority and the purposes for which it ought to be exercised. As Christians we believe that the Bible teaches two basic things about the state: it has been established and ordained by God, and its basic purpose is to promote justice.

When Christ was on trial before the Roman governor Pilate and refused to answer some of his questions, Pilate asked him, "Do you refuse to speak to me? Surely you know that I have power either to free you or to crucify you?" Jesus replied, "You would have no power over me if it were not given to you from above" (John 19:10–11). This idea of governmental authority originating in God's ordering of human affairs permeates all of Scripture, from Moses' instructions to the Israelites concerning the appointment of judges, to Paul's description of governing authorities as possessing their authority by act of God and as fulfilling a divine institution (Deut. 16:18–20; Rom. 13:1–2). It is on this basis that Emil Brunner writes, "Thus power does not belong only to the state as a reality, but to the state as a creative ordinance of God."[4] British scholar

1. See *The Politics of Aristotle*, trans. Ernest Barker (Oxford: Oxford University Press, 1946), Appendix I, p. 355.

2. Quoted by George H. Sabine in *A History of Political Theory*, 3rd ed. (New York: Holt, Rinehart & Winston, 1961), p. 295.

3. Max Weber, *The Theory of Social and Economic Organization*, trans. A. M. Henderson and Talcott Parsons (New York: Oxford University Press, 1947), p. 154.

4. Emil Brunner, *Justice and the Social Order*, trans. Mary Hottinger (New York: Harper & Brothers, 1945), p. 212.

Alan Storkey has written that the state "was gradually established and took different forms under God's guidance in response to a definite social weakness and need."[5]

If the state was established by God in response to certain social needs and situations, the question of the state's purpose and goals arises. Why did God establish it? What purposes does he intend it to fulfill? Most Christians have responded that justice lies at the heart of the answer. As Brunner has written, "The power of the state exists in order to put justice into action wherever justice would not be done and injustice done without the intervention of its power."[6] The state must also act according to other normative principles such as open communication and stewardship, but its central task is to promote justice and suppress injustice.

To understand what God intends the nature of the state to be and what divine purpose it fulfills in his ordering of human affairs, one must understand justice and its relationship to the individual. Ethicist Henry Stob has written, "Justice, Christianly understood, demands that every human being be treated according to what he essentially is. And what he essentially is, is first of all a person, i.e., one who bears in his very being the image of God and who in addition has been mandated and commissioned by his Creator to perform an important task in this world."[7] In Chapter Four we argued that as image bearers of God human beings are knowing, self-consciously creative, responsible beings. Justice means that human beings are treated as such.[8] They thereby possess the freedom and opportunity to act in society as the knowing, creative, responsible beings God intended them to be. For a society to be marked by this sort of freedom and opportunity, it must be marked by the mutual acceptance of certain obligations. The individual's freedom and opportunity to worship God, to pursue a career, to buy a home, and so on are assured when society accepts the obligation not to interfere with worship, not to arbitrarily limit career opportunities, not to deny persons the right to buy homes in the neighborhoods they choose, and so forth.

Injustice then means that there are forces present in society that refuse to accept their obligations to others and thus limit or destroy freedoms and opportunities for persons to act as true image bearers of God. In-

5. Alan Storkey, *A Christian Social Perspective* (Leicester, England: Inter-Varsity Press, 1979), p. 294.

6. Brunner, *Justice and the Social Order*, p. 214.

7. Henry Stob, *Ethical Reflections: Essays on Moral Themes* (Grand Rapids: Eerdmans, 1978), p. 133.

8. The concept of justice can also be applied to creatures and objects in the sense that an animal or a tree, or even a natural feature such as a deposit of oil or a river, is to be given its due as such. But here we emphasize justice in relationship to human beings because this is the form of justice we see as being the focus of the state's role.

justice can be perpetrated by economic or social structures that deny equal opportunities for education, career advancement, or social interaction. Or injustice can arise when a social order is turned into a chaotic, lawless situation in which the strong prey upon the weak and all are subject to random violence. Even the state—instituted by God to promote justice—can become a twisted, demonic institution that serves injustice by denying freedom and opportunities through totalitarian actions. Whatever the source, injustice means men and women are oppressed, are robbed of the freedom, joys, and opportunities God intends for all his children, and are forced into confining molds they are powerless to change.

The state, as God's instrument for justice in this fallen world, is to struggle against those social structures and systems that would deny justice to all God's children. It is thereby called to fight against economic systems that confer inordinate wealth on the few through oppression of the many, against racist social attitudes that deny a racial group their rightful chance to live the free, opportunity-filled lives God intends for everyone, and against unjust laws that deny people the opportunity to freely choose how to worship God, educate their children, and pursue careers. In short, God expects the state to protect his children from oppressive, justice-destroying structures and systems, including oppressive, justice-destroying technological structures.

In the first chapter we noted that technology can take on—and often has taken on—an oppressive character that destroys shalom. Here it is important to note that justice and shalom are closely related yet distinct. Nicholas Wolterstorff explains that "shalom is intertwined with justice. In shalom, each person enjoys justice, enjoys his or her rights. There is no shalom without justice. But shalom goes beyond justice."[9] Justice is a precondition for shalom. Many of the conditions and circumstances that destroy shalom also destroy justice. A technology that enslaves children in textile mills, robs future generations of natural resources by using them profligately, or becomes a tool used to subjugate and terrorize an entire nation is as destructive to justice as it is to shalom. A society that has attained justice—has attained a situation in which freedom and opportunities are present because the members of society, in obedience to God's will, recognize and accept their mutual obligations to each other—has moved a long way toward shalom. All that needs to be added is a certain delight, a vibrancy, a joy that can flower only under conditions of justice but that even justice cannot guarantee.

9. Nicholas Wolterstorff, *Until Justice and Peace Embrace* (Grand Rapids: Eerdmans, 1983), p. 69.

If technology were being done in keeping with God's will and in accord with biblically based normative principles, it would be done in a just manner. Shalom would then be the final blessing. Within the technological structures and institutions themselves and within society in general there would be forces and processes that would block destructive technologies and open the way for technologies done in service to God's will and in keeping with justice and the other normative principles. If this were the case, political rule and authority would be unnecessary. In a sinless world, justice would mark human relationships, the result of men and women acting in a natural, spontaneous, and joyful obedience to God's normative will. Love would abound, and therefore justice would abound. It is only when human sin—an unloving selfishness, an attempt to put self center-stage—fractures human relationships and destroys justice that the state needs to intervene in an attempt to restore justice. Emil Brunner has spoken clearly on this point:

> The more forcefully state-free justice, the social *ethos,* has developed, and the more thoroughly it shapes society according to the law of justice by its own strength without state compulsion, the more state help can be dispensed with. The fundamental Christian realization is that the state has only to intervene where individuals, families, free social groups, the churches, the municipalities, [and technological structures, we would add] cannot perform their tasks. Any justice created by the state is a makeshift, a substitute for the justice which human society should create of itself. [10]

Therefore, when technology violates God's normative will, thereby violating justice and other normative principles, the state has the God-given responsibility to use its power, rule, and authority to guide technology back onto paths of justice. This does not mean that the state is unconcerned about the normative principles besides justice, or that its actions do not affect those principles. Indeed, the state must pursue all normative principles simultaneously. The *focus* of the state's concern is justice, but by reason of this concern it is necessarily involved in and concerned with other normative principles such as cultural appropriateness, stewardship, open communication, trust, and delightful harmony.

An unjust technology is the very type of structural evil that God intends the state to struggle against, to control, limit, and direct so that his children, his image bearers, may live as he intended—in creative and responsible usefulness with joy, delight, and harmony. In God's ordering of humankind's affairs, it is the state that has been given the

10. Brunner, *Justice and the Social Order,* p. 205.

power, rule, and authority with which to correct and direct technology when it becomes unjust.

The issue Christians thereby see when they look at the relationship between technology and government is that of direction. When should the state use its authority to intervene and blunt or block a particular trend in technological development? Or intervene to promote a certain trend? When is intervention unnecessary because the technological structures are following justice-promoting paths? How can the political system maintain the independence and distance from the technological structures that it needs to judge those structures? These are the kinds of questions we face when exploring the relationship between technology and government.

GOVERNMENT AND TECHNOLOGICAL PRACTICES AND INSTITUTIONS

The American government as well as those of other modern societies has the power—the legal, available means and leverage—to direct the movement of technology. The pervasive involvement of government in technological institutions and practices indicates that it has the means to significantly influence the pace and course of technological development. Indeed, it is not an exaggeration to say that without government, the current structure of technology would collapse. It follows, then, that government could redirect technology by changing its involvements with technology.

Because government and technology are so intimately intertwined and because this intertwinement has developed gradually over a long period of time, it is easy to overlook the pervasive role that government plays in technology. To explore this point more fully, we will concentrate on the American situation, recognizing that very similar situations exist in all modern, technologically oriented societies.

Government as a Subsidizer of Technology. Government heavily subsidizes the doing of technology. The public periodically complains about the ADC—Aid to Dependent Children—program, but there is another, less visible but more extensive kind of ADC: Aid to Dependent Corporations. To grasp the magnitude of the government's assistance of technologically oriented institutions, we will consider three forms of direct aid and three forms of indirect aid.

Most obvious is direct *government subsidies for research and development* (R & D). Research grants and contracts are available through such government organizations as the National Institute of Health, the

Office of Research and Development within the Environmental Protection Agency, the National Science Foundation, and the Defense Advanced Research Project Agency. In addition, many governmental laboratories are involved in R & D, such as the National Engineering Laboratory of the National Bureau of Standards and the Environmental Research Laboratory of the National Oceanic and Atmospheric Administration, as well as such well-known national laboratories as Los Alamos, Brookhaven, and Oak Ridge.

All of these R & D activities translate into enormous government expenditures. The American government spent some $37 billion for R & D in 1983, $43 billion in 1984, and the 1985 budget proposal of the Reagan Administration asked for $52 billion.[11] Even more instructive are the figures comparing government funding for R & D with private R & D funding: in recent years the government has spent more for R & D than the private sector has. In 1980, for example, the federal government spent $34 billion for R & D; the private sector spent $30 billion.[12]

But this direct subsidy of technology through R & D is only one form of government's support of technology. A second direct form is *a variety of tax incentives.* Tax laws—as they relate to capital gains, depreciation allowances, and R & D tax credits—are a powerful means with which to stimulate technological development. Based on a series of case studies, Richard Nelson has concluded, "Some of these [governmental] policies are broad in scope, although their influence differs from industry to industry. The tax codes are one of these. While the influence of the tax code is pervasive, particular features, such as the treatment of capital gains, appear to be particularly important in certain industries."[13] In its drive for technological development, Japan's government has followed suit, making extensive use of "tax credits and deductions for research, development, and pilot plant facilities."[14]

A third form of direct governmental support of technology is the use of *subsidized loans and loan guarantees,* often combined with tax incentives. These programs can be used either to encourage the development and implementation of new technologies or to support existing

11. Janice R. Long, Lois R. Ember, and David J. Hanson, "R & D Funding Will Rise 14% in 1985 Federal Budget," *Chemical and Engineering News,* Feb. 13, 1984, p. 8.

12. Richard A. Rettig, "Applying Science and Technology to Public Purposes: A Synthesis," in the National Science Foundation's *Five-Year Outlook on Science and Technology,* vol. 2 (Washington, D.C.: Government Printing Office, 1982), p. 397.

13. Richard R. Nelson, "Government Stimulus of Technological Progress: Lessons from American History," in *Government and Technical Progress: Cross-Industry Analysis,* ed. Richard Nelson (New York: Pergamon Press, 1982), p. 477.

14. J. Herbert Holloman, "Government and the Innovation Process," *Technology Review,* May 1979, p. 35.

firms that have chosen not to innovate and face stiff competition (usually from foreign businesses). According to Robert Reich, "American industries threatened by foreign competition have also been propped up by a wide assortment of government subsidies, special tax provisions, and subsidized loans and loan guarantees." Reich estimates that such support programs cost the United States government about $66 billion in 1980.[15]

This massive direct subsidy of technology is dwarfed by the indirect subsidies that government provides. Three are especially important. First is *education*. State, local, and federal governments spend billions of dollars annually to provide an educational system that goes from prekindergarten classes through postdoctoral research programs. This educational system produces a trained population from which the various technological institutions draw their researchers, designers, production workers, managers, and marketers. Without the public educational system and public support of private institutions of higher education, technological structures and processes would collapse for lack of trained workers. J. Herbert Holloman and his associates at MIT studied technological development in several countries and found that a source of educated, skilled workers is a key ingredient in technological development: "Most developed countries view the quality of manpower skills as a direct determinant of technological development. Manpower development policies are therefore a key feature of many nations' programs for strengthening technological change." Holloman and his associates conclude by suggesting that since "qualified manpower is essential to technological change," Congress should develop a policy that will incorporate job training in the general education program and also provide training for the present work force.[16]

Government trade policies also have a profound impact on technology and its path of development. Japan has effectively used protectionist trade policies to assist its emerging high-tech industries.[17] Robert Reich has argued, however, that American protectionist policies designed to shield American steel and automobile industries from foreign competition have retarded technological innovation in those indus-

15. Robert E. Reich, *An Industrial Policy for America: Is It Needed?* (Washington, D.C.: Government Printing Office, 1983), pp. 25–26. Although Reich clearly sees such supports in a negative light because they often retard technological innovation, no such value judgment will be offered here. If American firms would ever reject technological innovation out of broader, socially responsible considerations, some protection or help from the government might be in order. But the purpose here is to point out another form of governmental impact on technological development.

16. Holloman, "Government and the Innovation Process," pp. 39, 41.

17. Holloman, "Government and the Innovation Process," p. 34.

tries.[18] Thus it seems that trade policies can encourage or discourage technological change, or can direct it into certain channels; the effect depends on which industries are afforded what protections from what type of foreign competition. But in any case, the influence of government is present and real.

The patent policies of government must also be considered.[19] Patents have two effects, both of which are aimed at stimulating technological development. First, patents give innovators financial protection by granting them exclusive rights to market a new product for a certain period of time. A financial incentive is thereby created for the development of new technologies. Second, innovators must make their innovations public in order to to obtain patents, and thus patents encourage the rapid dissemination of information about new technology. A patent holder has exclusive rights to market his or her innovation for a given time period, but others can use the knowledge gained from the innovation to develop additional technological objects. Understandably, government policies concerning what is patentable and the length of patent life have profound impacts on the pace and direction of technological development.

Government also protects and supports technology by *limiting the liabilities of companies* involved with technology. We have grown so accustomed to the concept of corporations with limited liability that we hardly give them a second thought. But a corporation that is in some ways independent of its owners, officers, and employees is a legal creation that has had a profound impact on encouraging technological innovation and experimentation. Those involved in a corporate enterprise are protected from personal financial loss if the corporation experiences financial trouble. In addition, they are not personally liable in product liability suits. Thus personnel in such a corporation are guaranteed crucial protections from personal, catastrophic financial loss if the company introduces a new technological object into the marketplace and is confronted with financial failure of the product and/or with lawsuits.

In summary, government protects and subsidizes technology in countless ways. If these governmental protections and subsidies were removed or altered, the way technology is done today would collapse or be significantly changed.

Government as a Consumer of Technology. Government is also a major consumer of technology. Because it is a principal purchaser of

18. Reich, *An Industrial Policy for America,* pp. 25–26.
19. Regarding the effect of government patent policies on technological innovation, see Nelson's "Government Stimulus of Technological Progress," pp. 476–77.

certain technological tools and products it has an enormous impact on their development. The field of telematics—the integration of telecommunications and computing—provides an example. Dan Schiller has concluded that "the Federal Government has played a major role in the invention and innovation of telematics in U.S. society," largely because it has pumped so much money into telematic industries since World War II. Schiller determined that the government has purchased almost fifty percent of such equipment and the systems in which it is used.[20] Other examples abound. According to J. Herbert Holloman, "Government procurement has played a significant role in establishing aircraft designers as commercial innovators."[21] Similar statements can be made about the semiconductor and computer fields.[22] The government's defense and space procurement programs in particular have stimulated and directed development in the so-called high-tech area.

Government as a Regulator of Technology. Government also regulates technology by establishing certain standards or conditions that technological objects and technological research must meet.[23] Clear examples are the standards for energy efficiency and air pollution that the government has imposed on the automobile industry. Additional illustrations are found everywhere one looks, from recombinant DNA research, to the nuclear-energy industry, to drug safety and effectiveness, to toxic waste disposal, to the use of agricultural pesticides. Government regulation is pervasive in scope and far-reaching in impact. It can stimulate technological innovation, as it does when it sets certain standards for an industry, which then seeks to meet them by technological innovation (as happened when the automobile industry was required to meet energy and air-pollution standards). Or it can stifle innovation by setting standards that only existing technology can meet (many housing codes are of this nature). But in either case, the government's impact on the pace and direction of technological change is overwhelmingly strong.

All this means that the political system has legally available means to profoundly affect the way technology moves and develops. Through its direct and indirect subsidies, its purchases of technological objects, and its regulatory activities, government is a dominating presence in tech-

20. Dan Schiller, *Telematics and Government* (Norwood, N.J.: Ablex Publishing, 1982), pp. 191, 192.

21. Holloman, "Government and the Innovation Process," p. 32.

22. See Nelson's "Government Stimulus of Technological Progress," pp. 452, 459–62, and 471–72.

23. For a discussion of how government regulation affects technological development, see Nelson's "Government Stimulus of Technological Progress," pp. 473–74.

nological institutions and structures. And God has given government the task of shaping the pace and direction of technology in order to help promote justice and struggle against injustice. Government is thereby intended to help bring about a society in which responsible technology, done in obedience to God, will flourish. A God-given role and the capability to fulfill that role seem, happily, to meet.

Yet this is not the whole story. Government does not operate in a pristine environment free of pressures from organized interests, partisan considerations, officeholders' self-interests, and public prejudices and biases; nor is it free from certain pressures emanating from the technological structures themselves. The next section of this chapter explores the reasons why the political system—despite its enormous power and its God-given role to promote justice—is often ineffectual in fulfilling its task of moving technology toward greater justice.

BARRIERS TO A PROPER RELATIONSHIP

The argument made thus far leads naturally to a conclusion that is often drawn: government should control technology, and only government can do so effectively. Samuel Florman has argued for governmental control of technology over voluntary self-control: "Voluntary good works are to be admired wherever they occur. But in the world of industry, compulsory good works, *ordered by legislation,* provide much better protection for society, and for men of conscience within industry as well."[24] The image such a position conjures up is that of a car and driver. The driver is clearly separate from the car and in control of it. He or she determines how fast and where the car is to go. Similarly, government can be seen as being separate from technological institutions and structures, and as possessing the means to control them. The discussion thus far could very well lead one to this conclusion, but the picture is far from complete.

The relationship between the political and technological systems is far more complicated than that suggested by the image of a car and driver. It is not a matter of inanimate, passive machinery being controlled by a self-directing, volitional person or social structure. Instead, one is dealing with two volitional social complexes or systems that are rooted in the same society and that interact with each other. This section considers the dynamics of the interrelation of government and technology, and thereby reveals several formidable barriers to government's playing a proper, justice-promoting role in relation to technology.

24. Samuel C. Florman, *The Existential Pleasures of Engineering* (New York: St. Martin's Press, 1975), p. 26; italics ours.

Weaknesses Inherent in Government. First, we need to keep in mind certain problems or weaknesses inherent in the very nature of government in a sinful, broken world. These are relevant to government's relationship to technology as well as to all other social and economic structures in society.

Weaknesses inherent in government have been considered elsewhere,[25] so we need not go into detail here, but a few brief points may be helpful. Most basic is the fact that the state, the God-given institution to work against the effects of sin in society and to bring about a measure of order and justice, is itself infected with sin. As noted earlier, the state is needed because of humankind's tendency to do technology in a sinful, unjust manner. But political processes are no more spared the contaminations of sin than are technological processes. Thus at the outset we know that the hubris, the selfishness, the drive for autonomy apart from God that often leads technology astray is also likely to lead politics astray.

More specifically, one must understand the role that self-interest often plays in public-policy decisions. Re-election, career advancement, and public recognition are goals earnestly sought after by most public policy makers. If any of these conflicts with the pursuit of justice, there is no guarantee that justice will win. Compounding this problem is the role of interest groups. There is no guarantee that government will respond to justice and not to powerful special-interest groups, including those with a powerful self-interest in having technology develop along certain lines that may be far removed from justice and other biblically based normative principles.

This is not to suggest that we cannot expect government to play a positive role in promoting just public policies. The American government and the governments of other modern democracies often do act as instruments of justice. The point is that they are fractured, imperfect instruments. But as we turn from the general nature of government to the specific way in which government relates to technology, we will note other barriers that hinder government from fulfilling its true task.

Common Societal Roots. Technological and political institutions both spring from the same culture, with its constellation of assumptions, values, and beliefs that are often technicistic. The implications of this are seldom clearly understood. As we noted in Chapter Four, technicism seeks human autonomy from God and thereby reduces all things to the

---

25. See, for example, Duane Lockard, *The Perverted Priorities of American Politics* (New York: Macmillan, 1971); Elizabeth Drew, "Politics and Money," *The New Yorker,* Dec. 6, 1982, pp. 54–149; Stephen V. Monsma, *The Unraveling of America* (Downers Grove, Ill.: Inter-Varsity Press, 1974), pp. 65–71, and *Pursuing Justice in a Sinful World* (Grand Rapids: Eerdmans, 1984), pp. 55–82.

technological, seeing technology as the solution to all human problems and needs. The belief that society's salvation lies in technology pervades modern culture and is a crucial force driving technology. And it sometimes propels technology to violate justice and the other biblically based normative principles.

But—and this is the crucial point—technicism permeates political processes as deeply as it permeates technological processes. Our Christian perspective leads us to expect the state to protect society from the consequences of the excesses of technicism, but the state itself is infected by the disease. All of the literature cited earlier in this chapter that considers the role of government in relation to technology examines that role in order to determine how government can more effectively develop technology and increase the pace of technological change.[26] It is assumed that more rapid technological change and greater technological sophistication constitute progress. Human progress and technological progress are seen as being one and the same, and government is assumed to play a crucial role in achieving that "progress." None of these assumptions or beliefs is questioned. This spirit is reflected in the Stevenson-Wydler Technology Innovation Act of 1980, thus described:

> It was designed to *promote United States technological innovation* for the achievement of national, economic, environmental, and social goals by (1) establishing organizations within the executive branch to study and *stimulate technological innovations;* (2) *promoting technological development* through the creation of certain incentives for industrial technology; (3) *stimulating* improved utilization of federally funded technological developments by State and local governments and the private sector; (4) *providing encouragement for innovation* through the recognition of individuals and companies which have made outstanding contributions in technology; and (5) encouraging the exchange of scientific and technological personnel among academia, industry, and the Federal laboratories.[27]

In short, government is a product of the same mind-set and the same set of beliefs that have given rise to technological institutions and processes. Both are rooted in the same faith. This constitutes a formidable barrier to the state's maintaining a proper, justice-promoting relationship with

---

26. We especially have in mind the works cited earlier by J. Herbert Holloman, Richard R. Nelson, Richard A. Rettig, and Robert E. Reich.

27. U.S. Congress, House Committee on Science and Technology, Subcommittee on Science, Research and Technology, *Implementation of P.L. 96-480, Stevenson-Wydler Technology Innovation Act of 1980* (Washington, D.C.: Government Printing Office, 1982), pp. v–vi; italics ours.

technology. The political system tends to reinforce and abet existing technological emphases and directions instead of evaluating, judging, and redirecting them in keeping with biblically based normative principles.

Political Decision Makers' Dependence on a Technological Elite. A third crucial factor that hinders the political system from properly judging and influencing the direction and pace of technology lies in the fact that the political system's decision makers usually do not possess technical expertise. They must rely upon technical experts for the information they need to judge the proposals and recommendations of those very experts. This creates an obvious problem. What compounds it is the tendency for huge sociotechnical structures to emerge with a small technically skilled elite at the top. This technological elite then dominates the political decision makers. Technocracy replaces democracy.

Such developments stem from the fact that modern technology is built upon specialization, with a small number of people possessing a great deal of highly specialized knowledge about very small areas. This means that public policy makers, who are generalists by nature and of necessity, do not possess their own independent knowledge with which to judge the information the technological experts give them. Thus it is hard for them even to tell if all relevant information is being provided, much less to evaluate its quality and accuracy. This being the case, how are they to properly judge the meaning and implications of this information for public policy and public justice?

Langdon Winner, the author of *Autonomous Technology,* has reviewed works by Don Price and John Kenneth Galbraith, and reached this conclusion:

> The guiding assumption is that in a society based on sophisticated scientific technologies, the real voting will take place on a very high level of technical understanding. The voice that one has will depend directly upon the information, hard data, or theoretical insight one is able to supply in a group decision-making process. One may register to vote on this level only by exhibiting proper credentials as an expert. The balloting will be closed to the ignorant and to those whose knowledge is out of date or otherwise not directly relevant to the problem at hand.[28]

Obviously, this kind of voting excludes most ordinary citizens. As David Dickson notes in *The New Politics of Science,* "A gap has been successfully maintained between public participation in decisions about

28. Langdon Winner, *Autonomous Technology: Technics-Out-of-Control as a Theme in Political Thought* (Cambridge: MIT Press, 1977), p. 170.

science and technology and the placing of such decisions under direct democratic control."[29]

Adding to this picture of technocracy is the alleged existence of a highly centralized structure of technological institutions and processes, dominated by a few gigantic technical conglomerates and the elite that runs them. This new elite possesses both technical and political power, as Jacques Ellul explains: "There is a limited elite that understands the secrets of their own techniques, but not necessarily of all techniques. These men are close to the seat of modern governmental power. The state is no longer founded on the 'average citizen' but on the ability and knowledge of this elite."[30] A technocracy is thereby established, with the result that the political system loses control to technological institutions and processes.

But there are indications that this view is overly pessimistic about the ability of politicians without technical expertise to make policy decisions involving technological issues. Political decision makers often have their own technical experts who evaluate and comment on the technical issues the decision makers face. In the United States, Congress has created the Office of Technology Assessment, and the president has the Office of Science and Technology. The executive branch of government also has its own technical experts in almost every field of activity. Public policy makers, therefore, have means by which to evaluate and weigh technical issues that are independent from the technological structures themselves.

Even more important, the position that argues that a technological elite reigns over the world of technology and dictates its will to the political system is too simple. Various studies by political scientists have questioned the very existence of a tightly knit elite of this nature; other analysts such as Jean Meynaud who do not rule out its existence nonetheless have difficulty describing it with any precision.[31]

It is in fact clear that technical experts often disagree among themselves. When this occurs, political decision makers are in a position to choose among contending options and to seek out additional perspectives and information with which to make technological choices. Edward E. David, Jr., has written, "The public and its representatives

29. David Dickson, *The New Politics of Science* (New York: Pantheon Books, 1984), p. 220.

30. Jacques Ellul, *The Technological Society,* trans. John Wilkinson (New York: Knopf, 1965), p. 274.

31. See, for example, Robert A. Dahl, *Pluralist Democracy in the United States: Conflict and Consent* (Chicago: Rand McNally, 1967); Robert A. Dahl, *Who Governs? Democracy and Power in an American City* (New Haven, Conn.: Yale University Press, 1961); and Jean Meynaud, *Technocracy,* trans. Paul Barnes (New York: Free Press, 1964).

have discovered what those inside the [scientific and engineering] community have known for many years, and indeed have taken for granted as a desirable and essential feature of the research and development process: the community is seldom of a single mind, even on questions at the core of scientific knowledge, particularly when these have social and economic consequences.''[32] Whenever experts publicly disagree, new options are brought to light, weaknesses or gaps in data exposed, and possible consequences of contrasting courses of action debated. The tough questions that the nonexpert might not have the knowledge even to ask are discussed. The nonexpert political decision maker and even the interested citizen are suddenly in a better position to make informed judgments concerning the social, political, and economic implications of rival public-policy choices.

This is not to suggest that the lack of technical knowledge of political decision makers and their consequent reliance for much of their information on an elite composed of the very experts they are seeking to control is not a problem—only that it is not an incapacitating problem. If this was the only barrier to government's effective promotion of justice in relation to technology, it could be overcome.

Technological Structures That Have Co-opted Government. Although the dependence of political decision makers on a technological elite poses an obstacle to the government's promotion of justice in technology, government also faces another, more challenging barrier. Langdon Winner has articulated it cogently, and we begin by summarizing his view.

Winner argues that the way technology is done carries within it certain imperatives that compel political decision makers to reach certain policy decisions, whether or not there is a technical elite pressing them to do so. His argument begins with what he calls the technological imperative and the phenomenon of reverse adaptation. The technological imperative states that "technologies are structures whose condition of operation demand the restructuring of their environments."[33] There is a logic in technologies which demands that certain conditions be met:

> If you desire X and if you have chosen the appropriate means to X, then you must supply all of the conditions for the means to operate. To put it differently, one must provide not only the means but also *the entire set of*

32. Edward E. David, Jr., "On the Dimensions of the Technology Controversy," *Daedalus* 109 (Winter 1980): 171. On the frequent disagreement of technical experts and its significance for policy makers, see also Allan Mazur, *The Dynamics of Technical Controversy* (Washington, D.C.: Communications Press, 1981), pp. 10–42.

33. Winner, *Autonomous Technology*, p. 100.

means to the means. A failure to follow the correct line of reasoning in formal logic brings an unhappy outcome: absurd conclusions. Failure to follow the dictates of the technological imperative has an equally severe outcome: a device produces no results (or the wrong one). For this reason, once the original choice has been made, the action must continue until the whole system of means has reached its proper alignment.[34]

The technological imperative may demand that certain economic conditions be met—for example, that certain raw materials be supplied or certain types of factories be built—but it may also demand certain social or cultural attitudes or forms of organization. On this point Winner quotes W. W. Rostow, who notes that the technological imperative often demands the modernization of traditional societies: "Psychologically, men must *transform or adapt* the old culture in ways which make it compatible with modern activities and institutions. . . . In their links to the nation, to their professional colleagues, to their political parties, to their labor unions, *men must find* a partial alternative for the family, clan, and region."[35]

Also key to Winner's position is his concept of reverse adaptation, which he defines as "the adjustment of human ends to match the character of the available means."[36] Usually one would expect means to be adapted to one's chosen ends. But in reverse adaptation the means are determinative. Winner gives two examples of the concept:

Efficiency—the quest for maximum output per unit inputs—is, no one would question, of paramount importance in technical systems. But now efficiency takes on a more general value and becomes a universal maxim for all intelligent conduct. . . . Similarly, speed—the rate of performance and swiftness of motion—makes sense as an instrumental value in certain kinds of technological operations. But now speed is taken to be an admirable characteristic in and of itself. The faster is the superior, whatever it may be.[37]

Having explained his concepts of the technological imperative and reverse adaptation, Winner goes on to argue that there does not need to be a technological elite in order for the technological structures in a society to totally dominate the government. He writes, "The approach we have now taken traces the fundamental source of important decisions in matters involving technology beyond the role of any particular class

---

34. Winner, *Autonomous Technology*, pp. 101–2.
35. Cited by Winner in *Autonomous Technology*, p. 103; Winner's emphasis.
36. Winner, *Autonomous Technology*, p. 229.
37. Winner, *Autonomous Technology*, pp. 229–30.

or elite—technical, scientific, administrative, or political—to the configuration of technological conditions themselves."[38]

These "technological conditions," rooted in the technological imperative and reverse adaptation, are what come to govern political decision making:

> The influence of socially necessary technical systems begins to constrain rather than liberate political choice. The technological imperatives appear in public deliberations as generalized "needs" or "requirements"—for example, the need for an increasing supply of electrical power—which justify the maintenance and extension of highly costly sociotechnical networks. Reverse adaptation takes the form of more specific goals and projects—the needless crusade for a new manned bomber, for instance.[39]

In other words, because of the constraints of the technological imperative and reverse adaptation, political decision makers are forced to move down very narrowly defined technological paths. They appear to be in charge, to be making real decisions, but in fact their decisions have been preordained. As a result, Winner claims, "no matter who is in a position of control, no matter what their class origins or interests, they will be forced to take approximately the same steps with regard to the maintenance and growth of the technological means."[40]

The substance of Winner's argument is correct. There is abundant evidence that what Winner calls the technological imperative and reverse adaptation are very much present in modern societies. When the chairman of the board of TRW-Fujitsu declares, "Civilization must adapt, the impact of technology must be absorbed"—that is, issues the technological imperative—few objections are raised by mainstream Western culture. Reverse adaptation is equally apparent and accepted. How else can one explain such projects as the Concorde, the British-French SST that has been a steady financial drain on both nations? Speed has come to be an end in itself instead of an appropriate, carefully thought-out means to some equally appropriate, well-conceived end.

The result is tight constraints on government; it is co-opted by the technological structures of society. A good example is the commitment American society made in the 1950s to the automobile as a major form of private transportation. With this commitment, wedded to a worship of speed and efficiency as ends in themselves and not simply as means, the construction of a vast network of freeways in post-World War II

38. Winner, *Autonomous Technology*, pp. 261–62.
39. Winner, *Autonomous Technology*, pp. 258–59.
40. Winner, *Autonomous Technology*, pp. 263–64.

America became inevitable. The outcome would have been no different if other political decision makers had been in power at the time.

This co-opting of the state by technological structures is indeed a formidable barrier to the state's playing its God-given, justice-promoting role in relation to technology. The following section considers what needs to happen if the state is to free itself and reassert its proper role.

FROM TECHNICISM TO BIBLICALLY BASED NORMATIVE PRINCIPLES

The results of the state's inability to effectively fulfill its justice-promoting role in relation to technology are readily apparent. It is estimated that 2,400 chemicals that may be carcinogenic are being used in the workplace, with unknown health consequences for workers. Of the thirty to forty million tons of hazardous waste generated annually by American industry, eighty to ninety percent is being disposed of improperly. We continue to generate electricity by using nuclear power even though there is no known way to safely dispose of the highly radioactive waste products. We build weapon systems of increasingly destructive capacity despite the fact that we already have all the destructive capacity we could conceivably ever need.[41]

To begin to understand how we can break the cycle of a technology gone wrong and reassert societal control through the state as God intended it to be, we need to recognize that technology has gained its powerful hold on the state because of technicism. That is the heart of the matter. Winner's technological imperative and reverse adaptation work as they do because of society's unthinking faith in technology as progress, as the way of salvation. Society clutches new technologies to its bosom without asking any questions about consequences and costs. As we noted in Chapter Three, technology is not neutral. Any new technology carries with it certain assumptions, implications, and consequences. Yet technicism plunges ahead without asking what they are. And once a new technology starts to gather momentum, technicism does not allow anyone to call a halt to it, despite certain negative consequences that may gradually become apparent. That would be opposing

41. On the above points, see the introduction to *Risk in the Technological Society,* ed. Christoph Hohenemser and Jeanne X. Kasperson (Boulder, Colo.: Westview Press, 1982), p. 5; William J. Librizzi, Jr., "Love Canal: A Review of Government Actions," in *Risk in the Technological Society,* p. 73; Susan Fallows, "The Nuclear Waste Disposal Controversy," in *Controversy: Politics of Technical Decisions,* ed. Dorothy Nelkin (Beverly Hills: Sage Publications, 1979), pp. 87–110; and Ralph E. Lapp, *Arms Beyond Doubt: The Tyranny of Weapons Technology* (New York: Cowles Book Company, 1970).

progress. Animals, the natural environment, people, society, the state—all must respond to the technological imperative.

Similarly, reverse adaptation rests upon technicism. Speed, efficiency, increased complexity and sophistication—all of which should be means to carefully thought-out ends—become ends in themselves to which humankind must bow down. Why? Because technicism says that such means involve change, and change is progress. A faster bomber is a better bomber. A computer is a better means of keeping a family budget than a ledger book. Everywhere we are confronted by a never-say-die faith in "progress."

Because society as a whole has adopted the faith of technicism, government is unable to play an effective role in justly directing technological structures. The heart of the problem turns out to be religious. The command to love God above all and one's neighbor as oneself needs to be followed. Not that technology and its fruits are always evil. In fact, they are often good. What is needed is a means to properly evaluate and judge technologies, and that comes from following biblically based normative principles. Such principles need to replace technicism as humankind's guiding standards.

With technicism's hold on society broken and at least certain large segments of society seeing technology within a framework of biblically based normative principles, government would regain the freedom to raise questions concerning ends, means, costs, risks, and purposes. The old cliché that you can't stop progress would lead immediately to the question, "But what is progress in this situation?" This question could then be debated in legislative chambers, executive branch offices, courtrooms, and the news media. Government would continue to come up against problems and barriers inherent in a fractured, sinful world. But it would be freed at last to begin to play a justice-promoting role in relation to technology. It would still fail sometimes, but it would have the potential to push and prod, to limit and encourage technology in a way that it currently cannot. The state would play a significant role in picking and choosing among technological options. A certain caution would replace the headlong plunge into every new technological possibility that comes along.

Breaking technicism's hold on society would mean that both those active in technological structures and the general public—not only as citizens but also as consumers and users of technological objects—would also be freed to raise the same questions of ends, means, costs, risks, and purposes that government would be raising. This triple impact—of self-correcting, self-policing forces within technological structures themselves, a market composed of responsible consumers, and a government freed from the distorted perspective of technicism— would lead to a fundamental change in the modern way of doing technology. The way would thereby be opened for a responsible technology, done in response to justice as well as to all the other biblically based normative principles.

CHAPTER NINE

A Design Philosophy

THE DOING OF MODERN TECHNOLOGY IS A SELF-CONSCIOUS ACTIVITY. Modern technological products such as television sets, home computers, and intercontinental missiles result from long, intricate, self-consciously planned processes of development and execution. Both our definition of technology (in Chapter Two) and our consideration of how modern technology differs from premodern or classical technology (in Chapter Six) have taken technology's nature into account. In Chapter Two we also noted that doing technology involves the two stages of design and fabrication, closely linked as two interacting parts of the production process. They are also linked by the fact that the fabricating facilities and procedures are themselves the result of a design activity. In light of the central role that design plays in both planning and fabrication, this chapter and the next focus on this activity.

Adding to the importance of the design activity is our concern with what normative principles are directing technology. The normative principles that one consciously or unconsciously relies upon and works out in design deeply affect the values that are embedded in the technological products and tools finally produced. It is at the design stage that the value-ladenness of technology—which, we have noted, is a necessary characteristic of technology—is given content and form. It is at the design stage in the automobile industry, for example, that decisions are made such that a car will be produced and marketed either as a solution to a basic transportation problem or as a solution to the ''need'' for a status symbol. How fabrication is done, of course, also has a normative dimension. Whether or not a given technological object is mass-produced or handmade, for instance, is affected by the normative principles one follows. But such decisions are usually made in the planning or designing process. Our concern for the value-laden character of technology, therefore, drives us to carefully consider the design aspect of doing technology.

This chapter goes about developing a philosophy for technological design by first considering the nature of design and ways to study it. Next it argues that design must be holistic, must take into account all the aspects of reality within which a technological object will function. This approach must be properly guided, and thus certain normative principles that should direct the design activity are discussed. Following that, a section on design specifications focuses on the holistic application of normative principles within the design process itself. Finally, the idea of sufficient design is introduced as a concept that encapsulates all these elements of our philosophy for doing technological design—holism, normative principles for design, and proper design specifications.

TECHNOLOGICAL DESIGN: AN INTRODUCTION

A Definition. We have made general references to technological design, but now more precision is called for. Design is that structured, innovative activity whereby people creatively use theoretical and practical knowledge and available energy and materials in order to specify the size, shape, function, and material content of a technological object. Theoretical knowledge arises from the activities in the various scientific disciplines such as physics, chemistry, engineering, economics, biology, psychology, and sociology. Practical knowledge includes various rules of thumb that designers have developed over the years and that are based somewhat on the sciences but in large measure on experience. Newton's laws of motion or the measured values of the viscosity of oil are examples of theoretical knowledge. The conclusion that, for a certain type of building, the heat loss to the environment on a winter day is "so many energy units per building surface area" is an example of practical knowledge.

Design depends not only upon theoretical and practical knowledge but also on the availability of energy and materials. It assumes the existence of the physical creation, and utilizes both knowledge and available energy and materials in its activity.

Design is also a "structured, innovative activity," a series of steps needed to creatively develop new or existing ideas into tools and products that fulfill a particular need. These steps consist of recognizing a need among a broad spectrum of groups (from public-policy makers to consumers), specifying in detail how to fill that need, developing and evaluating the various ways to meet these specifications, and deciding which design to detail and fabricate. The outcome of this process is the specification of "the size, shape, function, and material content of a technological object," seen as an innovative solution to meeting the need. Design results in a blueprint or set of detailed instructions for the physical characteristics of a technological object—either a product or a tool. Instructions for facilities and procedures needed to fabricate the object are included in these specifications.

It should be noted that although the design process is a structured activity, it is rarely if ever carried out in a rigid, linear way. One step does not follow another in lockstep fashion until the tool or product "automatically" emerges. Feedback plays an important part in the process. The results of one step—for example, certain design specifications—may lead to changes in prior steps, such as redefining an identified need. Furthermore, this kind of structured thinking about design may enhance rather than inhibit creativity in that it more clearly focuses people's attention on the broad range of tasks that must be accomplished.

The Design Itself. The outcome of the design activity is the design itself. Egbert Schuurman has argued that a design is expressed in formulas and drawings that represent the "laws" of technological objects and that serve as guidelines for fabrication.[1] Mario Bunge elaborates on the idea of the "laws" of technological objects: "Because artifacts [technological objects] are under intelligent control or are endowed with control mechanisms which have not emerged spontaneously in a process of natural evolution, they constitute a distinct ontic level characterized by properties and laws of its own—whence the need for elaborating a technological ontology besides the ontologies of natural and social science."[2] In other words, technology's development of laws can be compared to science's discovery of the universal laws of nature—for example, the laws of the conservation of energy, gravity, and momentum. The modern design activity consists of developing the "laws" or concrete embodiments of cars, planes, washing machines, and other technological objects. Nevertheless, there is a difference between the design process used to develop the "law" of the technological object and the scientific method used to discover laws of nature. Whereas science discovers the laws of what is embedded in natural, created reality, design embeds into reality the "laws" of various tools and products. In short, science describes the natural while design develops the artificial.[3]

1. See Egbert Schuurman, *Technology and the Future: A Philosophical Challenge* (Toronto: Wedge Publishing, 1980), p. 362. We have purposely put "laws" in quotation marks to indicate that the "laws" being discussed here are quite different from the laws of natural science, which are seen as universal.

2. Mario Bunge, "Philosophical Inputs and Outputs of Technology," in George Bugliarello's *The History and Philosophy of Technology,* ed. Dean B. Doner (Urbana, Ill.: University of Illinois Press, 1979), p. 271.

3. One can also note the difference between invention and design. Invention strikes upon the idea of airplane, computer, and so forth; design deals with the development of the idea, the "blueprint" for a particular, concrete embodiment or "law" of that idea.

Studying Design. This leads to the question of how best to study the design process in order to understand it and the normative principles it follows. One possibility would be to observe individuals doing design in a few specific industries and then analyze their work in detail. This method would certainly lend itself to an explication of some of the details of design. The problem with this approach, however, is that one would tend to accumulate mountains of information about specific design activities, but only slowly—if at all—uncover the basic patterns present in design activity. Also, making design decisions and doing the actual work of designing—even within a specific design project—are tasks usually performed by many persons, and thus an enormous number of individual activities would need to be considered in detail before patterns useful for analysis would emerge. This method of analysis, which may have its place within a given industry, ends up being somewhat akin to studying a forest by studying the individual trees.

A better method—the one followed here—analyzes general patterns of design. This broader approach is helpful both to the general public, who need to understand technology better, and to the decision makers within the design activity, who need an overall perspective on their work. To achieve this broader approach, it is helpful to employ what Hans Lenk and Gunter Ropohl (following Max Weber) refer to as an "ideal type" analysis of design.[4] Instead of making a close scrutiny of a few individual efforts, this approach involves observing the design activity from some distance so that overall patterns can be seen more clearly. This approach takes a general perspective on the design activity based on an amalgamation of a wide range of experiences and analyses of design. It has to do with the concept of design, not with individual design activities.

It is true that procedures observed from a distance do not apply in every design situation and that even where they do apply they are not always consciously followed by those involved in the design activity. But this does not negate the value of formulating a broad picture of design.

A HOLISTIC APPROACH

Those involved with the design activity use the concepts of, say, airplane, gun, and microwave oven in order to design the particular embodiments of these concepts—a Boeing 747, an M-16 rifle, a model EZ oven. The question thus arises, Exactly what design philosophy is

---

4. See Hans Lenk and Gunter Ropohl, "Toward an Interdisciplinary and Pragmatic Philosophy of Technology: Technology as a Focus for Interdisciplinary Reflection and Systems Research," in *Research in Philosophy and Technology*, vol. 2, ed. Paul T. Durbin and Carl Mitcham (Greenwich, Conn.: Jai Press, 1979), p. 32.

being followed? What approach to the design process is taken—what approach *should be* taken—when instructions are developed for fabricating the specific technological tools and products of our age?

What is needed is a holistic approach to design. For our purposes, holism is the view that the integrated whole of a technological object has a reality independent of and greater than both the sum of its parts and its particular function. For example, a commercial bread-baking oven is more than merely the assembly of its parts—burners, hearths, motors, timers, and so forth—and more than merely its particular function of baking bread. To describe it at all adequately, one must consider such aspects of it as the baking process, the experiences of the operator, the economic value of its function, the tastes of the consumer for certain types of bread, its effect on homemaking (no longer is a parent's love associated with the smell of fresh, homemade bread), and its effect on employment since its function became partially automated. In short, a commercial oven as a technological tool touches all of life. A holistic approach says it must be viewed accordingly.

This holistic description of tools and products relates to how we actually experience most if not all such objects. In practice we experience concrete reality as a unity. Herman Dooyeweerd (from a Christian perspective) and Robert Pirsig (from a perspective of Eastern religion) have reminded us that there are two realities: one's abstract models of reality, and the concrete reality of everyday experience.[5] Nevertheless, we do not distinguish between the two in daily life; we experience things as unities. For instance, we seldom experience a car as a variety of individual parts, or even as a form of transportation; we usually experience it as a means of interaction, mobility, or even social status. Donald MacKay illustrates this kind of perception when he describes a signal flashed from ship to shore as a complex unity of the physics of light and communication.[6] What is experienced is a unity: the concrete reality of message. We can analyze the light using physical laws and analyze the receiver— the human being—in terms of psychological principles, but these abstract models of reality do not do justice to defining or describing the experience of receiving a message.

The case for a holistic approach to design rests primarily on the fact that the technological tools and products produced by design and fabrica-

---

5. See Herman Dooyeweerd, *Roots of Western Cultures: Pagan, Secular and Christian Options* (Toronto: Wedge Publishing, 1979), p. 44; and Robert M. Pirsig, *Zen and the Art of Motorcycle Maintenance: An Inquiry into Values* (New York: Bantam Books, 1974), p. 54.

6. See Donald M. MacKay, "Man as a Mechanism," in *Christianity in a Mechanistic Universe,* ed. Donald M. MacKay (Downers Grove, Ill.: Inter-Varsity Press, 1965), p. 57.

tion enter everyday experience as unities. This being the case, design itself should be holistic. Indeed, people's lives are affected not by technological objects per se, but by how these objects function in all aspects of reality. A car not only conforms to the laws of physics and chemistry, but is also an object of proud ownership, has a value relative to that of alternate purchases, and is a focus of trust, because the buyer believes that if it is used correctly, it will not be harmful. If an object is to function well in all of its aspects, they must be taken into account in its design. And that is what holistic design seeks to do.

Confirmation of the importance of a holistic approach comes from those concerned with legal problems in the area of product liability:

> It is clear that today, under strict liability, a manufacturer's design process can be considered inadequate if based solely on the traditional criteria of cost, engineering adequacy as to function and manufacture, prescriptive adequacy as to regulations, codes and standard industrial practice, and marketability. If the design process is narrowly limited to satisfying the traditional criteria identified above, the elements of hazard identification and risk analysis which focus on the realistic interaction of the user and the device will be bypassed.[7]

Indeed, practical experience with the performance and safety of products has resulted in the call for a broad approach to design. At one level, this call could certainly be construed as self-serving, as no more than a way to avoid costly lawsuits. However, at a deeper level it expresses concern for safety and usability while recognizing the essential character of the holistic interaction between technological objects and human beings in everyday experience.

Proper, responsible design is holistic design. It recognizes that each designed and fabricated object functions in a rich variety of ways and should be designed with respect to each of these. Victor Papanek, a noted industrial designer, has called for this type of design in specific instances. For example, he has specified that the team that designs a high chair "should include furniture makers, pediatricians, child psychologists, babies, and mothers in addition to a product designer well-versed in materials and processes."[8] Papanek clearly recognizes that the design of technological objects must take the diversity of reality into account if those objects are to function well.

Holistic design of this nature involves making value judgments in all of

---

7. L. C. Peters et al., "Design Engineering and the Law," *Mechanical Engineering* 99 (Oct. 1977): 46.

8. Victor Papanek, *Design for Human Scale* (New York: Van Nostrand Reinhold, 1983), p. 32.

the various aspects of reality. Taking these value judgments into account in designing the object is the creative challenge for the designer. But is this enough? Does holism provide sufficient content for a design philosophy? One only has to imagine a horrific product—a gas chamber for the wholesale murder of innocent victims that is "well-designed" and "functional" in all aspects of reality (at least from the viewpoint of a Hitler)—to realize that a proper design philosophy requires something more than holism. One still must determine what normative principles should be followed in the practice of holistic design.

NORMATIVE PRINCIPLES FOR DESIGN

In Chapter Three we argued that technology is necessarily and intrinsically value-laden. Technological objects embody valuing, involve making decisions concerning knowledge, resources, and materials for which there are no neutral or purely objective bases. In addition, technological objects have embedded in them properties and capabilities that open up certain consequences and possibilities for interaction with their environments and close down others. And there are no neutral bases on which to decide which properties and capabilities to embed in technological objects. Technology, in short, is value-laden. As we have noted, valuing is not simply a matter of expressing human preferences; it is responding to God's will, to his normative standards.

These considerations lead us to consider the question of normativity in the design process. In design, a host of decisions are made about which knowledge, materials, and resources should be used and which properties and capabilities should be embedded in technological objects.[9] When technology is done responsibly, these decisions are made carefully, thoughtfully, and self-consciously, and they are made in keeping with biblically based normative principles. Holistic design is important, but it needs to be undergirded by normative principles that take into account all of the aspects of reality within which the technological object is to function.

The eight normative principles we set down in Chapter Five are the ones we believe should guide technological design. As we seek to apply these principles specifically, it is helpful to keep in mind the concepts underlying them: we should develop and make use of God's creation as he intends, thereby showing it proper respect; and we should seek to

9. For a study that argues, as we do, for the role of values in technological design, see Robert E. McGinn's "What Is Technology?" in *Research in Philosophy and Technology*, vol. 1, ed. Paul T. Durbin (Greenwich, Conn.: Jai Press, 1978), p. 196.

increase the opportunities for all people to be the loving, joyful beings God intends. We thereby show love to God and our neighbor. Even though we will discuss these normative principles individually, they are to be followed simultaneously, not in isolation from each other.

Cultural Appropriateness. All those involved with design must make sure that their designing results in culturally appropriate technological objects. This means making appropriate decisions in regard to the five sets of opposites defined in Chapter Five: continuity and discontinuity, differentiation and integration, centralization and decentralization, uniformity and pluriformity, and large scale and small scale. Those involved in design must not design technological objects that totally embrace one or the other of each of these five pairs of opposites, nor should they simply strike a balance midway between them. Victor Papanek's concept of "telesis"—from the Greek *telein* (to complete)—directly supports the idea of cultural appropriateness: "The telesic content of a design must reflect the times and conditions that have given rise to it, and must fit in with the general human socioeconomic order in which it is to operate."[10]

This norm is not simply one of accommodation to anything that works in a given cultural setting. But it recognizes that many aspects of a given culture are gifts of God, evidence of the working out of his will in that particular setting. These important cultural manifestations should not be destroyed by an intrusive technological object. Indeed, the culturally appropriate tool or product is one that both alleviates human burdens and preserves what is wholesome and good in a given culture. In this way it strikes an appropriate balance between continuity and discontinuity.

It is also important to balance the opposites of centralization and decentralization. Should our culture be more centralized and homogeneous or more decentralized and heterogeneous? This is a very complicated question to which there is no simple answer; we need aspects of both centralization and decentralization. For example, decentralized modes of living might depend on inexpensive electricity from solar sources, but cheap solar electricity is often dependent on microchip-based products that can be inexpensively manufactured only in centralized design-and-fabrication facilities.[11]

Those involved in design should consider such matters of balance in following the normative principle of cultural appropriateness. Determining what is and what is not appropriate in a given situation is not easy. It

10. Victor Papanek, *Design for the Real World: Human Ecology and Social Change* (New York: Bantam Books, 1973), p. 34.

11. This is an example that Papanek uses in *Design for Human Scale*, pp. 110-11.

demands a communal discernment of what is right in a given culture, of what comports with the will of God for that people. As we noted in Chapter Five, this discernment should be guided by the simultaneous following of the other normative principles, the great command to love, and a basic respect for and understanding of the God-created and God-willed diversity found within creation and humankind.

Openness and Communication. Uniting the normative principles of openness and communication results in the principle of open communication. In technological design, open communication means at least two things: (1) there should be no secrets about the value judgments being expressed and the knowledge being used in the design process, and (2) there should be no secrets about the known possible effects of the designed tools or products. These two standards should apply both within organizations involved in the design process and in their relationships to the general public, the ultimate users of the objects being designed.

Peter Drucker, author of *Technology, Management and Society,* has emphasized that "communication, in organizations, demands that the masses, whether they be employees or students, share in the responsibility of decisions to the fullest possible extent."[12] In addition, a designer or a team of designers must be completely open with other designers and with management concerning the design options that have been selected, others that have been rejected, and the potential or actual problems of the design. In a competitive atmosphere it is often difficult to admit to others—even within one's own organization—the weaknesses and problems in one's own work or in a colleague's work or, worse yet, in a superior's work, but the principle of open communication demands precisely this. To do otherwise is dishonest and risks violating other normative principles such as justice and caring.

The issue of openness becomes even more controversial when this principle is extended to the general public. Should the decision-making process within a given organization be open to public scrutiny? Should those making design decisions freely share their ideas, expressions of values, warnings, and decisions not only with each other but also with the public? Prevailing practice certainly dictates otherwise, as Jordan Baruch points out:

> Technology is developed in secret. Publication is anathema, the final test of validity is public use. . . . So strong is the drive for secrecy that early public policy created the U.S. patent system. Society went so far as to grant a

12. Peter F. Drucker, *Technology, Management and Society* (New York: Harper & Row-Colophon Books, 1970), p. 22.

monopoly to the technologist in exchange for revealing the technical knowledge embodied in the patent's disclosure. Engineers and technologists often work in teams and share knowledge within the host organization, but outside lie the competitors. Technologists work very hard to prevent the spread of their new knowledge.[13]

Some secrecy might be necessary in technological design, particularly when certain issues of national security are involved. However, these instances should not set the standard but rather should be necessary exceptions to the rule of open communication with the general public. If people are to be responsible with respect to technology—if consumers, for example, are to be more than mere passive receivers of products, are to participate responsibly in decisions that transform their culture—they must have appropriate information about the design process and, where possible, participate in it. The patent system is a reasonable vehicle for encouraging such openness while maintaining a way to compensate for work done. Disclosure laws are also helpful. Disclosure laws regarding such things as dangerous toxic chemicals being used in the workplace and the energy consumption of various products—such as energy-use data on new cars and new electrical appliances—help meet the normative principle of open communication.

In addition, if a design purports to solve a particular problem in a certain culture, designers have a responsibility to clearly communicate that value to the culture. Cultural appropriateness cannot really be properly judged unless people know what they are getting into when a particular tool or product is introduced into their culture. Those involved with design should see to it that these objects have no hidden consequences. Consumers should understand the proper use of an object and the consequences of its use, including any possible dangers.

This aspect of open communication is part of the Christian's responsibility to love one's neighbor by not "bearing false witness against" him or her. Meeting this responsibility means providing accurate information about a variety of technological objects. Within a highly literate, modern culture, the best way to communicate how to safely use a given drug is to print this information on the label of its container or in an accompanying leaflet. Workers need to be properly told how to safely use the technological tools of their trade, and the public needs to be properly told how to safely use technological products. Consumers who buy lawnmowers, for example, should be given easily graspable instructions and cautions. For example, the danger of a stone's hitting the rotating blade of a mower

13. Jordan J. Baruch, "The Cultures of Science and Technology," *Science,* Apr. 6, 1984, p. 7.

could be graphically illustrated by comparing the force of a stone thrown off the blade with the force of a stone dropped from a several-story building.

Stewardship. The normative principle of stewardship as it applies to design activity focuses first of all on the proper, limited use of finite resources. Making and using technological objects means utilizing finite materials such as natural resources and energy. Design specifies the kind and amount of materials and energy to be employed in the fabrication and use of technological objects. In light of both the short-term and the long-term problems of resource depletion and environmental damage caused by the careless acquisition and cavalier use of these resources, the design community must see to it that designs are economic in terms of stewardship—that is, frugal out of respect for the nature and finiteness of the resources used.

Second, stewardship means that proper respect is paid the objects and creatures God has created, including humankind. Technological tools and products should be designed in such a way that the nature of materials, plants, animals, and human beings is brought out and enriched, not trampled upon and ignored. Humankind thereby "tills" the creation by encouraging it to blossom and be fruitful. To build a dam that stops up a wild, free-flowing river and floods valuable agricultural land is not to act as a good steward of either the river or the land. Someone who instead designs a series of smaller dams in different locations might increase the cost of the project, but by locating the dams in nonagricultural areas and maintaining the river as a thing of beauty and grace, he or she is following the normative principle of stewardship.

Third, stewardship means that the natural environment is protected from pollution and other degradations. Therefore, one should design agricultural equipment so as to minimize erosion, cars and electrical generating plants so as to minimize air pollution, and sewage-disposal systems so as to minimize water pollution. Technology must not be allowed to destroy God's good creation.

Fourth, stewardship means that technological objects must be designed so that they can be easily repaired or rebuilt when certain parts wear out and so that they can be easily recycled when their useful life is over. To design objects according to a throwaway mentality or the modern creed of planned obsolescence violates the normative principle of stewardship. To do so wastes the valuable materials of creation, and stewardship unequivocally demands something better.

Delightful Harmony. In Chapter Five we noted that the normative principle of delightful harmony means three things: a harmonious technological object must be effective in the sense that it does well what it purports to do, it is pleasing and satisfying to use, and it promotes harmonious relationships between humankind and God, between differing cultures and societies, among people within the same culture or society, and between humans and the natural creation. This means that those involved in design must ask questions about the quality of the interaction between the object and its user. The user's ideal response is that the object is good—even a joy—to use. To elicit this response, the technological object must be designed so that it works well and gives its user a sense of accomplishment and satisfaction. The designer must take human abilities and needs—physical, aesthetic, and emotional—into account. The designs that encourage a harmonious relationship between object and user are born out of a kind of experience and intuition akin to that of craftsmen of an earlier time. These craftsmen intuitively followed certain rules, including the following:

(1) The product, object, or artifact should work well with a minimum of repair or maintenance.

(2) The designed object should meet the expectations of the end users.

(3) Most things should be made at the direct request of the people, to fulfill a specific need or want. [14]

In fact, both the design of a technological object and the designing activity itself should promote harmonious relationships. This of course makes harmony a very broad concept in this context, and one that is intertwined with the other normative principles, especially stewardship, justice, and cultural appropriateness. This intertwinement points up the real sense in which normative principles must be followed either simultaneously or not at all.

Justice. Designers must see to it that their work promotes justice, that each person receives his or her due as an image bearer of God, and that the rest of creation receives proper respect. This means, among other things, that designers should work to meet the other normative principles already discussed. It is unjust not to show a culture proper respect, not to freely provide accurate information about a technological object, not to respect the human need for harmony, not to conserve resources, and not to practice a proper respect for the creation. But none of these foregoing normative principles by itself would really prevent injustice—for in-

14. Papanek, *Design for Human Scale*, pp. 70–71. The idea of quality—Pirsig's central theme in *Zen and the Art of Motorcycle Maintenance*—although too elaborate a concept to describe here, may cast some additional light on the meaning of harmoniously delightful tools and products.

stance, the wrongful use of a technological object as a symbol of exclusivity by a small social group or even as a means of repression by one group over another. It certainly is possible that objects can be used by some to manipulate others—intentionally or otherwise—into wrongful positions of powerlessness.

This lack of power is evident in the field of computers, where one can be confronted with problems ranging from the inability to correct a computer-caused error in one's credit rating, to a feeling of helplessness in the face of highly sophisticated computer-controlled data banks containing a great deal of personal information that would be very harmful if misused. In both cases, nonexperts are definitely at a disadvantage: their financial and personal fate lies in the hands of those who understand computers and computer programming. The call, then, is to design computers and computer systems so that they are culturally compatible, economical with respect to resources, pleasant to use—and so that they discourage the discriminatory use of information. Computer systems that encourage the invasion of privacy certainly discriminate against those whose lives are then open to wrongful public scrutiny. The normative principle of justice is given its due when designers of computer systems take steps such as making them easier to understand and use so that everyone can deal with them more easily. Upholders of justice would also discourage the building of huge networks of interconnected computers, which particularly invite the invasion of privacy.[15]

Caring. Interactions among those involved in design must be of a caring nature—a genuine concern and love must be shown among those making design decisions. This care must also be extended to the fabricators of technological objects. The design of the workplace should show concern for the well-being of the worker, and worker input should be provided for as the design process progresses. When this process develops sensitive, caring designs, it provides the worker with a variety of meaningful tasks, both mechanical and mental, rather than creating work situations devoid of real challenge and responsibility. Recent experience shows that high technology coupled with increased employee responsibility actually works. This came as a surprise to a General Motors executive interviewed recently. He noted that "auto makers must use robots, lasers, and computers to improve our ability to creatively manage our technical resources." But he also stressed the important role that workers play: "The odd thing about all this is that moving decision-making down

15. On the problems posed by computers in regard to the invasion of privacy, see, for example, Abbe Mowshowitz, *Conquest of Will: Information Processing in Human Affairs* (Reading, Mass.: Addison-Wesley Publishing, 1976).

in the workplace . . . and creating a sense of ownership in the workplace are simple ideas that really work.''[16]

Those involved with design are also called upon to make sure that the technological objects they produce promote loving, caring relationships. Certainly designing computer systems that promote love and understanding among people is a particularly difficult challenge. It is very probable that when individuals work with a computer all day they develop a kind of machine mentality that spills over into their personal relationships; others become statistics, ciphers that can be ''stored and manipulated.'' Guided by the principle of caring in concert with the other normative principles, those who design computer systems should be sensitive to integrating computer-oriented interactions with people-oriented interactions so that work with the computer is more humanized.

Trust. The final normative principle suggests that those who design technological objects must do so in such a way that consumers can trust those objects to perform safely and dependably. Designers should not cut corners if doing so means creating an unreliable or unsafe technological object. In addition, designers should make sure that form is congruent with function: what a technological object looks like should reflect what the object is and how it should be used. Otherwise the object invites users to put a misplaced trust in it.

Trust also means that those who design technological objects must ultimately do so out of a faith commitment to God, the Creator of all, not out of a faith commitment to technicism or any other false god. It is easy for someone involved with design—who daily manipulates material, determines specifications, and finally sees the result of his or her work in concrete form—to experience hubris, a sense of pride and power that denies God and enthrones humankind and the work of its hands. But design done in keeping with the normative principle of trust recognizes that only in God's strength and wisdom do men and women find true strength and wisdom. Only then will all the other normative principles be followed. Only then will technological design be truly responsible.

DESIGN SPECIFICATIONS

The actual detailed work of design is done in response to design specifications that stipulate what the tool or product is to be and do, what performance standards it is to meet, and what other characteristics or

16. ''GM Executive Looks to More Joint Ventures,'' *The Grand Rapids Press,* Nov. 20, 1983.

qualities it must possess. Writing these specifications is a crucial stage of
the design process because it lays the groundwork for the remaining
steps.

It is therefore important that our design philosophy be properly applied
to the foundational activity of design specification. It is here that a design
philosophy is concretely expressed. Our concern is to specify those areas
that should be taken into account in establishing design specifications. It
is impossible to say what the specific content of these areas should be
because the content varies with the particular situation. Nevertheless,
briefly examining the various areas that design specification should take
into account and indicating how our design philosophy relates to these
areas will help clarify the nature of the specification activity and how it
should be guided by biblically based normative principles.

The first area with which design specification must deal is the definition of the problem or need that the technological object is to meet. A
technological object is then designed to meet that problem or need or to
achieve a goal to which the problem or need points. The need may be to
move large groups of people safely and quickly between a large conven-
tion center and a nearby shopping mall. Design specifications for such a
project usually include specific information about the number of people
to be transported, the length of the trip, the estimated peak levels of
activity, and so forth. The design process then develops the technological
object to meet the need. In this case an underground moving sidewalk, an
overhead monorail, and shuttle trams are all possible answers.

But this is not the end of the design specification process. According to
the holistic approach to design, the entire life-cycle of a technological
object must be considered when developing design specifications. Morris Asimow suggests that this cycle be broken into four distinct phases for
design purposes: production, distribution, consumption or use, and recovery.[17] Besides meeting needs, technological objects must perform
appropriately in each of these four areas. Thus, in each of these areas—as
well as in the definition of the need or problem to be addressed—design
specifications should be developed according to biblically based normative principles.

Definition of the Need or Problem. Before developing design specifications to address a problem or need, two basic questions need to be
asked which the normative principles in our design philosophy help
answer. The first question concerns what is a problem or need and what is
not. A particularly tragic episode from human history illustrates the

17. See Morris Asimow, *Introduction to Design* (Englewood Cliffs, N.J.: Prentice-Hall,
1962), p. 9.

point. In the early 1940s Hitler decided that millions of European Jews were a problem he wanted to "solve." His design specifications posed the question of how to quickly and efficiently kill these Jews and dispose of their bodies. But anyone following the normative principles of justice and caring would have defiantly shouted that there was no problem here for the design process to address.

A second question—assuming that a need or problem in keeping with biblically based normative principles has been articulated—is whether or not the need or problem should be given a technological solution. We might, for example, agree that there is a need for additional leisure-time activities, but also believe that normative principles such as stewardship, delightful harmony, and cultural appropriateness indicate that this need should be met by personal creative efforts, not by the production of more video games or snowmobiles.

Production. Two major concerns enter in when developing specifications for the production phase. First, the tool or product must be, in Asimow's words, "physically realizable."[18] The parts of the object must fit together properly, work together as intended, and be of high quality, whether handmade or mass produced. A second important concern is that the fabrication facility itself be designed properly. Specifications for it should be as carefully developed within our normative principles of design as the specifications for the object itself. Just as technological objects have great societal impact, so the workplace itself has a broad societal impact. It affects the availability of employment opportunities and the physical and psychological welfare of the worker in the workplace, and in turn the overall quality of national life is deeply affected. A decision to automate a certain fabrication process may have a negative impact on employment opportunities. Writing specifications for production that focus on the product and de-emphasize concerns for the workers doing the fabrication are, at the very least, ignoring the normative principles of caring and justice. A product may work well, but if it has been fabricated under adverse, dehumanizing conditions or uses materials extracted under these same conditions, it violates the normative principles for design.

Distribution. Design specifications for distribution are often ignored or downplayed. But in modern technology the producer and the user are usually separated by geographic distance. Therefore, products must function in certain ways—while in transit and on display—prior to their actual use. Asimow suggests four important specifications for distribu-

18. Asimow, *Introduction to Design,* p. 12.

tion: ease of transport, suitability for storage, long shelf-life, and attrac-
tiveness in display.[19] These are the sorts of issues that the design
specifications must address, guided by normative principles.

Stewardship, for example, says the specifications must call for a minimum of energy and resource consumption during distribution. Container
waste, in terms of both material and energy resources, should be minimized. Another major normative concern is that of justice. The specifications for distribution should be such that the product is as widely
available as possible and does not discriminate against certain groups of
users. For example, the design specifications for a new piece of farm
equipment for a developing society should be such that the new equipment is inexpensive and not dependent on an elaborate support system of
repair facilities and energy supplies, thereby assuring that it is available
to and usable by the mass of ordinary, poor farmers, not only by a
wealthy land-owning elite. Clearly, stewardship and justice—as well as
cultural appropriateness and the other normative principles—enter in as
standards that should guide design specification at the distribution stage.

Consumption or Use. Like specifications for distribution, specifications for consumption must be given careful attention. This is particularly true when there is a significant interaction between person and
machine. Inattention to specifications for use is evident everywhere,
from the convoluted instructions on how to use a home computer, to
military aircraft so sophisticated that the pilot cannot control the system
because human reflexes cannot handle its performance characteristics.
This latter problem is an example of the violation of the norm of delightful harmony. Where there should be a joyfully harmonious relationship
between human being and aircraft, there is instead dissonance and un-
certainty—the pilot is really not sure who or what is in control.

The call to those involved with design, therefore, is to take seriously
all facets of the human element when writing design specifications. This
is particularly important in the area of use, broadly conceived as the use
of both technological products and fabricatory tools and facilities. The
biological, psychological, social, and moral characteristics of human
beings are critical here. Noise, for example, must be kept below certain
decibel levels in the workplace so that conditions are healthy and safe
and workers can function creatively. Other human factors such as the
temperature, humidity, illumination, and color intensity must also be
properly specified.

Clearly, proper specification should be guided by biblically based

19. Asimow, *Introduction to Design*, p. 9.

normative principles for design. What people feel comfortable with in a given culture, how they process symbols, and how they interact socially—all these factors have to be taken into account and weighed when writing specifications if a delightful harmony is to be achieved. Doing so is an act of caring and justice, especially if this holistic philosophy of specification is applied equally to all interactions between people and technological objects, irrespective of the type of fabrication facility involved, the workers employed there, and the product and the consumers who use it. The technological tools used by the assembly-line worker must be designed with as much care as those used by the corporation president; the tools must be appropriate for the users and enable them to function effectively and joyfully.

The normative principle of trust speaks both to safety and to dependability. It is clearly important that technological objects be both safe and reliable. Designing tools and products that work properly during their intended lifespan is a challenge for the designer. Some deterioration is inevitable, but consumers should be provided with products that do not demand undue maintenance and repair. This surely has implications not only for trust but also for the proper stewardship of time, as Bob Goudzwaard appropriately reminds us: "Every consumption product automatically takes our time. We need time to buy it, to maintain it, and to replace it. For that reason, . . . a culture which becomes richer materially becomes poorer in terms of available time."[20]

The foregoing examples make it clear that the biological, psychological, and social characteristics of human beings must be taken into account in design specification. But a final example helps to illustrate that the moral aspect of human nature must also be weighed. One of the design specifications for rocket armaments mounted under the wings of carrier aircraft is that they must be able to fall fifty feet without exploding, although they do not still have to be operational after such a fall. However, they must be able to fall six feet without exploding and still be operational. These design specifications have been developed in response to the activities of the on-deck crews who mount the rockets. If they dropped a rocket while mounting it, it would fall about six feet. Rather than report the mistake and risk being disciplined, the crew often simply retrieved the dropped rocket and put it back under the wing, not caring if the fall had rendered it nonoperational. However, if a dropped rocket rolled away—which it would often do—it might fall down the

---

20. Bob Goudzwaard, *Capitalism and Progress: A Diagnosis of Western Society*, trans. and ed. by Josina Van Nuis Zylstra (Toronto: Wedge Publishing; Grand Rapids: Eerdmans, 1979), p. 148.

elevator shaft some fifty feet. When such an obvious mistake was made, the crew retrieved the rocket and discarded it; thus it did not need to still be operational. Consequently, the Navy developed design specifications for the rocket that compensated for this irresponsibility; it recognized the necessity of insuring the safety of the pilots, who in a combat situation were dependent on operational, effective rockets.

Recovery. The next stage in the life cycle of the technological object is recovery. Here too the design specifications must consider all of the normative principles for design. This is probably the stage most easily forgotten in design specifications, but significant nonetheless. Therefore, an important part of our design philosophy is that design specifications should include provision for eventual recovery of the technological object's materials after its useful life is over. The original design must be such that the tool or product can be easily refurbished and reused or its materials recycled, particularly if it contains scarce materials that are energy intensive in their extraction and manufacture. Storage batteries have long been designed for recovery, but many other technological objects such as home appliances—stoves, refrigerators, washing machines, and clothes dryers—have not. Designers should prepare these objects for eventual recycling by providing certain assembly specifications that simplify disassembly of reuseable components and certain specifications for enameling of the metal for easier metal extraction. In addition, designers should indicate how any nonrecyclable materials could be properly disposed of—even though disposal is not, strictly speaking, related to recovery. Asimow suggests that the rate of obsolescence can be reduced if designs anticipate technical developments, match an object's physical life to its service life, ensure that the object can be used in different ways during its lifetime, and specify how viable components and materials can be recovered when an object reaches the end of its useful life.[21] The norm of stewardship plays an especially prominent role in guiding design specifications in this area.

SUFFICIENT DESIGN

At this point we should sum up the design philosophy developed in this chapter. The processes of developing design specifications and then designing to meet those specifications are to be guided by a holistic perspective, the view that a technological object is experienced as an integrated whole which functions in all aspects of reality. In addition,

21. Asimow, *Introduction to Design,* p. 17.

our philosophy demands that these decisions be guided by normative principles for design that are rooted in a Christian understanding of humanity, God, and the creation.

The pursuit of these three things together—holism, proper design principles, and appropriate design specifications—is what we call sufficient design. This concept of sufficiency in design is meant to supplant the much too narrow concepts of technical, financial, and marketing efficiency, which are often used as guides for the development of design specifications. We have seen that these criteria are not adequate for the proper specification of a tool or product used in everyday life. Our philosophy calls for a broad consideration of the entire life-cycle of technological objects, with the concomitant, appropriate development of a broad range of specifications guided by biblically based normative principles.

But can such a design philosophy actually be practiced? Even if we acknowledge that it is necessary for responsible design, isn't sufficient design too high an ideal to be realized? It is certainly true that in a sinful, broken world, sufficient design will never be fully realized. In fact, it is unlikely to be realized to any great extent in our present technicistic age. But it is also important to recognize that through God's grace the possibility of significant headway remains. Barriers can be broken down; significant aspects of sufficient design can be realized. Sufficient design is meant to be an ideal model of responsible design towards which we strive. Working towards an ideal should come as nothing new to the Christian who, although imperfect, is commanded to seek perfection.

Although the analogy is not exact, this working toward an ideal model can be compared to the practice of working toward idealized models of technological objects themselves. For example, a technical designer of a steam power plant can calculate an ideal or maximum efficiency based on an idealized scientific model of that plant. That this ideal is never fully attainable does not stop the designer from using it as a gauge of and goal for actual efficiency of the design. He continues to upgrade the design to remove those obstacles that stand in the way of approaching the ideal, even though the ideal itself can never be fully attained.

Though we see imperfectly, our vision for all designers is that they work together holistically in light of the normative principles for design. The movement is away from a narrow concept of *efficiency* and toward the larger concept of *sufficiency* in design. Employing this concept means that we, in obedient response to God's command, can refine those purposes towards the joy, harmony, justice, peace, and vibrancy that mark God's kingdom of shalom.

CHAPTER TEN

Design and Fabrication in Practice

IN THE PREVIOUS CHAPTER WE DISCUSSED SUFFICIENT DESIGN, WHICH IS the ideal, the standard that technological design should pursue. Design should be holistic, should consider all facets of the reality within which the technological object will function. In addition, it should be done in obedience to the normative principles for design that are rooted in a Christian perspective on humanity and the world. But this ideal must be placed in the context of the real world of design and fabrication—in the real world of nuts and bolts, transistors and electrodes, of men and women who have strengths and frailties, hopes and fears. If our vision of sufficient design is to be fulfilled, we need to examine and clearly understand the nature of the arena in which it is to be pursued. That is the purpose of this chapter.

More specifically, the first section of the chapter deals with some intrinsic characteristics of design and fabrication. Sufficient design must take place in a context shaped by these characteristics because they are inevitably and necessarily present. Next the chapter discusses three characteristics of design and fabrication that are real and identifiable but not intrinsic. They must be altered if sufficient design is to be achieved. The final section of the chapter presents an illustration of the application of sufficient design.

INTRINSIC CHARACTERISTICS

Complexity. To understand the actual doing of sufficient design, one must understand the enormous complexity of the world within which it operates. Here we consider five aspects of that complexity. The *first* aspect lies in the large number of specialists involved in design and fabrication. As we noted earlier, modern technology is marked by a highly specialized division of labor. In actual practice, the general tasks of design and fabrication are broken down into a host of specialized tasks: engineering, research, model building, drafting, prototype development, machine-tool design, systems construction, quality control, testing, and more. In addition, the tasks of public-policy formulation, scientific research, marketing, economic analysis, and distribution are involved in the total technological process. All these specialized activities must be properly coordinated.

A *second* facet of the enormous complexity in design and fabrication results from the fact that a given design problem may raise a variety of complex issues and questions. An example can be found in *Design: Serving the Needs of Man,* by George Beakley and Ernest Chilton. In considering the design of a system of personal but publicly owned vehicles for central city transportation, the authors ask the following questions: Where and by whom will the vehicles be used? Are they to effect random movement, or are they to be part of a larger, more organized transportation system? How does one make such vehicles safe? What happens when it rains heavily and everyone wants to use one? What happens when they are concentrated at, say, a sporting event? What new rules and regulations need to be devised? What is the risk of nonacceptance by the public?[1] These are difficult questions to answer, but they must be addressed if the design process is to move forward—or is to be terminated if the project is not deemed feasible.

In the same vein, Mario Bunge emphasizes the complexity of issues in design: "Just think of the problems posed by the design of any new product. Is the relevant scientific knowledge realizable, and is it likely to be sufficient? Will the new product be radically new—that is, will it exhibit new emergent properties—or will it be just a rearrangement of existing components? Shall we design the product so as to maximize performance, social usefulness, profit, or what?"[2] Assigning relative values to the various factors in design specifications such as reliability, maintainability, and safety adds to the complexity of the task.

That the computer is ubiquitous in design and fabrication facilities is a *third* indication of the complexities involved in doing technology. Design problems in electronics, structures, and energy conversion involve thousands of variables and can be practically handled only by the modern digital computer. It is virtually impossible to mass-produce high-quality products without its aid. The computer handles thousands of variables with precision, directing the intricate, high-speed movements of machine tools and assembly devices.

1. See George C. Beakley and Ernest G. Chilton, *Design: Serving the Needs of Man* (New York: Macmillan, 1974), pp. 172–73.

2. Mario Bunge, "Philosophical Inputs and Outputs of Technology," in George Bugliarello's *The History and Philosophy of Technology,* ed. Dean B. Doner (Urbana: University of Illinois Press, 1979), p. 263.

The highly complex nature of the technological objects produced by the design and fabrication processes constitutes a *fourth* aspect of the complexity of these processes. A technological object usually works because of a very intricate interaction among its parts. Problems arise when improvements in one aspect often cause other aspects to perform poorly. The modern car provides an example. The improvement of its pollution-control equipment initially resulted in engine problems: the car was difficult to start and ran poorly when the engine was cold.

Many complicated systems are being designed and built today, such as nuclear power plants, space shuttles, and satellite communication systems. The popular media has been focusing on this complexity, especially with regard to the nuclear power plant and the space shuttle. The difficulties experienced in proper construction, operation, and decommissioning illustrate the technological complexity of nuclear power. Problems with the makeup and complexity of the space shuttle have been a major concern for the public since the Challenger tragedy of January 1986. The complexity in the area of communications is obvious: simply consider the large number of people and systems needed to utilize communication satellites. These systems range from the rockets needed to put the satellites into orbit, to the vast network of electronic apparatuses needed to send and receive signals.

This manifold complexity could be somewhat reduced or made easier to handle if, as a given design progressed, it would move toward or evolve into a single, well-defined solution to a problem. But the problem-solving activity of design never yields a single right answer, as Victor Papanek reminds us in *Design for the Real World.*[3] This is the *fifth* and probably the chief facet of complexity in the design and fabrication of technological objects. Any one of numerous different paths can be taken to solve a particular problem, which itself may be inadequately defined. Deciding which one to follow requires those involved with design to make value judgments. The normative principles for design that we have outlined should help guide designers in distinguishing between appropriate and inappropriate paths. Those solutions that cannot give each of the normative principles its due should be eliminated from consideration.

The complexity of the design and fabrication activities means that in practice they are not precise, fully rational activities leading to certain, fully knowable results. Thus the doing of technology is shaped not only by valuing but also by errors, estimates, and hunches. As Ralph

3. See Victor Papanek, *Design for the Real World* (New York: Bantam Books, 1973), p. 25.

Gomory tells us, "The most important point about technology is that it tends to be very complex. . . . The computer itself is complicated, . . . [and] no one has yet designed a large computer completely right. . . . In dealing with technology, things are sufficiently complex that much is done by rule of thumb and not by precise knowledge."[4]

Trade-offs. Experience has shown that making trade-offs is a second characteristic intrinsic in design and fabrication. Trade-off involves a compromise between two conflicting desirable features or goals. Of course, in an ideal world we would want to maximize both simultaneously. But in the real world it is often the case that the more one attains or provides for one desirable feature in a technological object, the less one can obtain of some other desirable feature.[5] One feature must be traded off against another.

Airplane design provides an example. The windows for the pilot in a supersonic aircraft must be large enough for good visibility, but small enough to assure the structural integrity of the plane while traveling at supersonic speeds. Closer to everyday experience is the trade-off involved in making a good bicycle, as Donald Baxter, Jr., explains: "To make them economically attractive, tradeoffs are made in weight and performance, the degree depending on the model. . . . [T]he higher strength-to-weight ratio of the chromium-molybdenum steel makes weight reductions possible, but at a dollar premium."[6] Many such trade-offs involve human safety. In an investigative article on airplane safety, Jean Heller explains the difficulty of making commercial aircraft tires safe:

> The FAA's response to blowout problems was to order tire pressures increased. . . . [W]ith lower levels of inflation, the tire sidewalls deflect more and build up more heat, which does make them more prone to blowout. But higher inflation dramatically increases the distance an airplane needs to stop in the event of an emergency. There was a safety tradeoff.[7]

The computer designer faces a more sophisticated trade-off problem. As microchips become smaller and smaller, fewer external connections are needed in assembly, which in turn means higher overall quality. At the same time, however, microchips of these very small sizes are more susceptible to voltage fluctuations and thus require a very stable but

4. Ralph E. Gomory, "Technology Development," *Science* 220 (1983): 576–80.

5. For more on the concept of trade-offs in technology, see E. V. Krick, *Introduction to Engineering and Engineering Design*, 2nd ed. (New York: Wiley, 1969), pp. 80–81.

6. Donald F. Baxter, Jr., "The Bicycle," *Metal Progress* (July 1973), pp. 63–64.

7. Jean Heller, "There's No Ironclad Guarantee That a Jetliner Will Be Fail-Safe," *The Denver Post*, Nov. 26, 1980, p. 17.

expensive voltage supply to operate properly.[8] Here there is a trade-off between quality and cost. The two desirable criteria of low cost and high quality cannot both be maximized.

In all of these cases there is a need to make an optimal trade-off between desirable but conflicting features in the design. And this necessity for compromise entails valuing. E. V. Krick puts it succinctly: "Once the [designer] knows the relative values attached to criteria [design specifications] he can determine the tradeoffs that must be made in order to optimize the overall design. The assigning of a relative value to a criterion is . . . a value decision."[9] Hans Lenk and Gunter Ropohl make the same point from a more philosophical perspective: "The discussion of conflicts between technical and economic goals and the consideration in so-called value-analysis of the qualitative categories of utilization and utility, etc., draw attention to the normative aspect of technological activity."[10]

The trade-offs necessary in design make a strong argument for the role of the normative principles that are at the heart of our concept of sufficient design. The ubiquity of trade-off decisions in design and their value-laden nature mean that everyone involved with design is constantly called upon to make value judgments. Our concept of sufficient design says that these decisions should be made from a holistic perspective and in response to such normative principles as cultural appropriateness, open communication, stewardship, caring, and justice. These and the other normative principles of sufficient design must all be given their due in design and fabrication activities. This is at the heart of the simultaneous pursuit of normative principles in the doing of technology.

Gaps. The doing of technology is a process in which the development of a technological object moves from the identification of a problem for which there might be a technological solution, to design, and then to fabrication. One of the important characteristics of the process is that gaps exist between and within each stage. Whenever we try to make or do something, it seldom turns out exactly as we had envisioned it. This is true of the perfect wedding that parents plan for their daughter; it is no less true of the technological object that was painstakingly researched, designed, modeled, and tested.

8. See Glenn W. Preston, "The Very Large Scale Integrated Circuit," *American Scientist* 71 (1983): 470.

9. Krick, *Introduction to Engineering and Engineering Design,* pp. 82–83.

10. Hans Lenk and Gunter Ropohl, "Toward an Interdisciplinary and Pragmatic Philosophy of Technology: Technology as a Focus for Interdisciplinary Reflection and Systems Research," in *Research in Philosophy and Technology,* vol. 2, ed. Paul Durbin (Greenwich, Conn.: Jai Press, 1979), p. 32.

One way to view the doing of technology is to perceive it as moving from an image in the designer's mind to its concrete manifestation. In his discussion of the fabricating of a motorcycle in *Zen and the Art of Motorcycle Maintenance,* Robert Pirsig claims that the machine is primarily a mental phenomenon because it emerges as a shape previously conceived in someone's mind.[11] Carl Mitcham offers a less mystical definition of design. He suggests that a modern design is first sketched on paper, then tested on the computer in graphic representation, next developed into a full-scale model, and finally fabricated.[12] Both Pirsig and Mitcham—even though their descriptions differ and are perhaps incomplete—lead us to conclude that the doing of technology is a progression from the abstract to the concrete.

As this progression takes place, gaps occur because our mental images just do not seem to correspond neatly to the real steps of implementation. For example, one's idea of how a technological object solves a problem is not quite what appears in its written description. As one moves through the design process, gaps between perception and reality continually occur. As a finite set of design specifications is developed, some concerns about the technological object's purpose and function are necessarily left out. Often qualitative aspects akin to a holistic approach are lost. Once the specifications are set, ideas for alternative solutions are generated, but no single idea meets all the specifications exactly—and thus another gap appears. When the selected design is fabricated, the resultant object never turns out exactly as planned (as anyone knows who has worked in a shop). Finally, when the object is used, it often inadequately meets its intended functions, or other unanticipated problems arise.

Evidence of these gaps can be seen in the cost overruns often experienced in the design, fabrication, distribution, use, and recovery of many technological objects. Additional evidence of gaps can be seen in the large number of product liability lawsuits. In both cases, design predictions concerning cost and what will happen when a tool or product is used or misused do not always match concrete reality. Further evidence of these gaps are the margins of safety that experience suggests should be applied to calculated predictions of the behavior of technological objects. According to Aaron Deutschman and his associates, safety factors in mechanical design are needed to bridge the void (created by gaps

---

11. See Robert M. Pirsig, *Zen and the Art of Motorcycle Maintenance* (New York: Bantam Books, 1974), pp. 94–95.

12. See Carl Mitcham, ''Philosophy of Technology,'' in *A Guide to the Culture of Science, Technology and Medicine,* ed. Paul T. Durbin (New York: Free Press, 1980), p. 311.

in knowledge) between performance predictions and the actual performance of machines.[13]

Extensive testing programs undertaken by various manufacturers before making products available to the public also testify to the existence of gaps. Before planes are certified for public use, they undergo extensive testing for several years, testing jointly undertaken by the manufacturer and the FAA. The main purpose of such testing programs is to see how well a particular product fulfills performance predictions. Testing is a necessary means by which to compensate for the omnipresent gap between theory and practice.

The existence of these gaps indicates first of all that many decisions in design and fabrication cannot be based on purely quantifiable, rational knowledge. What is an adequate safety margin? Will a product prove dependable enough that consumers will purchase it? What effect will a proposed technological tool have on the workers who will use it? The biblically based normative principles present in sufficient design speak to one's approach to these and a host of other questions. The principles of caring and trust lead one to build in a bigger safety margin than one otherwise might. Cultural appropriateness, justice, stewardship, and the other normative principles similarly affect how one deals with the gaps that will always be present in design and fabrication processes. In addition, the normative principles of openness and proper communication should guide those involved with design when they are confronted with gaps. These gaps must be openly acknowledged. Some of the problems that now plague the nuclear power industry are no doubt due in part to the lack of openness and proper communication among designers and fabricators and the power companies about how difficult it is to properly design and fabricate safe nuclear power plants.

Risks. The inability to make absolutely sure predictions about the performance of technological objects leads to major uncertainties about how the product will function. Unintended consequences result. That these are intimately and necessarily bound up with doing technology is noted by Victor Papanek: "The results of the introduction of a new device are never predictable."[14] Langdon Winner puts it even more forcefully: "Unintended consequences are not—not intended. This means that there is seldom anything in the original plan that aimed at preventing them."[15]

13. Aaron D. Deutschman, Walter J. Michels, and Charles E. Wilson, *Machine Design: Theory and Practice* (New York: Macmillan, 1975), pp. 8–9.

14. Papanek, *Design for the Real World*, p. 31.

15. See Langdon Winner, *Autonomous Technology* (Cambridge: MIT Press, 1977), p. 98.

The unintended effects of the computer provide an example. It has been noted that improvements in computer technology "have been brought about, on the supply side, by a remarkably diverse body of new technology and on the demand side, by the emergence of new, massive, and diverse applications of computational resources, which for the most part bear little resemblance to those for which the general-purpose computer was originally intended."[16] Winner provides an interesting and sobering perspective on these unintended consequences: "Technology is most productive when its ultimate range of results is neither foreseen nor controlled. To put it differently, technology always does more than we intend—both positively and negatively."[17] Experience has indeed shown that in such areas as computer technology, transportation, communications, space exploration, and medical technology, most of the effects—beneficial and otherwise—have been realized only after a given product has been used, even if only in rudimentary form.

Because those involved with design can never fully predict how a technological object will perform, doing technology is a risk-taking activity. Even when informed by past mistakes and successes, the task of prognosticating is filled with uncertainties and pitfalls—as experience has taught time and again. In light of this very real risk factor, the normative principles of sufficient design act as a guide to whether or not particular risks should be taken.

These four intrinsic characteristics of doing technology—complexity, trade-offs, gaps, and risks—set the stage upon which the philosophy of sufficient design is to be practiced. These characteristics are present any time technological objects are designed, fabricated, and eventually introduced into society. They form the real-life context within which any design philosophy—and its underlying normative principles—is practiced.

EXTRINSIC BARRIERS TO SUFFICIENT DESIGN

Our discussion thus far has clearly indicated that modern technology is often done in an irresponsible manner. If this is so, and if the design stage of doing technology is as crucial as we believe it is, there must be something fundamentally wrong with the way technological design is done. In some limited ways the characteristics intrinsic to design and fabrication can be seen as barriers to a fully responsible technology, but they are not at the heart of the problem. Sufficient design, based on

16. Preston, "The Very Large Scale Integrated Circuit," p. 466.
17. Winner, *Autonomous Technology*, p. 98.

holism and the following of biblically based normative principles, could guide design and fabrication activities so as to enable responsible technology to develop despite the limitations of the intrinsic characteristics.

But there are other barriers to responsible design and fabrication—extrinsic barriers. These barriers are largely the cause of the irresponsible, destructive ways in which technology is often done in modern societies, and technicism underlies all three of them. As noted earlier, technicism is the pursuit of technology for technology's sake; technology is its own justification, and technology is simplistically equated with progress. It is this faith—for technicism is indeed a faith—that has led to a technicistic mind-set, narrowness in design, and the imposition of severe time constraints on design and fabrication processes. It is to these that we now turn.

A Technicistic Mind-set. Because technicism is prevalent in modern society, most of those involved with design approach their task with a technicistic mind-set. This mind-set is marked by three characteristics.

First, it eschews any self-conscious reflection on the proper guides for doing technology and instead champions the possible; as Egbert Schuurman has put it, "Anything that can be done should be done!"[18] Alan Drengson also describes those guided by such a norm as essentially technical anarchists for whom anything goes: their maxim is "explore all and do all."[19] Walter Vincenti, a former engineering professor, has decried the fact that "many scientists think philosophically about what they do, but engineers are by definition doers, they want to get on with the job."[20] He is concerned that engineer-designers often overlook the philosophical implications of their work, and hence do not develop any discerning sense about the direction their work should take.

The second characteristic of the technicistic mind-set is an ego-satisfying drive for power and status. Those involved with design are all too often captivated by the power and status that comes with designing planes, cars, space shuttles, and computers. This work can become a source of ego satisfaction, particularly as it gives them an inordinate sense of power. Jacques Ellul describes this aspect of the technicistic mind-set in *The Technological Society:*

> There is associated with [technique] the feeling of the sacred, which expresses itself in different ways. The way differs from man to man, but for all men the feeling of the sacred is expressed in this marvelous instrument of

18. Egbert Schuurman, *Technology and the Future: A Philosophical Challenge* (Toronto: Wedge, 1980), p. 359.

19. Alan Drengson, "Four Philosophies of Technology," *Philosophy Today,* Summer 1982, p. 106.

20. "Interview with Walter Vincenti," *Stanford Observer,* Nov. 1982, pp. 10–11.

the power instinct which is always joined to mystery and magic. The worker brags about his job because it offers him joyous confirmation of his superiority. The young snob speeds along at 100 m.p.h. in his Porsche. The technician contemplates with satisfaction the gradients of his charts, no matter what their reference is. For these men, technique is in every way sacred: it is the common expression of human power without which they would find themselves poor, alone, naked, and stripped of all pretentions. They would no longer be the heroes, geniuses, or archangels which a motor permits them to be at little expense.[21]

Satisfying ego needs for power through technology negates faith in God. The work of design then involves placing one's trust not in the Creator but solely in oneself. Human autonomy displaces faith in God.

The third characteristic of the technicistic mind-set is a narrow, presumptuous commitment to an absolutized rationality as the one correct approach to design. If one were to ask particular designers to identify their most important personality trait, almost all of them would point to their rational, "straightforward" way of thinking. They would say that when they make decisions, they stick to facts. This kind of mind-set sees no place for valuing or for biblically based normative principles. Nor does it recognize that decisions are necessarily made in the face of missing information and uncertain consequences.

In short, a technicistic mind-set avoids any philosophical contemplation about the proper direction for design, uses design as a means to gain power and status, and possesses an overweening rationality. The first of these characteristics emerges directly out of technicism's blind faith in the benign nature of technology as an inevitable path to human progress apart from God and his will. Much the same can be said for using design to fulfill the drive for power and station. And Chapter Three—which argued that a neutral, value-free technology is a myth—speaks to the illusion of a fully rational, purely factual design process.

Peter Drucker rightly reminds us of the real nature of decision making: "It is not the facts that decide—people have to choose between imperfect alternatives on the basis of uncertain knowledge and fragmentary understanding."[22] The technicistic mind deludes itself into thinking that the decision was based on a straightforward, well-thought-out analysis—

---

21. Jacques Ellul, *The Technological Society,* trans. John Wilkinson (New York: Vintage Books, 1964), p. 145. The meaning of *technique* as Ellul uses it is not fully captured by the English word *technology.* As Robert Merton points out in the foreword, Ellul uses *technique* to mean "far more than machine technology. Technique refers to any complex of standardized means for attaining a predetermined result" (p. vi). See our more complete discussion of this point in Chapter Eleven.

22. Peter F. Drucker, *Technology, Management and Society* (New York: Harper & Row-Colophon Books, 1970), p. 138.

that it was fully rational—when in fact it was directed by such things as a prideful nationalism, an unqualified profit motive, a desire for peer approval and personal recognition, cultural traditions, a reverence of technology for its own sake, and a thoughtless following of the latest fad. These are poor substitutes for biblically based normative principles for sufficient design. Yet they are often unconsciously followed under the guise of an allegedly rational, objective approach.

Thomas Schelling's concept of a critical mass indicates that a strong motivation for human action is the behavior of others.[23] Essentially, he suggests that people persist in acting a certain way only when enough others continue to act that way. Rationality or "the facts" play a limited role in this type of action. For example, the public may think that the designers of a particular computer developed the most efficient option in terms of cost, production, and use, when in fact the designers simply followed others. Often what is perceived as creative design rationally arrived at actually has more to do with personal and corporate security based on peer approval.

The three characteristics of a technicistic mind-set—by leading one away from reflecting on the proper direction of technology, emphasizing power and station, and ignoring the valuing and the uncertainties inherent in design—combine to form a barrier to the practice of sufficient design. The way to remove this barrier is to depend on God; this reliance frees one to pursue the practice of holistic design guided by normative principles based on his will. This is a radical proposal. It strikes at the root of the matter and would fundamentally alter the way design is done and, consequently, would also fundamentally alter the role and effects of technology in modern society. Those who follow such a path will often feel like exiles in Babylon. Nevertheless, it is their design efforts that— because they serve God—will ultimately also serve humankind.

Narrowness in Design. In Chapter Six we noted the hegemony of science in technology—the tendency of technology to take on the mind-set and many of the methodologies, approaches, and findings of science. This hegemony of science in technological design results in a narrowness that destroys holism and ignores the normative principles at the heart of sufficient design. The problem is that science is marked by a methodology that emphasizes abstract knowledge and that breaks reality into small parts and then concentrates on studying those parts separately. In addition, science is too often overrated as a social force—seen as more rational, powerful, and beneficent than it actually is.

23. See Thomas C. Schelling, *Micromotives and Macrobehavior* (New York: Norton, 1978), pp. 91–96.

These characteristics of science—given the hegemony of science in technology—lead to technological design marked by narrowness, not holism. And without that holism the normative principles essential for sufficient design cannot be adequately weighed and applied, and are often ignored. Robert Pirsig pinpoints what is lost by taking a scientific, abstract approach to design: "The scientific method is good to find out where you've been but creativity, originality, inventiveness, intuition, imagination, 'unstuckness' are completely outside its domain."[24] For Pirsig, the narrow approach of using only scientific models—a result of the overreliance on the scientific method—simply does violence to the creativity needed if one is to be a holistic designer.

We should also note that the tools used by those concerned with the details of a given design also contribute to this tendency toward narrowness. These tools, essentially used to translate ideas into reality, often force the technical designer to think in limited ways, as Jack Ryan has pointed out: "People who work with their minds but express the idea on paper are the designers, whose orthographic [perspectival] drawing has shaped much of the world. Most things are designed so they can be drawn in plane view and simple elevations. This is very limiting, and it's hard to do a good design that way."[25] This limitation has been somewhat reduced by the use of computer graphics, which can quickly provide various three-dimensional perspectives of the object being designed. But using this tool entails adapting to its limitations. Specifically, it means that design specifications must be put in numerical form. If a designer is not careful, he or she will begin doing only those designs that can be numerically translated.

This narrowness can be overcome by designing holistically. To do so, those involved with design must recognize the real limitations of quantifiable, scientific information when making decisions about technological objects that must function in the real world. This reality is not the abstract reality of rationalized science but the concrete reality of everyday experience. Properly using the results of science in design is indeed a creative challenge, one that involves removing the barrier that the misuse of science imposes. The challenge comes in writing design specifications with a creativity that captures all of the functional aspects of a technological object rather than just those that can be numerically defined.

It is as one escapes the clutches of this narrowness that the normative

24. Pirsig, *Zen and the Art of Motorcycle Maintenance*, p. 273.

25. Jack Ryan, "You Can Consciously Stimulate Your Creativity," *Engineering Education*, Jan. 1974, p. 292.

principles of sufficient design can come into play and be given their due. A scientized tunnel vision in design and fabrication prevents one from asking questions of justice, stewardship, and cultural appropriateness. But when science and its methodologies are put in their proper place, holism can be practiced and normative principles that reflect God's will can be given their due. Technology is then freed to be practiced responsibly.

Inappropriate Time Pressures. The competitive nature of the institutions involved with technology often leads to designing under very severe time pressures. Increasingly complex technological objects are being designed and fabricated within increasingly short periods of time. One business may be trying to develop a new product or tool before its competitors do in the hope of having the market to itself for a while. And if one of its competitors has already come up with a new tool or product, often the pressure is on to produce an equivalent or slightly more advanced tool or product as soon as possible. Particularly in the areas of weapons systems and space technology, one nation is often fearful of being outpaced by a rival nation, and therefore races against time to make new, more sophisticated technological advances. Other fields are plagued with similar pressures. Take medical technology. One medical research center may often be under pressure to possess a particular technological device as soon as possible so that the recognition, prestige, and research dollars will be awarded to it rather than a rival medical center. This pressures the designer and producer of these devices.

There are three reasons why these time pressures constitute a significant barrier to the doing of sufficient design. First, such pressure leaves little if any time to be concerned about the long-term effects of design activities. Those involved with design simply do not have time to step back from their work and ask the fundamental questions of purpose, direction, and meaning. They are always working under the gun of some immediate deadline.

Second, pressure leaves too little time to obtain and properly evaluate information pertaining to design. Even when information is readily available, it can be so abundant or so ambiguous that time is needed to uncover the insights and truths embedded in it. Peter Drucker comments on the problem this creates for a business manager, but what he says also applies to those involved with design: "The amount, diversity, and ambiguity of the information that is beating in on the decision maker have all been increasing so much that the built-in experience reaction that a good manager has cannot handle it." He or she breaks down in one of two ways, Drucker says. "One is withdrawal from reality, i.e., 'I know what

I know and I only go by it. . . .' Or there is a feeling that the universe has become completely irrational so that one decision is as good as the other, resulting in paralysis.''[26]

In his popular book *Future Shock,* Alvin Toffler makes a similar point, noting that one way people react to an overload of information is to withdraw from it, to deny it even exists. Another reaction is a retreat into narrowly defined specialties. Thus professionals such as doctors and financiers—and, we would add, designers—are unable to consider the broader societal issues that impinge on their professional practice.[27]

Third, pressure leaves too little time to creatively expand the range of alternative solutions to a given problem. The press of time often means that the conventional wisdom about a given situation prevails and solutions more in keeping with the normative principles of stewardship, caring, and justice are overlooked. Sufficient design calls for a broader purview of design than that compatible with the current emphasis on doing technology quickly.

Similar points need to be made in regard to fabrication. Fabrication, if it is to be done properly, also needs more time than is usually afforded it. Making quality products means allowing adequate time not only for manufacture but also for the fabricator's input into the design process itself.

This, in summary, is the world within which the philosophy of sufficient design is to be practiced. Certain characteristics of design and fabrication are intrinsic; others are extrinsic. The intrinsic characteristics need to be fully understood and taken into account by designers and fabricators, but they are not barriers to sufficient design. The extrinsic characteristics, however, constitute all-too-real barriers to the practice of sufficient design. A technicistic mind-set often sets the tone and direction of design and fabrication. This and the misuse of science turn the doing of technology into a narrow, scientized design process. The pressure of time makes the holistic development of design specifications extremely difficult. This pressure also negates any substantial effort to think more thoroughly about the consequences of introducing a particular tool or product into society. The results are apparent in the evils that technology has given the world, from dehumanized workplaces to rising cancer rates in certain localities because of toxic chemicals that are carelessly developed, used, and disposed of.

Thus it is important to look at the doing of technology from a critical distance so that the extrinsic barriers stand out in sharp relief. Once identified, these barriers can be broken down with the help of holistic

26. Drucker, *Technology, Management and Society,* pp. 136–37.
27. Alvin Toffler, *Future Shock* (New York: Bantam Books, 1970), p. 359.

design and appropriate, biblically based normative principles. This is not easy to accomplish. To do so requires going against the prevailing stream of modern culture and practice. Therefore, headway will usually come—when it comes at all—slowly and sporadically, and there will be setbacks. But the task is not without hope. By God's grace, the possibility of making progress, of breaking down barriers, remains. And when progress is made, it brings peace and joy in its wake.

AN ILLUSTRATION OF RESPONSIBLE DESIGN

The idea of responsible design can be illustrated by analyzing a certain design in light of the normative principles for sufficient design.[28] For some people, especially children and those confined to wheelchairs, the usual height of a sink installation is too high. General Motors has responded to this need by developing an electrohydraulically operated sink that costs $6,000, plus an additional $700 for installation. Converting two bathrooms and a kitchen with this product would cost over $20,000. However, a group in the industrial design department of Leeds Polytechnic in England has developed a design that shows the do-it-yourselfer how to convert an ordinary sink into one accessible to children and handicapped persons. The cost? Only thirty dollars. General Motors is selling an expensive product; the English design group is offering an inexpensive concept. Measuring each design against the normative principles is enlightening.

Perhaps each design is culturally appropriate in its own way. Those accustomed to an expensive life-style would probably opt for the General Motors product. Those more practical or less well-off would probably opt for the design of the English group. What is culturally appropriate must also be judged in light of other normative principles such as stewardship and caring. Indeed, all eight normative principles should be simultaneously achieved in design. If both designs come with instructions about proper usage, both comply with the principles of openness and trust with respect to safety. The English group's provision of a drawing for the do-it-yourselfer is an example of proper communication. Victor Papanek indicates that "General Motors unveiled their adjustable sink with all the advertising hoopla conceivable."[29] One wonders if this constitutes proper communication about a needful product.

The large difference in cost between the two designs seems to indicate

28. This example is taken from Victor Papanek's *Design for Human Scale* (Princeton, N.J.: Van Nostrand Reinhold, 1983), pp. 27–29.
29. Papanek, *Design for Human Scale*, p. 27.

that the simpler approach would better conserve energy and material resources, to say nothing of financial resources. Stewardship is relevant here. Although the inexpensive adaptation might not be as visually pleasing as the General Motors model, both would probably meet the aesthetic criterion of delightful harmony. Both designs would probably satisfy the principle of harmony between user and product, and both seem to be an expression of caring in that they each address the needs of children and the handicapped. But the high cost of the General Motors product would for the most part run counter to the principle of justice because the number of handicapped persons who could afford such a device would probably be limited. The English design would be available to a much larger group because of its low cost.

This example, though simplified for purposes of illustration, shows what is meant by a creative design that comports well with the normative principles for design. That the English design group solved this problem with a design that calls for a minimum investment of resources and that is almost universally available indicates their high level of creativity. It illustrates that holistic design, responsibly guided by normative principles, can be done.

CHAPTER ELEVEN

Prophetic Witness to a Technicistic Society

THE CADENCE OF OUR CULTURE IS SET BY THE BEAT OF THE TECH-
nological drum. In and of itself, this basic fact should be cause for neither
great rejoicing nor great alarm. The crucial question is, if this is so, who
or what is determining the beat? The central message of this book is that
in modern society this beat is largely determined by a drive for power, for
human mastery apart from the will of God. Humankind has revolted
against its Maker, has declared its independence from him and his will,
and all too often drives ruthlessly for a salvation of material prosperity
brought about by technological prowess.

In contrast is a technology done out of love and in response to God's
normative will. A sharper contrast is hard to imagine. Throughout this
book it has been argued that technology, as a part of the cultural task
given humankind by God, must be done as a form of serving others and of
caring for the rest of creation. Love is the motive; God's norms are its
guide. True, our efforts are hampered by the continuing effects of the
Fall, and therefore we cannot bring about God's kingdom of shalom by
human efforts alone. Nevertheless, a technology done out of love and in
obedience to God's will is certainly a part of the vision of this kingdom,
which we are commanded to seek (Matt. 6:33).

Of course, how we view technology affects how technology relates to
science, the economic and political worlds, and the design and fabrication processes. In our present culture, science, economics, politics, and
design and fabrication are all pulled under the spell of technicism. All
serve the same god—a god that fails.

Clearly, the question to be answered is, how does one live a responsible life of faith in God and obedience to his will in a technological world
committed to the belief that God is irrelevant and that human technology
is the way of salvation? One response is as old as God's confronting
Adam and Eve in the Garden after their fall into sin: prophetic witness,

bearing witness to the truth in the face of lies, evasions, and false promises. It is this type of response we will explore in this chapter, first by considering the nature of prophetic witness, next by considering the content of the prophetic message that needs to be brought to our hurting world, and finally by discussing the role an activated conscience plays in prophetic witness. The final chapter considers more specific, action-oriented strategies.

THE NATURE OF PROPHETIC WITNESS

Prophecy Defined. Many people today recognize the need for a prophetic witness in a technological age. Ralph Nader is often hailed as a prophet to today's industry. People everywhere have noted with interest George Orwell's prophecy of doom, *1984*. Our appeal for prophetic witness, however, arises from the belief that it has been basic to God's work in the world throughout human history. The line of prophetic witness can be traced from Old Testament times through the centuries of church history to the present.

The historic line of prophetic witness has been marked by prophets who have functioned more as messengers than as predictors of the future: they tell forth more than they foretell. A *prophet* speaks *on behalf of* God. Prophecy is a form of communication couched in the imperative that calls men and women to their cultural responsibility and challenges them to make righteousness and faithfulness to God's will their guide. Prophecy is, therefore, an inspired communication representing God's interpretation of a particular historical moment.[1] The heart of prophecy lies in a divine word addressed to actual situations. The prophet is God's proclaimer and announcer. "I will put my words in his mouth," God declares in Deuteronomy 18:18, "and he will tell them everything I command him."

As Yahweh's messengers, biblical prophets sometimes indicated what the future held for society, economics, and politics. The Messiah's future was also plainly foretold. But prediction was never the prophets' principal function, either in the Old Testament or the New. Special knowledge of the future surfaced only occasionally when the prophets fulfilled their primary role of conveying God-inspired messages. Paul confirms the predominantly ethical and educational character of Old Testament prophecy, using the term to denote teaching, admonishing, convicting, and authoritative assessment. (See 1 Cor. 14:1-3, 31, for example.)

---

1. See Abraham J. Heschel, *The Prophets*, 2 vols. (1962; rpt., New York: Harper & Row-Torchbooks, 1969, 1971), 1: xvi.

"Official" prophets—those through whom God revealed his inspired word—existed only during the biblical period from Samuel to John the Baptist. But down through the centuries such prophetic voices as those of Tertullian, Augustine, Saint Francis of Assisi, John Calvin, John Wesley, William Wilberforce, and Charles Finney have spoken God's truth in the specific situations of their times. Today, contemporary prophets—who are found throughout Christ's church—apply scriptural truth to particular needs and situations. They also need to speak to society's technological aspects and activities. But given the enormous complexity of technological issues, it is foolhardy to assume that the responsibility for prophetic witness should be shouldered by a small group—the ordained clergy, for instance. As heirs of the Protestant Reformation, we insist on the universal office of believer, an office that bears a prophetic dimension to be exercised according to the individual believer's gifts and tasks. The task of prophetic witness today thus belongs to all believers in varying degrees and ways as they live as engineers, academics, ministers, politicians, and corporate executives. James Houston calls the Christian community to a fresh sense of its mission:

> I appeal to evangelical Christians to use the whole range of their professional skills to speak prophetically about our times. We need deeper analyses of the pathology of scientific, technological, social and political evils in our contemporary world, in light of the eternal realities revealed in God's Word. A new missionary enterprise is involved: to go virtually into every professional area of life, just as in the past we have emphasized the geographical penetration of our world with the gospel.[2]

While all believers as officeholders must live and speak prophetically, some possess the prophetic gift in special measure. All of us must speak the truth in a technological age, but some of us have the special gift of prophecy. This prophetic gift is largely exercised by way of the written or spoken word. But words can never be divorced from actions. Thus prophetic witness can also be carried out by deeds in those cases where actions effectively illustrate, dramatize, and confront. And always the prophet's deeds must mesh with his or her words. The next chapter centers on our calling to lives of simple obedience and faithfulness, often seemingly far removed from the attention of others. But here we consider

2. James M. Houston, "The Judgment of the Nations," in *Prophecy in the Making*, ed. Carl F. H. Henry (Carol Stream, Ill.: Creation House, 1971), pp. 360–61. Also see Richard J. Mouw, *Called to Holy Worldliness*, ed. Mark Gibbs (Philadelphia: Fortress Press, 1980), pp. 71–72, 132–33.

prophetic witness, which involves confronting the evil powers of the present age.

The Need for Prophetic Witness. With modern societies in the grip of technicism, the need for prophetic witness has never been greater. The pitfall is that we will merely accommodate present culture rather than trying to change it. The old adage "To get along, go along" can become the unconsciously adopted rule even of Christians. Because we live in a technicistic society, there is an almost overwhelming danger that we will assimilate its attitudes, outlooks, and assumptions without even being aware of it. That which is unnatural and unbiblical comes to seem natural and proper.

To break out of this mold—the accretion of outlooks and attitudes that society subtly and alluringly presses around us—we need the prophetic witness who mounts the watchtower to speak God's truth. Idols must be smashed, assumptions laid bare, and consequences exposed. In light of this urgent need we share the pained grievance of Nicholas Wolterstorff, who has noted that "the vision of the Christian community as always an alien presence in human society, as always the witness, the agent, and the evidence of something lost but to be regained has been sadly lost."[3] It is this vision that must be regained if the Christian community is to bear witness in a technicistic society to the meaning of faithful obedience to God's normative will.

Biblical Prophecy. Writing about prophecy seems somehow totally foreign to our modern, secularized culture—somewhat akin to introducing the Greek myth of Icarus and Daedalus into a scientific paper on "Wing Strength and Stress Management in Supersonic Aircraft." Therefore, we need to be especially clear on the type of prophetic witness that we are calling for. The nature of biblical prophecy helps us understand prophecy and its relevancy for modern culture.

The biblical account of prophecy stresses that God is personally involved in historical events. Abraham Heschel's monumental study, *The Prophets,* uses the word *pathos* to describe God's intimate, heartfelt concern for all the affairs of humanity, an emotional involvement that must also characterize prophetic communication about technology today if such witness is to be authentically biblical. According to Heschel, divine pathos is the basic, underlying spirit of biblical prophecy: "This notion that God can be intimately affected, that He possesses not merely intelligence and will, but also pathos, basically defines the prophetic

3. Nicholas Wolterstorff, "How Does Grand Rapids Reply to Washington?" *Reformed Journal,* Oct. 1977, p. 14.

consciousness. . . . God is not conceived as judging the world in detachment. . . . In the biblical view, man's deeds may move Him, affect Him, grieve Him, or, on the other hand, gladden and please Him."[4] As prophets communicate God's interpretation of history, they are constrained to represent him as more than an authority figure expecting sheer obedience. His pathos—his deep concern and love—must reverberate in their voices.

Unlike "neighboring" deities, the God of the Old Testament prophets was not indifferent and unknown. Mystery and transcendence shrouded God's sovereign acts in history, yet the prophets constantly portrayed God's participation in the predicament of humankind. The elemental fact was God's engagement with Israel—his fundamental stake in its destiny. Thus the final determinant of prophetic authenticity was how the prophetic agents expressed God's concern. Prophets declared God's heartfelt, reconciling concern for people, not merely abstract truth about God's being. They communicated not only his will but his love and his will combined. As Heschel notes, "The theme of prophetic understanding is not the mystery of God's essence, but rather the mystery of His relation to man. . . . The fundamental experience of the prophet is a sympathy with the divine pathos. . . . The typical prophetic state of mind is one of being taken up into the heart of divine pathos. . . . The prophet hears God's voice and feels His heart."[5]

For the biblical prophet, history is not a derelict arena where lonely humanity struggles on its own to survive. History reveals God's ongoing providential care of humankind. Heschel makes the point forcefully: "For the biblical understanding of history, the idea of pathos is as central as the idea of man being an image of God is for the understanding of creation. . . . Man is not only an image of God; he is a perpetual concern of God."[6] Wicked acts, therefore, do not merely abuse those who live in historical space and time; they affront God. Evil works among men and women are a humiliation of God. And, as Heschel notes, righteousness "is the mold in which God wants history to be shaped. . . . God needs mercy, righteousness. . . . Justice is His line, righteousness His plummet (Isaiah 28:17). It is not one of his ways, but in all his ways."[7] Injustice, which wantonly defies the divine purpose of history, filled the biblical prophets with dismay. On the other hand, visions of righteous and prosperous societies inspired them to exalted and dramatic poetry.

Present-day prophets who confront the evils of a technicistic society

4. Heschel, *The Prophets*, 2: 4.
5. Heschel, *The Prophets*, 2: 264; also see vol. 1, p. 26.
6. Heschel, *The Prophets*, 2: 58, 6.
7. Heschel, *The Prophets*, 1: 198.

must show the same sorrowing, loving concern, the same involvement with society and its failings as the biblical prophets did. Only then will they be faithful to the nature of the God for whom they speak.

Jacques Ellul as a Prophet. These generalities concerning a reconciling, loving concern as the underlying spirit of prophecy can be sharpened by reference to Jacques Ellul. Dale Brown has applauded Ellul's ''Amoslike ministry to the technological society,''[8] and the prefaces of Ellul's most recent books all label him prophetic. As a lay theologian, Ellul in fact develops the biblical content more explicitly than other present-day critics of our technological culture who also operate from a Christian perspective, critics such as E. F. Schumacher, Paulo Freire, and Ivan Illich. Ellul's voice has been long raised and consistent: he established his basic thesis already in 1948 and outlined his fundamental concept of *la technique* in 1954.[9] Not surprisingly, prophecy is among Ellul's exegetical interests. He calls himself a ''watchman on the walls'' (a self-designation he takes from Ezekiel), and he appreciates the prophetic mode of writing both in theory and in practice. In this section, therefore, we pay special attention to Ellul. Perhaps by understanding his approach and contrasting our own with it, we can cast additional light on the nature and scope of prophetic witness.

Some of Ellul's detractors refuse to consider him a prophet in any sense. Many complain that his pessimism and fatalism destroy his credibility as a social analyst and a prophetic witness. Lewis Mumford deplores Ellul's ''ingrained fatalism,'' and Harvey Cox speculates that the ''endless humdrum of the Paris suburbs and the glacial immobility of the French bureaucracy'' may have made Ellul revengeful. Rupert Hall stings him mercilessly: ''Ellul lives on black bread. . . . The [so-called] prophet whose cry is only 'Woe, ye are damned' walks unheeded.'' Others implore him to stop acting as though he must single-handedly suffer for the world's unrighteousness.[10]

But charging Ellul with unrelieved pessimism misjudges his spirit and objective. ''I have no mechanical, fatalist, or organicist view at all,'' he insists; ''I only say that most of the time, in our day, things are that way.''[11] Ellul consistently uses the redeeming phrases ''only if'' and

8. Dale Brown, ''Critique: New Demons,'' *Sojourners* 5 (Nov. 1976): 37.

9. See Jacques Ellul, *Presence of the Kingdom* (1948; rpt., New York: Seabury Press, 1967), and *The Technological Society,* trans. John Wilkinson (New York: Knopf, 1965).

10. These quotations and a summary of other literature condemning Ellul as a pessimist can be found in Clifford Christians' ''Ellul on Solution: An Alternative But No Prophecy,'' in *Jacques Ellul: Interpretive Essays,* ed. Clifford Christians and Jay Van Hook (Urbana: University of Illinois Press, 1981), pp. 147-73.

11. Jacques Ellul, *The Political Illusion* (New York: Knopf, 1967), p. 34. Also see Ellul's foreword to *The Technological Society.*

"only then." "I am convinced," he declares, "the situation is not completely hopeless." Only if we fail to act will today's forces be "transformed into inevitabilities."[12] True, Ellul's dialectical method often functions erratically. His *Meaning of the City* provides an example. In the overarching dialectic between Babylon and Jerusalem, Ellul emphasizes Babylon throughout, but does not give the City of God its due until the final pages of the book. But those who find only judgment without grace in Ellul's works fail to understand how his dialecticism usually operates, or they read far too selectively and superficially. Ellul himself has explained,

> When I write a book or article I always think about my audience. It is never abstract. . . . Thirty or forty years ago everyone was sure the world was progressing. Everything was tremendous, life was wonderful, etc., etc. At that time, I said, "No, be careful." Now everyone I meet, especially young people, are uptight, nervous, afraid. In this environment, I tell them to listen, that there is a chance. There are few possibilities, but one should never lose hope.[13]

In sharp contrast to those who simply dismiss Ellul as being overly pessimistic are those who believe that Ellul's message comports so well with the Bible's message and his analysis of modern society is so perceptive that nothing further need be said. David Gill, for instance, concludes that Ellul's work is unassailable and that Christians can best witness in this technological age by interpreting, defending, and promoting Ellul's writings.[14]

But those who totally embrace Ellul's message do not give sufficient weight to the fact that the intense, loving concern that should infuse the prophet's message—a sense of divine pathos—is essentially missing in Ellul. Instead, he espouses an apocalypticism that is at odds with the transformational emphasis that should mark the modern prophet's witness. This point requires some explanation. It is useful to begin by noting that Ellul's theological framework rests upon the work of Karl Barth—not uncritically so, but in a fundamental way nonetheless.[15] For our

12. Ellul, *The Technological Society,* pp. xxix, xxxi.

13. Ellul, quoted by Berta Sichel in "New Hope for the Technological Society: An Interview with Jacques Ellul," *Etcetera: Review of General Semantics,* Summer 1983, p. 206.

14. See, for example, Gill's foreword in Ellul's *Money and Power* (Downers Grove, Ill.: Inter-Varsity Press, 1984), pp. 5–8, and his introduction in Ellul's *Living Faith* (San Francisco: Harper & Row, 1983), pp. xi–xvi.

15. For an overview, see Geoffrey W. Bromiley, "Barth's Influence on Jacques Ellul," in *Jacques Ellul,* pp. 32–51.

purposes here, the Barthian distinction between *Historie* (actual historical events) and *Geschichte* (the interpretation of those events) is crucial. Based on this distinction, Barth denies that human history has meaning or value. God as Wholly Other is free to invade history, as he did in Jesus Christ, but full meaning and salvation lie outside history and are experienced only through faith. This entails a gulf between secular and sacred histories, the latter culminating in an eschatological climax at the final judgment.

For Ellul, this apocalypse at the end of time anchors both freedom and revolution. He argues that technology impinges on our faith and freedom in an overwhelming manner; even though people consider themselves free, they actually suffer from the illusion of freedom and conform to the demands of the technological society. Ellul does not believe that the illusion can be uprooted by any strategy that arises from the flow of human history. History as human activity is ruled by necessity; it is not subject to human control. Society's only hope for an authentic freedom, therefore, rests upon a terrible cataclysm at the end of historic time, one that reaches back to shatter our everyday illusions and totally disrupts the flow of history with a solution rooted outside it. The result is a permanent revolution that delivers humankind from slavery into freedom. Darrell Fasching has described Ellul's position as "apocalyptic revolt," a phrase that precisely indicates Ellul's dialectical intention. The freedom of the apocalypse beyond history revolts against the lack of freedom we experience within history. Ellul thereby presents an alternative that confronts the technological era without a hint of compromise, while at the same time he protects the radical distinctiveness of the solution. He opposes all middle-level compromises within the existing historical process.

Ellul's apocalypticism thus stands in contrast to biblical prophecy, which emphasizes God's involved, loving concern for men and women living in history. According to Ellul's view, divine compassion is not the governing spirit; before the final consummation, society is nothing more than a lair for demonic powers, or—according to those with views similar to Ellul's—a wasteland where technological forces rule unchecked. Making an apocalyptic moment dominant leaves only one option: a total and indiscriminate revolt against the present system. No meaningful change incremental or otherwise, can be effected through the everyday workings of the historical process. The adherents of apocalypticism think their view is a positive one, but it may actually prove destructive of human responsibility by engendering a fatalistic attitude toward the existing technological situation.

The prophetic transformation advocated in this book is no less radical in intent; it both resists and employs revolutionary language. It speaks out against the tragic failure of the human race and calls for righteousness. Prophets must be confrontational when society's basic ideas and motives become deeply and uncritically entrenched, as is the case with technicism in today's culture. But prophetic transformation differs from Ellul's vision of the apocalypse; it is built on a different premise. Prophetic witness should be animated by divine concern, not only divine judgment. Prophets must carry a burden in their souls for both those who plunder and those who are trampled by human greed. Prophets are often compelled to condemn their society's complacency and waywardness, but always with the aim of reconciling men and women to God and to each other. They do not invoke timeless abstractions but echo the voice of God imploring humankind to turn back. As Abraham Heschel notes, "It is not a world devoid of meaning that evokes the prophet's consternation, but a world deaf to meaning."[16] History has meaning and purpose because God is Lord of history, though he may often be ignored or scorned.

What may appear to be words of doom in biblical prophecy are actually exhortations to repentance. Jonah's message to Nineveh is a prime example. Judgment is not absolute, but conditional: disaster will strike only if the people do not renounce their wicked ways. Since history is not a blind alley and since returning to God offers a way out, the prophets' attitude is always one of heartfelt concern, not disparagement. True, the prophets make sweeping allegations on occasion, but the thrust of prophetic witness is particular circumstances and specific wickedness; their aim is not to condemn history wholesale but to redirect it. We can take our cue from them. We must resist certain evils without compromise, but we must also work for and anticipate change within the historical process. In his book about John Calvin, W. Fred Graham calls the sixteenth-century Reformer "the constructive revolutionary"[17]—a label that should also describe us in our commitment to prophetic transformation.

The end of time is certain; the role it is presumed to play forms the core of the debate between Ellul's apocalyptic revolt and our prophetic transformation. Both views recognize that the future is not a simple continuation of the present. But apocalyptic thinking advocates a realized eschatology wherein the kingdom of God is to be fulfilled here and now following a cataclysmic shattering of existing historical patterns; prophetic transformation does not. Nor does it deny the possibility for reform within present history, although it also recognizes that history always and necessarily falls far short of God's kingdom of shalom. The final victory must yet occur. As Karl Lowith writes,

16. Heschel, *The Prophets*, 2: xv.
17. W. Fred Graham, *The Constructive Revolutionary: John Calvin and His Socio-Economic Impact* (Atlanta: John Knox Press, 1978).

The Kingdom of God is already at hand, and yet, as an eschaton, still to come. This ambiguity is essential to all history after Christ: the time is already fulfilled and not yet consummated. . . . On account of this profound ambiguity of the historical fulfillment where everything is "already" and what is "not yet," the Christian believer lives in a radical tension between present and future.[18]

Since the God of pathos remains the Sovereign of the fallen world, our prophetic witness to this world must always have a redemptive, transformational focus.

BASIC THEMES OF THE MESSAGE

The specific message of prophetic witness to technology varies with circumstances. However, three themes are always prominent and together form the basic characteristics of the message: it always warns against the idolatry of technicism, calls for liberation from an accommodation to the status quo, and condemns outrageous evils—all with the purpose of ensuring that a responsible technology guided by God's normative will can prosper.

A Condemnation of Technicism. First, the prophetic witness confronts the idolatry of technicism and insists on desacralizing it. The issue here is the technicistic perspective (as described in Chapter Four and elsewhere throughout the book) that largely animates the technological process today. Technical activity has been turned into the Myth of Technique, which Arend Van Leeuwen defines as "a pseudo-messianic pretension" that technology possesses "the ultimate key to all problems."[19] This ideological construct manifests humanity's will to power in the technological sphere and uncritically presumes that technology has a sacred character, that it is worthy of an ultimate allegiance. Of course, many individuals, companies, and technological objects are not imbued with this spirit; nevertheless, technicism is predominant in industrialized societies and leads to overconfidence in the fruits of technology. In Dietrich Bonhoeffer's terms, something of penultimate value—human technical effort—becomes deified into something of ultimate status.

One essential condition of prophetic responsibility, therefore, is destroying technicism as unacceptable worship of a modern god. Prophetic witness exposes the idolatrous attitudes, intentions, desires, and aims

---

18. Karl Lowith, *Meaning in History* (Chicago: University of Chicago Press, 1949), p. 188.

19. Arend Theodoor Van Leeuwen, *Prophecy in a Technocratic Era* (New York: Scribner's, 1968), p. 19.

that are driving technology forward. Prophets condemn unqualified worship of the technological enterprise for its own sake. Against the overweening technical spirit that ridicules the spiritual as invalid, prophets articulate a biblical view of culture in which questions of meaning, life's purpose, and moral values predominate. To demythologize or desacralize technology effectively, prophetic radicalism severs at its root the blind faith that technological prowess will lead to one achievement after another.

Prophetic witness should be directed toward such extravagant claims as those of Emmanuel Mesthene, Simon Ramo, and Ronald Reagan, which were noted in Chapter Four. We fulfill our prophetic responsibility only when the mythologies held by such representatives of modern society are destroyed, and important questions regarding ends and direction are once again made central. The concepts presented in this book—the cultural mandate, humanity under the authority of God, technology done as a form of service, biblically based normative principles that guide technology—must be articulated and applied in a dramatic, forceful manner. We must drive home the contrast between a technology without limits and one under the authority of God's normative will, between a technology that is seen as humanity's best hope for the future and one of limited means to achieve certain limited ends, between a technology that becomes an end in itself and one that is an instrument to achieve chosen ends. The modern prophet must do this and more in order to shatter the mold into which technology—the centerpiece of modern culture in developed countries—seeks to force all of society.

Ellul's work, properly understood, serves as a provocative example of prophetic desacralization in a more general sense. His concern is not primarily with machines and tools but with the spirit of "machineness" itself. In Ellul's view, modern society is so beguiled by technical productivity that it unconsciously reconstructs all social institutions on this model. Society takes technical efficiency and turns it into a force so powerful that it casts aside all other imperatives. He notes that "in ancient days men put out the eyes of nightingales in order to make them sing better," and laments that today all other values are similarly sacrificed to that of maximum proficiency.[20]

David Gill correctly criticizes those readers of Ellul who conclude that he opposes technological efforts rather than confronting the "sacralized phenomenon, the ensemble of means, the way of thinking."[21] Ellul does

---

20. Ellul, *Presence of the Kingdom*, p. 75.

21. David W. Gill, "Interview with Jacques Ellul," *Radix*, Jan.–Feb. 1984, pp. 7, 28. Much of the misunderstanding has been perpetuated by the substitution of *technology* for *la technique* in a number of the English translations of Ellul's works—a substitution that Ellul

in fact castigate the mind-set that is "committed to the quest for continually improved means to carelessly examined ends"[22]—to the worship of what he calls *technique*. He opposes this powerful phenomenon as a dehumanizing force and exposes it as contrary to the biblical mind of love and justice. Earlier societies also engaged in technical activities and produced technological objects, Ellul notes, but modern society has taken a further, dangerous step by sacralizing the genius behind machines and uncritically allowing its rampaging power to control not just industry, engineering, and business but also politics, education, the church, mass media, and international relations.

La technique is somewhat different from the concept of technicism being developed here. It is narrower in that it focuses on the ultimacy of efficiency, and broader in that Ellul sees it as dominating many fields besides the technological process as we have defined it. From our perspective, Ellul overestimates the influence of *la technique:* it has not invaded society's thinking or its institutions as comprehensively or as deeply as Ellul suggests. Ellul can be legitimately criticized for his reductionism in which his obsession with *la technique* explains all modern evils. Langdon Winner correctly argues that Ellul seems intent on a view "deliberately designed to leave no passage out, . . . an ubiquitous concept of technique expand[ed] to encompass any subject and to resist contrary examples."[23] Despite such differences of definition and scope, Ellul's desacralizing of *la technique* stands as a clear model of prophetic witness. We can follow Ellul's example in analyzing, exposing, and attacking technicism.

Our technicism and Ellul's *la technique* come together in their shared conviction that technology so emphasizes technological means that ethical imperatives or norms are squeezed out.[24] Winner has labeled this reverse adaptation. The technical prowess of human minds and hands is worshiped so devoutly that questions of purpose, ends, and direction never arise. Under technicism society constructs a definition of the good based on means, which it has elevated to a position of genuine moral purpose. Thus we streamline methods, increase sophistication, and improve speed—all apart from God-directed ends or discernible purposes.

Computers, for example, invade classrooms without a clear philoso-

---

says he never approved. Harper & Row has now agreed to use *technique* (small *t*) when referring to individual technical acts and *Technique* (capital *T*) to designate the sacralized totality of means, the spirit of efficiency.

22. Robert Merton, foreword in *The Technological Society*, p. vi.

23. Langdon Winner, *Autonomous Technology: Technics Out-of-Control as a Theme in Political Thought* (Cambridge: MIT Press, 1977), p. 177.

24. See Ellul, *Presence of the Kingdom*, chap. 3.

phy of education to orient them. The rhetoric promises a decisive edge for schools equipped with the latest computer hardware. After all, computers are "modern," technologically sophisticated. A technicistic society makes the facile assumption that a computer-based education is a better education. But difficult questions about goals inevitably arise. Exactly how does computer-based education enliven an interest in the arts or sharpen critical insight into their meaning? Or, presuming that a key goal of education is to aid students in developing and articulating a world-view, how does the use of computers actually contribute to that goal? The answers to such questions are far from precise. In fact, the use of computers in education is not the major benefit that advertising hype claimed it would be. A recent article in *Newsweek* pointed out that "for most schools, the computer revolution is turning out to be a movement without a cause."[25]

Prophetic witness forces means back into their proper boundaries and restores biblical standards for humanity and society as the basis for establishing rightful goals and purposes. What we need to fulfill our call to prophetic witness is a penetrating discernment. As E. F. Schumacher insists, we must recognize means as merely means and recover non-utilitarian ends for the technological process, ends that do not barter away God's loving concern for humankind's unique entitlements as his image bearers.[26]

As modern prophets desacralize technicism, science will be freed to play its proper role, economics will be able to fulfill its proper ends, politics will be liberated to play its justice-promoting role, and design and fabrication can again be done in a holistic fashion. Society must be released from the grip of the superstition of technicism. Only then will all the aspects of the technological enterprise be free to respond positively to biblically based normative principles. Only then can there be a responsible technology. The prophets' attack on technicism, therefore, is absolutely crucial.

Liberation from an Accommodation to the Status Quo. The prophetic message also speaks against an unholy accommodation and complacency. In the biblical tradition, the prophet shatters indifference and disdains those caught up in false comfort and security. The prophet realizes that callousness must be cut away if history is to be changed. Certainly humankind needs structures that provide order and stability to prevent chaos, but these ordering structures can become master instead of servant

25. "Access Without Success," *Newsweek,* Mar. 19, 1984, p. 96.
26. E. F. Schumacher, *Guide to the Perplexed* (New York: Harper & Row, 1977), chap. 3.

and entrap men and women in the status quo. When this happens, people undergo a subtle transformation, conforming to prevailing cultural patterns, to the assumptions about reality which govern society at large. All too often we remain oblivious to human need and God's wondrous ability to use human efforts to accomplish great good, blissfully unaware of our own insensitivity.

In technological societies accommodation means being seduced by the compulsions of materialism. Schumacher makes the point that advanced industrial societies often press technology into the service of materialism. In his view, a materialistic culture thrives on the nonsense that those who consume more are automatically more fulfilled than those who consume less.[27] Materialism entices and paralyzes so subtly that wealthy people measure their worth by their material accomplishments, and the disenfranchised believe their salvation lies in getting their share of physical goods. Sins of omission are the most blatant evidence of a callous lack of concern. Captured by selfishness and consumerism, those in rich societies pay only scant attention to the radical inequities in the distribution of the world's resources. Sometimes they become frustrated with the quality of food and service at a restaurant, but they show little awareness of millions who have no food at all.

Materialism is one of society's enslaving evils, a principality (to use Pauline language) whose power was broken through Christ's resurrection. Paul makes it clear that history is woven together by such forces and structures (see Rom. 8:38; 1 Cor. 2:8, 3:22; Col. 2:8–10; Gal. 4:1–11). He teaches that apart from Christ, men and women are at the mercy of these powers. As Hendrikus Berkhof has written,

> They [the principalities] encompass, carry, and guide [our] life. . . . They are all our "guardians and teacher," the forces which hold together the world and the life of man and preserve them from chaos. . . . Yet precisely by giving unity and direction they separate us from the true God; they let us believe that we have found the true meaning of existence, whereas they really estrange us from true meaning.[28]

Because a loving compassion for others must characterize the prophetic witness, it is precisely this impersonal alienation from God that is the great travesty. A principality such as materialism appears to provide so much security that it makes God's preserving care seem irrelevant. But materialism actually results in a vicious enslavement that isolates indi-

---

27. The main argument is found in Schumacher's *Small Is Beautiful: Economics as if People Mattered* (New York: Harper & Row, 1973).

28. Hendrikus Berkhof, *Christ and the Powers* (Scottdale, Penn.: Herald Press, 1962), pp. 17, 25–26.

viduals from each other and from a personal God. Thus individuals fall far short of the divine purpose for them, and their lives are devoid of the Lordship of a personal Being.

Apathetic accommodation to the status quo can result from one of two causes; at times each feed upon the other. In countries of abundance, love of the world and its alluring baubles usually crowds out the Word of God. In countries with few economic resources to distribute among the population, the needy majority often suffers blatant oppression at the hands of a wealthy few. In the first circumstance, the prophet calls for the sleeper to awake; in the second, he or she calls for the oppressor to set the people free and repent of selfishness and greed.

Paulo Freire's plea for a critical consciousness demonstrates one way that prophetic responsibility can be exercised against acquiescence to the status quo.[29] His writing grows out of his experiences in his homeland, the state of Pernambuco in Northeast Brazil, the poorest region in the Western hemisphere. There the rural poor bear the scars of the exploitive ruling elite. Freire calls those who are consumed by their positions of material power to be set free. But the oppressed may also be locked into their negative role in this system, and thus they also need to develop a new consciousness in order to initiate the process of change.

In the face of technicism, the prophetic witness insists on desacralization; in the face of an insidious conformity and accommodation to prevailing cultural assumptions, the prophet cries for liberation. Both rich and poor must reexamine their accommodation to existing cultural patterns and assumptions. Materialism as the way to happiness needs to be challenged. Those who perpetuate oppressive structures must be brought under the judgment of God. Those who are oppressed should be awakened to their own ability to define a role for themselves in history commensurate with the gifts God has given them. Freedom would then be actualized in concrete societal situations, as the liberated, under God, would hold the reins for directing technology responsibly.

Condemnation of Outrageous Evils. On occasion the prophetic responsibility can be fulfilled only by a total rejection and condemnation of especially outrageous evils. The list of evils in the technological realm that are particularly outrageous is always subject to debate and will change over time. Thus the list is always illustrative, not ex-

29. For a summary of Freire's work and a basic bibliography, see V. A. De Lima and C. Christians, "Paulo Freire: The Political Dimension of Dialogic Communication," *Communication* 4 (1979): 133–55. See also Paulo Freire, *Pedagogy of the Oppressed*, trans. Myra Ramos (New York: Seabury Press, 1970), and *The Politics of Education: Culture, Power, and Liberation*, trans. Donaldo Macedo (South Hadley, Mass.: Bergin and Garvey, 1985).

haustive. However, in principle, prophetic witness includes the condemnation of a certain class of actions that have no redeeming value and are the opposite of the command to love God above all and others as ourselves. Therefore, the prophetic task is not complete without a total rejection of those evils that are especially destructive and clearly cannot be justified on biblical grounds.

Ivan Illich has sought to demonstrate theoretically why certain particularly outrageous evils exist. Built into technological development and other productive processes, he argues, is the disutility phenomenon. The continuing development of tools does not perpetually add to the attainment of certain human ends. He is convinced that at some point, without exception, technological processes and objects cease to provide any demonstrable improvement and either show spectacular negative consequences or transfer their counterproductive costs to another domain of society. Illich illustrates his theory with concrete examples. Thus he demonstrates that faster transportation does not necessarily save time, that medical "advances" at some point begin to generate more negative than positive benefits, that the increasing size of schools and pace of information-transfer will result in overload and the awarding of diplomas of incompetence, and that short-term agricultural benefits are outweighed by long-term disasters. In situation after situation, Illich argues, one eventually reaches zero productivity or total counterproductivity.[30] Although one can question the details of Illich's position—especially his insistence that there are no exceptions to his thesis—it does help explain why frequently outrageous, indefensible evils emerge in society.

In condemning such evils, the prophet's testimony of words will sometimes develop into a testimony of actions, as he or she calls attention to a particular evil and dramatizes the depth of its offense through acts of resistance. In this case, the prophet's steadfast rejection is born of holy impatience. Richard Mouw rightly warns that radical words and behavior should not be motivated by pride and anger. The audience and offenders to whom the prophet's action is directed ought not to hear angry self-righteousness but the pleas of a loving, caring God.[31] Prophets strive for transformation; they do not seek to make people desperate. They believe in the possibility of change through faith in God and his intervention in human affairs.

Nuclear weapons designed for first-strike capability provide one example of a technology on the modern prophet's list of outrageous evils.

---

30. Ivan Illich, *Tools for Conviviality* (New York: Harper & Row, 1973), chaps. 1, 3.
31. See Mouw, *Called to Holy Worldliness*, p. 118.

Christian pacifism and the just-war theory are united in their opposition to these weapons. The just-war theory, for example, condemns the concept of first-strike capability on the grounds of its intention to initiate war by destroying noncombatants indiscriminately. Not all nuclear weapons should necessarily be condemned; some are ordered, designed, and manufactured for the sole purpose of functioning as effective deterrents to enemy attack. In a complicated world, disagreements are likely to arise over the most effective nuclear policy—a nuclear freeze, a diplomatic compromise aimed at removing all potential first-strike weapons, a refusal to build a new generation of weapons with first-strike capabilities. Nevertheless, the prophet must speak out against developing the wrong kinds of defense. And the prophetic message is not limited to attacking first-strike nuclear weaponry. The evils of militarism, failures to honor peace treaties, sabre-rattling terrorism by military powers—prophetic witness also censures these signs of human wickedness.

Another example of a clear-cut, outrageous evil is the technology of mind-controlling drugs. Obviously, drugs have played a positive role in medicine, relieving pain and increasing life span. Physiological and psychological advantages have been achieved through electronic intervention and psychotropic and antipsychotic medications. Although attempts at behavior control raise profound ethical questions, one can argue that they are morally justifiable. However, as Hans Jonas observes,

> From the relief of the *patient,* a goal entirely in the tradition of the medical art, there is an easy passage to the relief of *society* from the inconvenience of difficult individual behavior among its members: that is, the passage from medical to social applications. . . . The troublesome problems of rule and unruliness in modern mass society make the extension of such control methods to non-medical categories extremely tempting for social management.[32]

Admittedly, the line separating enabling care from social domination is sometimes ambiguous. However, for a social institution—whether it be the government, the military, a business, or a hospital—to seek to exert mind control over any but those suffering from severe psychotic disorders is clearly not appropriate, responsible technology. Such destruction of human freedom and dignity is unthinkable within a biblical understanding of humankind, where an individual's responsibility for his or her behavior may not be contravened by another's technology.

---

32. Hans Jonas and Alvin Johnson, *Philosophical Essays: From Ancient Creed to Technological Man* (Englewood Cliffs, N.J.: Prentice-Hall, 1974), pp. 48–49.

Open-ended eugenics is a third example of a technological process clearly and unambiguously contrary to biblical principles. As with nuclear weaponry, prophetic witness does not speak against all forms of this technology. Human genetic research aimed at specific gene therapy and limited to human organs has many potential negative side-effects, but on balance it may be morally appropriate because it carries possibilities for eliminating genetically transmitted diseases. However, the purpose of open-ended eugenics is species engineering, modifications of the human genome itself that can be passed on reproductively. In its extreme forms it envisions semihumans created for slave tasks. The prophetic witness must be largely educative and persuasive in its response, recognizing that some research projects fall in the ambiguous area between species alteration and medicine, with long-term results unknown. Because of the complexities involved, Christians will not always agree on which public policies best sort out the permissible from the impermissible. But the uncertainties of gray issues do not preclude a condemnation of those immoral genetic experiments that wantonly disregard the sacredness of personhood.

Prophetic witness that is true to biblical form is animated and guided by a divine covenant with humankind. Whether desacralizing technicism or denouncing accommodation to the status quo or condemning outrageous evils, prophets speak out of a heartfelt, loving concern and are always motivated by a desire to help others fulfill their God-given destiny. Since God cares passionately about men and women and is intimately involved in their destiny, prophets love their neighbors with an equal passion. Therefore, they warn against all technology that violates the Great Commandment, that disregards the biblically based normative principles for technology.

ACTIVATING THE CONSCIENCE

As the voice of divine compassion regarding society, prophetic witness stirs the human conscience. Clinical appeals to reason and analysis are insufficient; justice is not merely a calculation whereby all parties receive their due. Justice is that, but it is more—a force that must surge forward like a mighty stream (Amos 5:24). This will happen only when we are touched deep within our psyches. God expects his children to have an insatiable thirst, a relentless yearning for mercy and love that parallels his own. Living in intimacy with God envelops prophets in divine compassion; they anticipate that their listeners will feel their consciences stirred by equal fervor.

For a biblical vision of prophetic witness to succeed today, the pivotal role of conscience must be recaptured. Conscience is a fundamental aspect of Christian ethical theory. In the twentieth century Freud has stifled the modern appreciation of the conscience by reducing it to a nagging voice, a repressive intruder producing unnecessary guilt.[33] H. Richard Niebuhr knows better: instead of reducing the conscience to a discrete "unit" of the person, he sees the whole self reflected in the conscience.[34] The conscience is more than merely an inner voice telling us to do right and shun evil; it is that dimension of our personality where God's correction and reconciliation take place, and where our duties to him and our neighbor are given shape. Conscience is that facet of our humanness where we apprehend moral truth and come under an obligation to follow it.

Those who understand conscience in terms of divine compassion—of God's pathos—correctly realize that prophetic witness does not seek a conscience that merely abides by a set of normative principles. "There is no dichotomy of pathos and ethos, of motive and norm," Heschel points out. "They do not exist side by side, opposing each other; they involve and presuppose each other."[35] Pathos and ethos are of one piece, and together they produce fruitful action. The attuned conscience is not governed by unreasoned emotion; it produces activity rooted in deliberate decision and charged with normative content. In particular cases, prophetic witness need not include elaboration; the murderous King Ahab, for instance, needed only to be shocked into a reminder of what he already knew about Naboth's rights. But prophetic witness usually includes explanation and instruction as well as proclamation. As Philip Hughes notes, "Even the regenerate conscience has much to learn and, in order to be liberated from the erroneous notions of his past, is in need of instruction in the revealed truth of God. The formation of conscience keeps step with the formation of one's understanding of the truth."[36] The prophetic aim must always be to offer explanation and teaching sufficient to prevent the hopeless self-flagellation and immobilization that comes from being uninformed, and to produce a responsive conscience.

33. For an overview of the manner in which conscience is presently treated in Christian ethics, see Edward LeRoy Long, Jr., *A Survey of Recent Christian Ethics* (New York: Oxford University Press, 1982), chap. 8.

34. For a valuable summary of the importance of conscience in the work of H. Richard Niebuhr, Gerhard Ebling, Helmut Thielicke, and Dietrich Bonhoeffer, see Eric Mount, Jr., *Conscience and Responsibility* (Richmond, Va.: John Knox Press, 1969). Donald E. Miller outlines in detail the psychoanalytic tradition and argues that religious belief frees the conscience rather than oppresses it. See *The Wing-Footed Wanderer: Conscience and Transcendence* (Nashville: Abingdon, 1977).

35. Heschel, *The Prophets*, 2: 5.

36. Philip E. Hughes, *Christian Ethics in Secular Society: An Introduction to Christian Ethics* (Grand Rapids: Baker Book House, 1983), p. 41.

Prophetic witness is a catalyst for obedient acts motivated by a conscience that is both informed and inspired. While the conscience is honed in community, it sometimes leads one to walk alone to do what's right. "A man is bound to keep faith with conscience," says Henry Stob. "Not to do so is to surrender one's inner personal integrity, to destroy character, and to subvert all morals."[37]

Whistle-blowing is one way in which such an activated conscience expresses itself in the world of technology. Whistle-blowing refers not to sounding a private alarm within an organization but to making public protest. It calls attention to negligence or abuses in company policy or activity that threatens the public interest. These alarms embarrass management and put anyone benefitting from the abusive practice on the defensive. Therefore, the engineer who discloses safety defects in braking systems and the factory worker who complains about hazardous chemical seepage are usually risking their jobs by doing so.[38] But often whistle-blowing is the only means—or at least the most effective and pointed one—by which the voice of conscience can be communicated.

Whistle-blowing is an outgrowth of prophetic witness. How we handle it is complicated by the fact that moral tensions are usually involved. On the one hand, employees are duty-bound to honor both explicit and implicit contracts with their company. Added to such contracts are pledges of loyalty, formal and informal, to colleagues and clients. Also involved are company policies regarding secrecy and security and the confidentiality of in-house discussions. On the other hand, the public's health and safety may be at stake. To live prophetically, we must not only desist from harmful acts but also prevent harm as well.

Although whistle-blowing is morally desirable, it must not be done hastily or recklessly. It is important to establish the validity of an accusation before a finger is pointed. Informants may lie out of paranoia or to promote their own interests; alleged product defects are often open to debate. Christian ethics justifies civil disobedience, however; in principle the right and obligation to speak out on matters of conscience are nonnegotiable if based on accurate information and if guided by the proper motivation and not by the desire for self-glory or revenge. Mat-

37. Henry Stob, *Ethical Reflections: Essays on Moral Themes* (Grand Rapids: Eerdmans, 1978), p. 155.

38. However, the sociological study undertaken by Myron Glazer contradicts the common wisdom that the fate of whistle-blowers is uniformly grim: "My evidence provides a more intricate mosaic. Virtually all individuals discussed here have been able to rebuild their careers and belief in their competence and integrity. . . . Ironically perhaps the diversity of American economic and social institutions provides opportunities to those who have dared defy the authority of the established order." See "Ten Whistleblowers and How They Fared," *The Hastings Center Report*, Dec. 1983, p. 40.

thew 18 requires that the offending parties be informed before a public declaration is made: thus going public can be justified only after failure to persuade those directly involved with the problem.

Whistle-blowing is usually initiated by an expert, but the obligation cannot rest only with him or her. In order for whistle-blowing to function meaningfully, it must be recognized and protected by the broader community. An important structural reform involves spelling out whistle-blowing procedures so that company policies encourage employees to speak up rather than putting them on the defensive. The largest professional engineering society (the Institute of Electrical and Electronics Engineers), among others, expects its members to speak out against abuses that threaten the public welfare. Without such explicit protection for legitimate complaints, the whistle-blower must bear too great a burden, and is often seen as a turncoat. Several years ago, when he was president of General Motors, James M. Roche complained,

> The enemies of business now encourage an employee to be disloyal to the enterprise. They want to create suspicion and disharmony and pry into the proprietary interests of the business. However this is labeled—industrial espionage, whistleblowing, or professional responsibility—it is another tactic for spreading disunity and creating conflict.[39]

While this complaint has some validity, the fact remains that superior-subordinate relationships are oppressive unless there are mutually agreed-upon policies for upward communication. The normative principle of open communication suggests such channels should be available and used when necessary. Fortunately, companies such as Xerox, IBM, and Polaroid now offer explicit resolution procedures—forums for employee complaints against management decisions and even provisions for outside arbitration.

Of course, courageous whistle-blowing is only one act of conscience. Others, less dramatic and less public, are equally necessary in people's everyday involvement in the technological enterprise. Responsible decision-making on all levels reflects an active conscience.

The prophet, traditionally a gadfly of the establishment, has usually operated on the periphery of society, at a distance from seats of power. But it is important that the prophetic witness speak to the mainstream. Thus we must strengthen our prophetic witness and its role in cultural transformation by bringing this form of communication more directly into the existing order.

39. Roche, quoted by Lea P. Steward in "Whistleblowing: Implications for Organizational Communications," *Journal of Communication*, Autumn 1980, p. 93.

To bring prophetic witness into the existing technological order, two things are essential. First, prophetic witness must be raised within the Christian community itself. Hearing God's Word as the people of God is essential in equipping the laity for ministry in the world, as Richard Mouw points out:

> The clergy perform a very special function in the community of God's people. . . . Prophetic preaching will often include admonition, criticism, and warning; it will often be characterized by a clear and bold "Thus saith the Lord!" . . . But we must not assume that the prophetic ministry that takes place within the Christian community is the unique calling of the clergy. All of us—clergy and laity—ought to admonish and correct one another. Prophetic "forth-telling " can take place within the family, at the church coffee hour, in the Sunday School class, in bull sessions and heated arguments.[40]

However, this internal prophetic witness can never be a substitute for the prophetic responsibility that Christians are to exercise within the larger human community. This brings us to the second essential condition that must be met if prophetic witness is to be brought into the existing technological order. Prophetic witness must consist of both word and deed; the two ought not to be divorced. Prophetic witness may never be a series of prescriptive statements only, doctrinaire assertions about the state of reality. In today's corporations, governmental agencies, and schools, acts of conscience—stimulated by a prophetic, loving concern—can often be the most strategic instruments available for transforming the technological process.

There is a great need for agreement within the Christian community on prophetic responsibility as outlined above. Those of us committed to a technological process directed by biblically based normative principles can no longer indulge in the luxury of debating the validity or meaning of prophetic witness. We must prayerfully nurture the exercise of such witness, especially among those with prophetic gifts. And as our consciences are set afire by divine grace, we will see significant institutional transformations which themselves are signs of God's kingdom. Aided by a vital prophetic witness against the human propensity to make technology serve the interests of power, our technological activity can be freed at last and inspired to follow the biblical path of loving God above all and our neighbors as ourselves.

40. Mouw, *Called to Holy Worldliness*, p. 72.

CHAPTER TWELVE

Technology and Mutual Responsibility

THIS BOOK HAS ARGUED THAT IN ORDER FOR TECHNOLOGICAL ACTIVITIES to be done in servant-like response to biblically based normative principles, science, economics, politics, and the design and fabrication of technological objects all need to be radically redirected. If this redirection is to occur, prophetic witness must speak out against the technicism that pervades modern society. But more is needed if responsible technology is to emerge. If the present-day beat of the technological drum is to be changed, many more people must recognize and accept their responsibilities in regard to technology.

It is easy to assume that the responsibility for a technology done according to God's normative will rests with those occupying positions of special power or influence—with governmental policymakers, researchers, engineer-designers, corporate executives, and a host of others directly involved in technology. Indeed, a very large measure of the responsibility does rest with them. Yet the burden of responsibility is not entirely theirs; all of us—as consumers, citizens, and contributors to society—share a collective responsibility for the proper doing of technology. This raises the question of who is responsible for what—which is the subject of this chapter. This chapter first considers the nature of responsibility, comparing collective responsibility with position-specific responsibility. Then it suggests how these two forms of responsibility should be implemented.

THE NATURE OF RESPONSIBILITY

In exploring the issue of responsibility, it becomes immediately apparent that knowledge, powers, and opportunities vary widely from person to person. Different people occupy different positions in relation to technology, depending upon their calling and gifts. The design engineer working in a large corporation, the government bureaucrat in a research-and-development grant program, and the ordinary person with no special knowledge of or involvement in technology differ widely in position—each possesses different occupational skills, knowledge, power, and opportunity. Nevertheless, they all are responsible, although the level of their responsibility differs.

In order to more fully understand the nature and apportionment of responsibility in relation to technology, we will consider the nature of responsibility itself, next explore the collective version of responsibility, and then examine how collective responsibility is altered—sharpened, focused, and deepened—for those with special positions of knowledge or power. Collective and position-specific responsibilities are integrated aspects of our responsibility as human beings.

Responsibility: A Basic Definition. Responsibility is inherent in our definition of human nature. As God's image bearers, we live in an ongoing relationship of accountability. Nonresponsibility is inconceivable. H. Richard Niebuhr has made it clear that we are "responsible selves" set in a particular direction and responding in either an acceptable or a blameworthy manner. We live in response, in responsibility, to a personal God; our response is not based on consequences alone or on an abstract imperative (such as doing the public good).[1] Circumstances condition the way we fulfill our responsibility, but responsibility can never be relinquished.

This concept of responsible personhood contradicts the prevailing notion of negative freedom bequeathed to the Western mind by the Enlightenment. Negative freedom says that true human freedom is found simply in the absence of restraints. The Enlightenment arrived at this distorted notion of freedom because at its heart it emphasized the cult of sovereign freedom—an arbitrary free will conceived as autonomous from the claims of all external allegiances. The Enlightenment began and ended with the assumption that human freedom could be cut away from the normative moral order but never integrated meaningfully with it. We have lived under the shadow of that pretension ever since, and as a consequence, many people today perceive responsibility as having a

---

1. See H. Richard Niebuhr, *The Responsible Self* (New York: Harper & Row, 1963). A major theme of his book regards the distinctiveness of this approach to Christian ethics, and he concludes, "The approach to our moral existence as responsible selves . . . makes some aspects of our life as agents intelligible in a way that the teleology and deontology of traditional thought cannot do" (p. 67).

practical value but not functioning as an inescapable imperative. Peter Berger concludes correctly that "individual autonomy is the most important theme in the worldview of modernity."[2]

Clearly, this spirit of individual autonomy dominates Western society's approach to technology. In reaction to this spirit of autonomy and the resulting individualizing and narrowing of responsibility, Christians must insist on a version of long-range responsibility commonly shared and in that way co-extensive with the range of contemporary power.[3] This call for large-scale change goes out both to those directly involved in doing modern technology and to the millions indirectly involved in it.

It is certainly true that moral possibilities are grounded in freedom, and that actions cease to be moral if one is not free. The importance of freedom is not debatable, but the nature of that freedom is variously defined. What we will develop here is a vision of positive freedom, of accountable freedom, of human freedom with responsibility as its integrating center. Graham Haydon refers to this moral outlook as an "ethic of responsibility," a view of "virtue-responsibility" required of people without reference to position or role. Advocates of an ethic of responsibility "treat the requirement of responsibility as an ever-present moral demand, necessarily incumbent on any person qua person (or qua moral agent) prior, logically, to particular responsibilities."[4] Thus the fundamental element of the moral life is fulfilling certain duties because they are incumbent on us as persons, not primarily as corporate executives, engineers, or legislators—nor, for that matter, as citizens or consumers. Even as radical a utilitarian as John Stuart Mill captured a glimmer of the primacy of our humanity over our roles when he said, "Men are men before they are lawyers, or physicians, or merchants, or manufacturers; and if you make them capable and sensible men, they will make themselves capable and sensible lawyers or physicians."[5]

Similarly, in an adequate view of calling, one's general vocation is not equivalent to one's specific occupation. Certainly our obedience to God is rendered through all occupations—ordinary ones as well as powerful and strategic ones—but it cannot be limited to them. Our God-issued calling is the entire sum of our activities in the sociopolitical context in

2. Peter Berger et al., *The Homeless Mind: Modernization and Consciousness* (New York: Random House, 1973), p. 196.

3. See Hans Jonas, "Technology and Responsibility: Reflections on the New Tasks of Ethics," in *Philosophical Essays: From Ancient Creed to Technological Man* by Hans Jonas and Alvin Johnson (Englewood Cliffs, N.J.: Prentice-Hall, 1974), p. 18.

4. Graham Haydon, "On Being Responsible," *Philosophical Quarterly* 28 (1978): 46–51.

5. John Stuart Mill, "Inaugural Address at the University of St. Andrews," *Dissertations and Discussions,* vol. 4 (Boston: Spencer, 1867), p. 388.

which we find ourselves.[6] The sum of our responsibilities as created image bearers of God provides the arena for our obedient servanthood. All who claim to practice their Christianity exclusively through their occupations—that is, persons who reduce their calling to their employment and therefore claim to have no duties in areas outside it—have fractured responsibility beyond all biblical guidelines.

Collective Responsibility. Collective responsibility is inherent in people as social, cultural beings, who together share obligations for cultural vitality. Admittedly, responsible technology in a collective sense is a vague concept in an individualistic society dominated by selfish interests. Moreover, to claim that we bear a collective responsibility for certain kinds of technologies—for example, for exotic and elitist medical technologies—introduces complicated problems regarding causality. Can we ascribe blame for harm and failure—or credit for success—when dealing with extremely sophisticated, highly specialized technological objects or processes? Despite such complications, however, we as social beings do share a common, general responsibility.[7]

Collective responsibility grows out of collectivities. These are powerful realities, even though their parameters are elusive and their embodiments vary widely. It is especially important to note the existence of distinct national or nation-based societies. Usually bound by such ties as language, religion, cultural traditions, and government, national societies are particularly important collective entities. Would the nuclear arms race be escalated by specific acts of a nation's political officials unless public sentiment ultimately endorsed such action? We are hesitant to make a direct causal connection, yet we realize that overweening nationalism and faith in more technologically sophisticated weapons play a critical role in a militaristic approach to world affairs. We also understand that materialism in some important sense is a collective responsibility of Western societies and that it fosters tragic inequities in the use of the world's resources. Although the concept of collective responsibility does not allow us to determine individual liability, it does prevent us from drawing the erroneous conclusion that societies are amoral entities.

Collective and Position-specific Responsibility. Obviously, each of us fulfills several roles in life simultaneously. A business manager, for

6. For a helpful debate on the relationship between vocation and occupation, see Vernard Eller and Nicholas Wolterstorff, "A Voice on Vocation," *The Reformed Journal,* May 1979, pp. 16–23.

7. See John Ladd, "Philosophical Remarks on Professional Responsibility in Organization," in *Designing for Safety: Engineering Ethics in Organizational Contexts,* ed. A. Flores (Troy, N.Y.: Rennsalaer NSK Study, 1982), p. 200.

example, is likewise a citizen, possibly a member of a local church, potentially a parent whose oldest daughter works for UNESCO, and possibly a second-generation immigrant from Mexico who has many relatives still living there. Each of these roles entails certain responsibilities. But—and this is what needs to be emphasized—the business manager, like all of us, is responsible not in a compartmentalized, role-by-role way, but as a whole person. All of us—designers, advertisers, scientists, government officials, economists, teachers—must develop a strong sense of collective responsibility as whole persons, as created image bearers of God. In fact, enlarging the scope of our responsibilities primarily means so intertwining our work-related duties with our communal relationships that our thinking and our actions are inseparably shaped by both our expertise and our general servanthood under God. Collective responsibility is not only essential; it is conceptually prior to and serves as the basis for position-specific responsibility. One must never be separated from the other.

In Chapter Ten we made the point that because of severe time pressures, technical experts often retreat into narrowly defined specialties and fail to consider the broader implications of their work. This is an improper, distorted fulfilling of one's position-specific responsibility. J. Peter Euben also lodges an appropriate complaint against a technical view of profession-specific (that is, position-specific) ethics that are isolated from the cultural and historical scene, and are so preoccupied with skills and training for practitioners that social structures in need of reform are left untouched:

> The tendency to concentrate on the ethics of the professions instead of on public morality as a whole is a dangerous reversal of priorities. The primary issue is how and where politically to educate the citizenry as a whole, since the resolution of this larger issue contains guidelines for the more particular matter of professional ethics. Getting these priorities straight is especially imperative for a democracy, in which government by the people demands a general and sustained moral education in, through, and about public life, rather than the teaching of ethics to a professional elite.[8]

Alan Goldman also contends that professional prerogatives ought never to be established on a discrete, profession-specific basis independent of a common moral framework.[9]

This brings us directly back to the biblically based normative princi-

---

8. J. Peter Euben, "Philosophy and the Professions," *Democracy* I (Apr. 1981): 120.

9. See Alan H. Goldman, *The Moral Foundations of Professional Ethics,* Philosophy and Society Series (Totowa, N.J.: Rowman & Littlefield, 1980), chaps. 1, 6.

ples that should guide humankind's technological activities. Being responsible comes down to obediently following God's normative will. This is true for a technical designer; it is no less true for a retired senior citizen. It is true for a technical designer as a professional with expertise in the doing of technology; it is no less true for that same technical designer as a parent, consumer, or citizen. People respond to God's normative will as whole persons, not as players of discrete roles. As whole persons they respond to normative principles for technology either in obedience or in rebellion. That is foundational.

But we also recognize that differing gifts, callings, and positions shape this response. The technical designer, because of his or her knowledge and calling, has a responsibility that takes a somewhat different form than that of the retired senior citizen. Nevertheless, these individuals do not have different responsibilities—they share the same responsibility expressed in different ways because of the distinct positions they fulfill.

STRATEGIES FOR IMPLEMENTING COLLECTIVE RESPONSIBILITY

Granted its importance, how is collective responsibility to be exercised? How is the often powerless-feeling public to fulfill its responsibility? Suggested below are three middle-level strategies (which fall between theory and detailed procedure) for enabling collective responsibility to significantly influence modern technology. The agenda that follows calls for developing a network of concern, for reforming the mass media, and for building renewed life-styles.

Developing a Network of Concern. The first item on the agenda for implementing collective responsibility is essentially an educational task: developing a network of concerned persons. Most of these people will probably be found within the Christian community, but by God's grace others will also be concerned to fulfill their responsibility by forming an effective network. The problem is that most people have a poor understanding of technology and its role in and impact on modern society. Thus it is crucial to educate people about technology so that they will clearly perceive the need to join together to change it. For the most part, technology as an area of concern is not even on the public's agenda— nor on the church's agenda. We need to have Christian churches, schools, and print media take the phenomenon of technology seriously and aid us in applying normative principles to it. The aim would be to develop a network of discussion and ideas among nonexperts who are inspired to join together to reform the technological enterprise.

Harry Blamires has complained bitterly that no vital Christian dialogue occurs on such issues as technicism, materialism, and the technological process in general:

> Except over a very narrow field of thinking, chiefly touching questions of strictly personal conduct, we Christians in the modern world accept, for the purpose of mental activity, a frame of reference constructed by the secular mind and a set of criteria reflecting secular evaluations. There is no Christian mind; there is no shared field of discourse in which we can move at ease as thinking Christians.[10]

Isolated academics lecture their students; a minister preaches courageously; an engineer or vice president performs acts of conscience. But all of these are only flickers of inspiration that die quickly because they burn alone. Blamires pleads for a flow of redeemed thinking within the Christian community, a pool of discourse, a reservoir of basic understanding that is nurtured by the insights of opinion leaders and that strengthens them in return by additional reflection and mutual interest. Christians are beginning to actively involve themselves in such issues as nuclear war, abortion, racism, and world hunger. They need to recognize the importance of becoming similarly involved in the major technological issues of today.

Ivan Illich considers the matter of vernacular discourse to be central to any significant transformation. He argues that culture is best interpreted as an ongoing attempt by powerful groups to dominate the life of the common people by controlling language. Most Marxist thinkers trace the character of modern life to the rise of big-business capitalism, the development of bureaucracy, or the introduction of powerful technologies. But Illich seeks to demonstrate that each of these changes rests on a more fundamental historical transformation of the modes of communication. The forms of political and economic control since the sixteenth century—whether those of the Roman Catholic Church, early capitalism, or twentieth-century professionalism—all rest on the domination of language. In each case, Illich argues, powerful groups expropriate the right to define human needs, claiming that satisfaction depends on meeting these needs. Language is used as a means to appropriate and control: "Good old words have been made into branding irons that claim wardship for experts over home, shop, store, and the space or ether between them. Language, the most fundamental of commons, is thus polluted by twisted strands of jargon, each under the con-

---

10. Harry Blamires, *The Christian Mind* (Ann Arbor, Mich.: Servant Books, 1978), p. 4.

trol of another profession."[11] Thus doctors define health, lawyers define justice, engineers define technology, educators define intelligence, urban planners define cities, and journalists define news. When elite groups insist on the symbols of expertise, the public is robbed of meaningful participation in these institutions and the social issues surrounding them.

Illich starts with the familiar Marxist argument that both capitalism and professionalism reduce human activities to mere commodities, but he pushes the thesis further by suggesting that the two are ultimately linked by the fact that both capitalists and professionals maintain their hegemony through communication. Both create artificial scarcities by symbolically constructing a set of needs that only they can satisfy. Illich thus transforms Marx's vision of history from one in which a new set of productive relations unfolds in each epoch to one in which successive areas of human consciousness are linguistically colonized by groups in search of wealth and status.[12]

One can question whether Illich overstates his case, particularly his frequent implication that groups try to maintain societal control through planned, self-conscious strategy. But without a doubt language is a powerful force in society, and jargon is frequently wrongheaded. Christians committed to cultural transformation, therefore, can best be inspired by plain language. Manifestos, pamphlets, books, educational materials, discussion guides, journals, films—all in the language of nonexperts—are vital to the formation of a network of concern. Martin Luther's pamphlets, Thomas Paine's tracts, and today the books of Charles Colson and Ronald Sider—all are indisputable evidence that the pen is mightier than the sword, that we can be deeply moved by plain words truthfully and powerfully spoken. At the very least, what we need is a comprehensive educational program that "addresses the patterns of laity involvement within the corporate structures. Laity education must deal with questions about what the Christian faith means for daily Christian involvement in the world. . . . Even considered altogether, our programs as presently constituted are woefully inadequate to meet the challenge of lay ministry."[13] If church members are to perform their daily activities in a more distinctively Christian manner, we need to significantly improve all aspects of religious instruction regarding technology.

11. Ivan Illich, *Shadow Work* (Boston: Marion Boyars, 1981), p. 29.

12. For further elaboration, see John J. Pauly, "Ivan Illich and Mass Communication Studies," *Communication Research* 10 (Apr. 1983): 259–80.

13. Richard Mouw, *Called to Holy Worldliness* (Philadelphia: Fortress Press, 1980), pp. 128–29.

Manfred Stanley reaches an identical conclusion about vernacular discourse and the forming of concerned networks, although not in the explicitly Christian sense developed above. At the top of Stanley's agenda is the formation of discussion groups or networks that enable participants to encourage each other in responsible thinking and action. He is not talking about schooling per se but education broadly construed: the development of a cultural competence "to attend to the world around us, to interpret what we see and hear; to name in our own voices the conclusions we are prepared to let inform our conduct."[14] In order to exercise our collective responsibility, we need to be able to make well-grounded judgments about the critical issues in our technological age.

Developing a network of concern in regard to technology would produce at least three tangible benefits. First, it would *increase accountability among those involved in the technological process.* Accountability, of course, is a key element in the Christian understanding of responsibility. According to Graham Haydon, no one has a "sense of responsibility" unless he or she is "informed by the realization that an account of this conduct can appropriately be called for." Those who gladly give accounts are responsible people "who can serve as model[s] for an ethic of responsibility."[15]

Accountability is brought into focus by interaction—debate and discussion—among members of a group. This is accountability as answerability, people being challenged, inspired, and exhorted to greater responsibility. Through such interchange, all Christians in their technological involvements—whether direct or indirect—are enabled by God's grace to mature in the exercise of their gifts, to become more discerning and responsible in whatever positions they occupy in life.

Second, a network of Christian concern about technology can *assist in raising appropriate questions about professionalism in technology.* Professions in complex societies—including those in technology—often become haughty and self-serving, more interested in their own status and prosperity than in the public good. A certain esprit de corps can develop that turns inward and centers on protecting the particular profession and its prerogatives. Responsibility exercised prophetically by professional experts will involve raising appropriate issues and offering intelligent resistance in those areas where the direction and purpose of the profession itself have become wrongheaded.

14. Manfred Stanley, *The Technological Conscience: Survival and Dignity in an Age of Expertise* (Chicago: University of Chicago Press, 1981), p. 221.
15. Haydon, "On Being Responsible," p. 55.

Social analysts have become increasingly interested in the crucial issues surrounding professional life in a contemporary industrial context.[16] Those with a Christian perspective on technology can effectively cooperate with sensitive professionals, Christian or not, to examine the substantive questions that are rarely addressed even in professional codes of ethics or at meetings of professional associations. In addition to being able to better serve their own members in the professions—such as science, business, engineering, law, and politics—Christian professional experts and Christian laypersons have a golden opportunity to contribute to the formulation of the broader agenda regarding professionalism itself.[17]

Third, a network of Christians concerned about the technological process can *ensure that the matter of ends and goals is more effectively addressed.* Technology done in response to God's will always proceeds toward biblically sound ends. But we often lose sight of these ends or never pursue them because they remain unarticulated and unexamined. Moreover, technicism traps us into allowing the technological order to work toward greater technical efficiency without considering definitive human ends. Goal-setting left in the hands of government decision makers and corporate officers often gets reduced to short-term objectives. Christians guided by a biblical vision of ideals and normative principles have a natural basis on which to develop worthwhile goals in a world dominated by means, averages, and consensus.[18] By God's grace, generating goals worthy of biblical teaching can have a cathartic and uplifting impact on the technological enterprise.

Reforming the Mass Media. A second essential ingredient for making collective responsibility viable is transforming the mass media by which many of the ideas about the technological world are shaped and through which technological innovations are announced and promoted. It will be difficult to carry out the educational goals discussed above if the mass media constantly undermine them and resist a clearheaded analysis of technology. The reason for this is obvious: most of what the

16. See, for example, Michael D. Bayles, *Professional Ethics* (Belmont, Calif.: Wadsworth, 1981).

17. For a significant attempt to initiate the discussion from a Christian perspective, see Dewey Hoitenga, "Christianity and the Professions," *Christian Scholar's Review* 10 (1981): 296–309. For a provocative response, cf. Raymond G. De Vries, "Christian Responsibility in Professional Society: A Reply to Hoitenga," *Christian Scholar's Review* 13 (1984): 151–57; and Hoitenga's response, pp. 158–62.

18. The need to maintain ends worth dying for has been central to Ellul's argument since 1948. See his definitive chapter "Ends and Means" in *Presence of the Kingdom* (1948; rpt., New York: Seabury Press, 1967), chap. 3. See also Chapter Five of this volume.

general public knows about technology it learns through news and advertising. The average American family today lives in a media-saturated environment: it owns two television sets and five radios, subscribes to six magazines, and feeds itself a steady diet of records, tapes, films, and video cassettes. And every indication is that the immediate future will offer an even larger number and greater diversity of media technologies. The question is whether this enormous information system will encourage technology to develop according to technicism or according to biblically based normative principles. If collective responsibility is to mature, mass communications must receive proper direction.

As a starting point, we must recognize the irony that as the wizardry of delivery and the amount of information increase, the ability to understand and critique decreases. According to Jacques Ellul, the information explosion produces a paralyzed person, not an informed one. The modern person inundated with information is like a frog incessantly subjected to electrical stimulation: "We know what finally happens to the frog's muscles: they become rigid."[19]

The media represent the "discussion edge" of the technological process. They exhibit the structural elements of all technical objects, but their particular identity as such inheres in their function as bearers of symbols. Just as cars are designed to transport and microwave ovens to cook, so televisions, computers, and radios are designed to communicate. Information technologies thus represent the properties of technology while serving as agents for communicating the meaning of the very phenomenon they embody. Thus Ellul calls communication systems the "innermost, and most elusive, manifestation" of technological activity.[20] All technological objects communicate meaning in an important sense, but the media carry that role as their inherent function.

The communicative dimension of God's universe is too important not to be thoroughly reformed for his service. When Adam was given his responsibility as a cultural being, the uniqueness of his task was indicated by his naming the animals. He also communicated with God, giving God an account of his stewardship. At the very beginning of human history, communication was the connective tissue of culture-building.

Today much of society's communicating is done through the media;

---

19. Jacques Ellul, *The Political Illusion* (New York: Knopf, 1967), pp. 57–58. This point is similar to the one made in Chapter Ten regarding information overload and the technological decision maker.

20. Jacques Ellul, *Propaganda* (New York: Knopf, 1969), p. xvii.

we see much of the world through their lens. Because the media are not neutral, their reform is especially urgent and challenging if collective responsibility is to take root in the so-called information age.

Ellul indicates the bias of the media by calling it "sociological propaganda." By the grace of God, his label does not accurately describe all the media, but it is still valid as a generalization. In his scheme, the principle of efficiency that characterizes the technological enterprise as a whole also dominates the communications apparatus. The mass media do not transmit neutral stimuli; both in makeup and in message, they help integrate members of society into a technological system. Ellul worries about such overt forms of persuasion as advertising in business, public relations in industry, and political propaganda in government. However, he is most concerned about the covert, subtle signals, the ubiquitous messages that present certain conceptions of life as truth. The language of technology provides an example: there is a tendency to overuse "breakthrough," "cure," and "major advance" in reporting technological innovations. This overstatement subtly advances technicism by attributing more to technological change than is usually warranted.

The metaphor Ellul uses in this context is the perfect adaptation of the fish to its environment. As the fish is surrounded by water, we are enveloped by data, surrounded by a monodimensional world of stereotypes and slogans and integrated into a homogeneous whole by the "propaganda of conformity." The mass media have become so powerful, Ellul argues, that the ways in which we adapt to technology in our everyday lives are considered normal, even desirable, and we claim that new ideas or alternative worldviews are ideologies or "just propaganda" (an ironic twist). From this vantage point, Ellul sees the mass media—whether news, advertising, or entertainment—as encouraging us to adapt to the existing culture. He sees the language of the media as championing a materialistic culture while it withers critical intelligence as a decisive force.[21]

Though valid in some ways, Ellul's view of media as propaganda is an overgeneralization that can be countered with a long list of meaningful exceptions. There are journalists who seek a truthful account of the day's events in a context that gives them substance and meaning. There are documentaries, commentaries, newspaper columns, opinion journals,

---

21. For a worthwhile reflection on living radically in a materialistic culture, see John F. Kavanaugh, *Following Christ in a Consumer Society: The Spirituality of Cultural Resistance* (Maryknoll, N.Y.: Orbis Books, 1981).

public broadcasting features, and mass paperbacks that resonate with a prophetic accent and lobby for important ideas.[22] Even while recognizing their limited audiences, we also recognize their impact. To some degree they serve as instruments for understanding and implementing our collective obligations. With the help of such instruments—free from the sheer pursuit of profit and audience ratings, and flexible enough for participatory control—technicism can be desacralized, accommodation attacked, and outrageous evils scourged.

Also encouraging is the profound uneasiness presently developing within the mass media about their contemporary mission. Historically the press and mass communications in general have thrived on First Amendment privileges and their status as the "fourth estate." Today their defensiveness and arrogance are turning to anxiety in the face of public disaffection and bewilderment concerning their guiding principles. Much of the unease festers beneath the surface, but recently some of the disenchanted have spoken out. As the titles of current articles indicate, media's lodestar and motivating ideal is being challenged: "Is Objectivity Possible?" "Is Objectivity Obsolete?" "Objectivity—a Forsaken Ideal." Such reassessment makes this an opportune time to press for structural change and radical redirection.

Despite such hopeful signs, Ellul's critique of the media is in many ways accurate. Their power is great, and their message is permeated by a secularized scientific technicism. The positive signs and exceptions noted above must grow into a general movement of reform if the mass media are to promote and not undermine the viable culture of discourse.

Paulo Freire has argued that the mass media have the ability—and therefore the responsibility—to develop four kinds of literacy: political literacy, which involves understanding human existence well enough to enable us to rise above human oppression; cultural literacy in entertainment, which involves the insight into the values, ends, and ultimate meaning of life; consumer literacy, which can be encouraged by supplying enough detail and information about technological products so that buyers can make informed choices; and civic literacy, which can be encouraged by news reports in which new developments in technology, the latest happenings in the workplace, and matters of health and safety are presented fully and fairly, positively or negatively, as the truth dictates.[23] We would never suggest that the mass media are to do all this

22. Consider magazines such as *Consumer Reports, Sojourners,* and *The Other Side;* television programs such as the "MacNeil-Lehrer Report" on PBS and (though less consistently valuable) "60 Minutes" and "20/20"; and high-circulation books that challenge existing cultural practices such as Rachel Carson's *Silent Spring.*

23. On political literacy, see Paulo Freire's *The Politics of Education* (South Hadley,

alone. But in industrial societies they cannot escape their responsibility to contribute to rather than undermine these tasks.

In modern societies the mass media are large, powerful businesses with close ties to the rest of society's corporate structure. Therefore, any call for reform will have to call for basic structural changes. While individual programs—a newspaper here and a key figure there—are important places to begin, the kind of wide-ranging reform that is necessary will involve redeeming the media structures themselves. Altering the way that mass media institutions hire employees, share profits, issue contracts, involve workers in management decisions, allocate money to news reporting, determine their audiences—all these changes and more are essential.

Ronald Sider has illustrated the importance of structural change with a compelling story about a small town at the bottom of a mountain. People taking the steep, winding road into the town often had accidents and were hurt, and the devout Christians among the townspeople banded together to provide volunteer ambulance service twenty-four hours a day. When a visitor recommended that they build a short, inexpensive tunnel through the mountain and close the treacherous road, the villagers refused. After all, the mayor owned a service station along the road, and their emergency service worked reasonably well. The church, they insisted, should preach the gospel, offer "a cup of cold water," and not get involved in political and economic matters. To this day, the story goes, the faithful laity help the victims of the accidents but take no steps to eliminate the accidents themselves.[24] The parallel is clear. Without undergoing fundamental structural changes, the mass media will be unable to play the reforming, liberating role we envisage for them. Those seeking to develop a responsible technology will need to work constantly to undo the damage being done by the media's pervasive technicism.

Models and opportunities for structural change abound. Public television in the United States is a precious resource, an alternative to the commercial structure. Cable television systems, with the possibility for greater diversity, offer potential for change. Governmental regulation, for all its weaknesses, can prevent misleading advertising, insist on public-service programming, and provide for different points of view on controversial issues instead of allowing those with enough money the

Mass.: Bergin & Garvey, 1985). On media reform, see Clifford Christians, "Redemptive Popular Art," *The Reformed Journal,* Aug. 1980, pp. 14–19; and William L. Rivers et al., *Responsibility in Mass Communication,* 3rd ed. (New York: Harper & Row, 1980), chap. 8.

24. See Ronald J. Sider, *Rich Christians in an Age of Hunger* (Downers Grove, Ill.: Inter-Varsity, 1977), pp. 203–4.

exclusive right of access. If local stations took more responsibility for programming based on community needs and perspectives instead of relying so heavily on national network programming, viewers would have a greater range of possibilities for action and change presented to them.

Examples of possible structural reform in the mass media could be listed almost endlessly. Discovering fruitful places for structural change and effecting such change produces far more powerful results than dealing with isolated details or externals. If the public is to have the perspective and knowledge it needs to exercise its collective responsibility effectively, such fundamental redirection is essential. The media must not be permitted to inculcate and celebrate technicism.

Renewed Life-styles. Those who have been inspired by the vision of technology in keeping with biblically based normative principles—a technology of love and servanthood—need to live lives transformed by that vision. This may mean getting along with one car instead of two, avoiding prepared ''convenience'' foods and making simple meals from scratch, having a backyard garden, recycling as many materials as possible, and restricting television viewing time (especially viewing of the commercial networks). Or a renewed life-style may mean making more radical changes: leaving a job in a corporation devoted solely to profit-making, teaching one's children at home, depending completely on public transit instead of owning a private car, growing virtually all of one's own food, and watching no television at all.

Whatever the specific content of a renewed life-style, it is important that we critically examine the way we live and self-consciously decide in light of God's normative will what is right and wrong. In so doing we throw off the shackles of a materialistic, technicized culture and look to God instead. The specifics of the Christian life-style cannot be dictated because of the variables involved—who we are, what God calls us to do, and the times and situations in which we find ourselves. But whatever their particulars, our life-styles must indicate our total obedience to God's will.

A transformed life-style is important for two reasons: it is a form of obedience to God, and it is a testimony to others. The first point is clear. Belief and behavior are always inseparably linked for the Christian. To recognize and understand the evils of a secularized society guided by the principles of technicism yet to live in that society exactly as everyone else does, without reflecting one's commitment to Jesus Christ and the command to love God above all and neighbor as self, is simply wrong. Obedience to biblically based normative principles necessarily means acting differently as a consumer, a citizen, a worker, and a parent.

Renewed life-styles also serve as testimonies to society, testimonies that God can use to help bring about needed structural changes. This form of obedience is concrete and situational, and therefore can serve as the basis for authentic witness. Those who live in peace can speak more vibrantly about peace and love in society and the world. Those who consciously change their eating habits because of world hunger bring an authenticity to discussions of new legislative proposals regarding it. The nonverbal communicates an incredible amount; only ignorance of the communication process allows one to see verbal communication as more powerful. The power of a life lived in radical obedience to Jesus Christ is greater than that of many sermons or books.

A transformed life-style must always be lived communally; it must be supported, encouraged, and held accountable by a Christian community. Although the Christian life is never to be lived in isolation from fellow Christians, Christian community is especially important for those attempting to live in a radically different way that goes against the cultural mainstream. Its influence is so strong and so pervasive that one needs the constant presence of a community that is both supportive and challenging if one is to avoid succumbing to prevailing cultural patterns.

Stanley Hauerwas, author of *A Community of Character,* underscores our point with a bold declaration:

> The most important social task of Christians is to be nothing less than a community capable of forming people with virtues sufficient to witness to God's truth in the world. Put as directly as I can, it is not the task of the church to try to develop social theories or strategies to make America work; rather the task of the church in this country is to become a polity [that is, a community, a body] that has the character necessary to survive as a truthful society. That task carried out would represent a distinctive contribution to the body politic we call America.[25]

Christians need not be physically separate from society to live truly transformed lives; they can be in society but not of it. Certain congregations living in the mainstream emphasize the importance of stewardship, and the life-styles of most of their members are distinctly consistent in word and deed with prophetic transformation. In other cases, strong family units, task forces designed to lobby for a position, separate organizations, and informal friendship groups provide a context for expressing a life-style that conforms faithfully to biblical teaching on collective responsibility.

Others seek and develop renewed life-styles in alternative commu-

25. Stanley Hauerwas, *A Community of Character: Toward a Constructive Christian Social Ethic* (South Bend, Ind.: University of Notre Dame Press, 1981), p. 3.

nities that are physically separate from society. Given the overwhelming commitment of Western culture to a materialistic, technicistic world-and-life view, and given the great strength of culture in shaping attitudes and outlooks, some Christians have concluded that the only way they can live in true obedience and bring up their children to do so is by joining alternative communities of fellow believers. Alternative communities can serve as a vital arena in which individuals achieve their potential without having their personal identity swallowed up by remote, impersonal institutions. Community members can in some ways be protected from the strength and pervasiveness of materialism and integrative propaganda. Living in carefully controlled contexts enables people to experiment and to work out in painstaking detail a response to the new challenges in the larger world that are as yet not fully understood.

Alternative communities do run the danger of withdrawing from interaction with society and thus becoming culturally irrelevant. At their worst they constitute a denial of cultural responsibility: members withdraw into an insular community offering them comfort and personal support, and they stop thinking and caring about a society filled with people being hurt and torn apart by a materialistic, technological culture. But alternative communities can also be powerful agents of cultural change. They can be such by clearly showing in word and deed exactly what living in obedience to Christ means in a modern, technologically oriented society, and by continuing to interact with mainstream culture. Illich argues for the alternative community not as a form of escape but as a way to choose ''joyful austerity'' as a life-style. They are a kind of self-imposed opportunity to free oneself to cultivate a deeper sense of self-consciousness and faithfulness.[26]

In summary, we can be freed to fulfill our collective responsibility as members of society by developing a network of concern, reforming the mass media, and living transformed lives. Then we will be free to develop responsible attitudes and opinions, make responsible product choices as consumers, and act as responsible citizens by voting, voicing opinions to political and corporate leaders, and forming citizen advocacy groups. Through these and other concrete actions we will be able to fulfill our commitment to collective responsibility.

POSITION-SPECIFIC RESPONSIBILITY

All of us share a collective responsibility simply by being part of a society. But some people, by virtue of their occupation or some other

---

26. See Ivan Illich, *Tools for Conviviality* (New York: Harper & Row, 1973), p. xxv.

special position they fulfill in relation to technology, have an additional responsibility. As noted earlier, responsibility differs in both extent and form, depending on whether one is a corporate vice-president for marketing, a design engineer with a computer firm, a researcher at an agricultural research center, a congressman on the Committee on Science and Technology, or a chemist in a large pharmaceutical company. But in exactly what ways do the responsibilities of these individuals differ?

The Conventional Answer. This question has a standard response, one that is often presumed without being articulated. Conventional wisdom says first of all that technical experts have a responsibility to act with professional skill and integrity in their area of expertise. The codes of ethics that have been drawn up by various professional societies whose members are active in technology reflect this type of responsibility.[27] According to this view, when technical experts speak as such in their fields of specialization, they do so with a certain authority or stature; but when they speak outside of this role, they have no more authority or stature than anyone else. A concomitant belief is that technical experts have a responsibility to speak and act with skill and integrity in their specific professional capacity, but have no special responsibility outside their area or even within their area if the issue at hand is not a narrowly defined "technical" issue within their purview.

Conventional wisdom also says that certain policymakers in some ways determine what the technical experts do. These policymakers are the corporate executives, government officials, and key research and academic leaders who decide what lines of technological development should be pursued and what technological objects should be produced by what processes. Conventional wisdom does not clearly spell out how much responsibility these individuals have. In some ways they are seen as having tremendous responsibility—they, after all, are the ones who decide what is to be done. On the other hand, they are often seen as not having as much power—and therefore not as much responsibility—as is sometimes assumed. They may be bound by their own lack of expertise and therefore need to rely on technical experts for advice and insight. But the most frequently made claim is that the power of these policymakers is limited because they must respond to forces present among the general public. Government officials—if they are bureaucrats or judges—claim that they are only following the law, not making it; if they are elected officials, they claim that they must follow public opinion or they will be

27. See, for example, "IEEE [Institute of Electrical and Electronics Engineers] Code of Ethics," as reprinted in George E. Dieter's *Engineering Design: A Materials and Processing Approach* (New York: McGraw-Hill, 1983), pp. 12–13.

out of a job. Corporate executives claim that in the final analysis they must respond to consumers, or they will soon be out of business. Research and academic leaders claim that the governmental and corporate sources of their funds direct the decisions they make.

Finally, conventional wisdom recognizes that the general public shares in this responsibility, because as voters and consumers they react to the decisions of the policymakers and either reward or punish them.

The Conventional Answer and Technicism. The way in which conventional wisdom views responsibility in a technological society presents serious problems. Seeking to parcel out responsibility according to the positions people hold in relation to technology—given the distorted understandings of roles and occupations that people tend to have today— limits and splinters responsibility almost to the point where no one is responsible. Everyone has a convenient basis on which to blame someone else. The heart of the problem lies in the technicism that we have discussed frequently. Technicism influences conventional wisdom, and technicism sees technology in a fragmented fashion. To have a true picture of position-specific responsibility, we must remind ourselves of what has gone wrong and how a technology directed by biblically based normative principles differs from the status quo.

Under the line of the Fall and secularization (discussed in Chapter Four), modern, secular societies pursue human power and mastery independent of God's will and norms. This drive for human mastery has developed into technicism, a belief in technology as the means to human progress and the answer to all human problems. Technicism has become a false god that has drawn science, economics, politics, and technological design into its orbit. These different areas of activity and responsibility have all become part of technologically oriented institutions and structures that obey the technological imperative.

The result is that people in all these fields tend to perceive their responsibilities too narrowly and apply them too broadly. Their perception is too narrow because it is based on a single criterion. They judge everything in terms of the technological imperative, the drive for greater and greater efficiency and technological sophistication. And it is precisely because they judge everything by this narrow standard, because they apply it too widely, that they carry out their responsibilities as experts too broadly.

The mechanical tomato harvester developed by the University of California in the early 1960s illustrates this problem.[28] Critics such as the

28. See Mark Kramer, "The Ruination of the Tomato," *The Atlantic Monthly*, Jan. 1980, pp. 72–77; and "Weighing the Social Costs of Innovation," *Science*, Mar. 30, 1984, pp. 1368–69.

California Rural Assistance League have blamed the tomato harvester for forcing small farmers out of business, replacing thousands of workers, and giving consumers tasteless, tough-skinned tomatoes (because a special kind of tomato had to be developed to withstand the rough handling of the harvester). One can argue whether or not all these charges are fully justified, but this case does demonstrate the multilevel issues related to technological innovation.

Several parties were guilty of supporting this "step forward." The university's research-and-design team simply did not consider such social consequences as the loss of jobs for seasonal workers and driving small farmers out of business. The university itself does not require that academic research consider the social consequences of its developments, because such guidelines are presumed to infringe on academic freedom. The state helped fund development of the picker (the legislature supports state universities with public funds), although the picker ended up benefitting only a few in agribusiness and harming thousands of laborers. The large canneries signed contracts with the tomato growers large enough to use the pickers, since one reliable major supplier met the needs of the canneries more efficiently than dozens of smaller growers. The tomatoes suffered too: developing hybrids that would not be damaged when mechanically picked and adding chemicals for uniform color change regulated the growing process but sacrificed the taste, texture, and quality of the tomatoes. Economists calculated that the picker's efficiency would reduce the price of tomatoes, but they failed to take heavy investments and a lack of competition into account, so consumers paid a high price for a mediocre product.

This story is more complicated than a summary suggests, and many aspects are open to alternative explanations. However, it gives a good picture of what usually occurs when the technological process follows the power motive instead of the goal of sufficient design, when social consequences are not integrated into planning. The university absolutizes academic independence, and the growers and canners absolutize efficient production. The curricula in science and engineering exclude the social and ethical aspects of these fields, as student training and professors' writing reveal. Public policy allows engineering at the university to proceed according to the technological imperative. The narrow framework in which responsibility is assessed and the absolutizing of one end such as profit or so-called technical expertise results in technological development contrary to appropriate normative principles.

Technological Activity Responsive to God's Will. What is needed is a return to the Creator and his normative will, represented in the line of creation and redemption. The cultural mandate is still in effect, a mandate to develop and bring out the riches and potentialities God has placed in his good creation. His command of love, embodied in the normative principles outlined herein, must be our guide. Heeding this command both broadens and narrows the responsibility of those involved with technology. It broadens responsibility because each individual involved in technology must approach his or her task with a concern for pursuing all the normative principles simultaneously. But responsibility is at the same time narrowed because one area is not to exert hegemony over other areas. All decisions do not become technological decisions.

This kind of responsibility must be implemented at all levels. While the scope of design activity must become holistic—must be broadened— it must simultaneously be narrowed so that technical efficiency does not exert hegemony over the needs of labor, or over government's concern for the public interest, or over the consumer's concern for high-quality products. Business executives must broaden their aims to see beyond financial returns and the security of investments, yet at the same time they must limit these aims so that the balance sheets do not have hegemony over social consequences and the environment of the workplace. We must urge government officials to take a broad view of their task of directing and monitoring technological activity on behalf of the public. Costs and burdens must be allocated, disputes adjudicated, evildoers restrained, and levels of responsibility assigned. The state, in other words, has an obligation to supervise, but also a prospective duty for vision and direction-setting leadership. Yet we must not lay all the burden on the state, as though its strong guidance is all that is necessary for responsible technology.

That the responsibilities of those involved with technology must be narrowed in one sense and broadened in another can be further illustrated by taking a close look at the responsibilities of economists. In the first place, the conception of economic activity must be enlarged to include nonmonetary aspects of wealth and income. Economists have a category of externalities—events that do not fit within the market framework— which has become so large that it is an obvious testimony to the reality and vitality of nonmarket economic events and aspects. Until we develop economic theories that allow us to see all the components of economic wealth—including such things as the natural creation and labor that is done without remuneration—we will be concerned with only part of the issue of resource use, that part made most visible to us by the conventional use of money. And no theory of optimal use of resources and no actual disposition of those resources can possibly succeed if they focus on only part of the domain. While we give our myopic attention to money matters, the real wealth of the world will be frittered away.

Like the definition of economic activity, the basis for participating in economic activity has been seen much too narrowly. The idea that individuals can maximize increments of pleasure by manipulating material goods does not give us the right starting point for economic activity. It is not the scarcity of the means for satisfying human desires that first and foremost gives us economic activity, but rather God's entrusting the creation to humankind for the purpose of meeting its needs and rendering him glory. Stewardly servanthood must replace human autonomy as the starting point of economics.

But this economic servanthood is not something we render in isolation, nor does it comprise the whole of our response to God and neighbor. Modern society often suggests that economic prudence is all a person needs. But this is not the case, not by any true definition of what constitutes the economic. Such a view does violence to the multiformity and coherence of our lives. True, the scope of economic concepts must be enlarged in the way just discussed, but the domain of the economic in our lives—as seen in both theory and practice—must be narrowed. Our definitions of progress—whether assessed at the national level in terms of the growth of the Gross National Product, or by families in terms of hopes for ever-increasing monetary incomes—have been too narrow. Developing economic wealth does not assure national or familial well-being. It does not and cannot fully tell us about growing in service to God and neighbor. It is necessary to reject the hegemony of economics in both theory and practice, and instead seek a proper place for it among other disciplines and professions and among the other aspects of our lives. Economics is to be broadened to include such normative principles as justice, care for one's neighbor, and stewardship, and at the same time it is to be seen as only a limited aspect of our existence, not one that gives full due to justice, caring, or stewardship.

The same point can be made about the design profession. Designers are to think beyond themselves and their specialties, beyond ego and power needs, beyond ''the facts of the matter.'' They are to perceive the complex, value-laden situation within which a technological object must ultimately function. Their responsibility thus goes far beyond the requirement of conventional wisdom—that they simply design well in a narrow, technical sense without concern for the broader social, cultural, environmental context. Yet in another way their responsibility is narrower than that usually assigned them by conventional wisdom. The narrow standard of highly specialized technical expertise is not to be applied indiscriminately to issues that are largely social, economic, or political in character.

* * * * *

The ultimate point to be made is this: responsible technology must rest upon a servant-like commitment to love God above all and one's neighbor as oneself. It is as all of us—designers, research scientists, consumers, public policy makers, citizens, fabricators, corporate executives, journalists, scholars, and others—seek to love as Christ loved us that we will be able to live in the line of creation and redemption. We will then broaden the standards by which our technologically relevant decisions are made to simultaneously include all the biblically based normative principles, and at the same time narrow the application of the economic, the technical, the scientific, and the political. In so doing we will responsibly fulfill the ancient cultural mandate. We will become builders who work with, not against, God's good creation to bring out and develop the riches he has placed there. As we do so we will often feel like exiles in a strange and threatening land. Yet we have God's promise that our efforts will not be in vain. Faithfulness will bear fruit. It will be a harvest of God's choosing and timing, but a valuable harvest nonetheless, one worth the struggle and the wait.

Recommended Reading

Ellul, Jacques. *The Technological System*. New York: Seabury Press-Continuum, 1980.

In this volume Ellul updates his best-selling book *The Technological Society*, published in 1954. Ellul develops two of his central themes here. First, he lodges a complaint against machineness. The harsh law of efficiency, *la technique,* has become the supreme value in industrialized societies. Second, he clarifies his notion of autonomous technology. In the chapters titled "Autonomy" and "Self-Augmentation" he demonstrates that technological systems grow by an intrinsic dynamic. This book is somewhat more systematic than his 1954 volume, and it also takes into account a larger number of scholars of technology.

Florman, Samuel C. *Blaming Technology: The Irrational Search for Scapegoats*. New York: St. Martin's Press, 1981.

As the title suggests, Florman contradicts those who would be anti-technology. He maintains that "it is not technology but 'fear' of technology that is running rampant." To check the fear of an autonomous technology, one that has a life of its own, he reminds us of various technologies that have not fared well—from the SST to the rotary engine to weather modification. An underlying thesis of this book and much of Florman's other writing is that the work of engineers, if governed by a proper combination of self controls and governmental controls, should not present a threat to humankind. Thus he relieves technology of the role of scapegoat and indicts the public sector, since we are all responsible, to varying degrees, for the decision making that affects technology. Since he speaks to all of us, we should perhaps heed his challenge to gain a more balanced perspective on the genesis of the ills and benefits brought about by modern technology.

Florman, Samuel C. *The Existential Pleasures of Engineering*. New York: St. Martin's Press, 1975.

The author, a practicing engineer who also has a master's degree in literature, proposes that "engineering is an expression of mankind's most elemental impulses and most sublime aspirations." He calls the engineer-designer and the layperson to more fully understand the pleasures of creating the artificial. He develops the idea that the technologist is still a craftsman at heart and thus should enjoy all the pleasures of craftsmanship. Florman is one of the few engineers who has taken up the task of commenting on the technological phenomenon. His stimulating viewpoint, widely known among those who study technology, is of value to both engineers and laypersons.

Giarini, Orio. *Dialogue on Wealth and Welfare: An Alternative View of World Capital Formation*. Oxford: Pergamon Press, 1980.

Giarini creatively demonstrates the importance of a correct perspective on the value of economic and technological activity. He argues that fundamental economic concepts such as wealth, income, cost, and productivity have been incorrectly defined. In particular, because we have developed an economics of industrialization, not an economics of true wealth, we have reduced our notion of value to that which is measured in monetary terms. In the process, Giarini argues, we have been using up a portion of our "dowry and patrimony" of nonmonetized wealth without considering the cost. Our distorted way of perceiving reality has led to misdirected actions and policies that frequently reduce rather than enhance total wealth. Distortion of technological change is one phenomenon that Giarini examines. He suggests new concepts and strategies for a proper development of wealth and welfare.

Goudzwaard, Bob. *Capitalism and Progress: A Diagnosis of Western Society*, trans. and ed. by Josina Van Nuis Zylstra. Grand Rapids: Eerdmans; Toronto: Wedge, 1979.

Goudzwaard looks at Western culture from the standpoint of the relation between faith in human progress and the development of capitalism as a particular societal structure. These have led to a distorted technical and economic notion of progress which in turn has precipitated a crisis in the form of an accumulation of interdependent problems. In redressing the error of Western ways, Goudzwaard wishes to avoid the typical superficial reaction that seeks piecemeal solutions to the intertwined problems. Instead, he sees the necessity of working toward the simultaneous realization of the norms that God gives for man's cultural activities. This would overcome, for example, the distortion created by the Industrial Revolution when it granted almost absolute priority to the advance of technology and industrial production in the development of Western culture. It means the transformation of a tunnel society, in which everything is valued only instrumentally, into an open society in which persons, cultural institutions, and societal forms regain the opportunity to develop according to their own unique possibilities.

Heidegger, Martin. *The Question Concerning Technology and Other Essays*. Trans. William Lovitt. New York: Harper & Row-Torchbooks, 1977.

This is a collection of the five most important essays on technology by Heidegger, who is probably the philosopher most cited on the question of technology. In this volume he introduces his terminology and line of argument. Though the language he uses is complicated, Heidegger conveys a dialectical vision in which man and nature encounter one another creatively in the process of doing technology. He aims to prove that technology is not merely the application of science but expresses man's poetic ability.

Illich, Ivan. *Tools for Conviviality*. New York. Harper & Row-Colophon Books, 1973.

In this book Illich warns that our development of technologies must not cross the borderline and become technologies that infringe on our individual liberties. Technology is convivial if responsibly limited to its natural scale, thereby allowing human beings control. Illich believes that each of our technologies has a natural scale, and if we go beyond it in design or usage, we will develop something destructive despite our best intentions. He believes the industrial mode of production is decaying and seeks to outline a technology appropriate for the postindustrial age.

Jonas, Hans. *The Imperative of Responsibility: In Search of an Ethics for the Technological Age*. Chicago: University of Chicago Press, 1984.

In this widely discussed book, Jonas examines the ways in which modern technology changes our conclusions about morality. He notes that media technologies have made the world into a single "unit," and that we are now capable of destroying ourselves with nuclear weapons; therefore, he argues, any theory of responsibility that we advocate must fully confront these realities. It is particularly important that we preserve the earth and give prophecies of doom priority over blue-sky blissfulness.

Mitcham, Carl, and Robert Mackey, eds. *Philosophy and Technology: Readings in the Philosophical Problems of Technology*. 1972; rpt. New York: Free Press, 1983.

This volume is a carefully edited anthology of twenty-six essays (many of them classics) on the philosophical problems of technology. In their introduction the editors analyze the scope of the readings. The essays themselves are divided into five categories: conceptual issues, ethical and political critiques, religious critiques, existentialist critiques, and metaphysical studies. The essays by Ernst Juenger and Friedrich Dessauer appear in English for the first time. The book also has a twenty-five-page bibliography.

Mitcham, Carl, and Jim Grote, eds. *Theology and Technology: Essays in Christian Analysis and Exegesis*. Lanham, Md.: University Press of America, 1984.

This collection of twenty essays supplements the philosophical readings mentioned above. The editors shaped the collection to indicate that ''the central question, even in the philosophy of technology, is ultimately theological in character.'' Among the authors represented are A. Malet, J. Ellul, P. T. Durbin, G. Grant, and E. Schuurman. The book has an invaluable bibliography (840 entries) on the theology-technology theme.

Mumford, Lewis. *The Myth of the Machine*. 2 vols. New York: Harcourt Brace Jovanovich, 1967, 1970.

In these two volumes one of the leading scholars of technology and culture gives us a radical interpretation of cultural development. Mumford develops in rich detail the thesis that man is not first of all a tool-using or tool-making animal, but rather ''pre-eminently a mind-making, self-mastering and self-designing animal.'' Consequently, the locus of all his activities lies in his own organism. In the beginning, man's technics were life-centered—a bio-technics. Our present culture, through a long historical process, has become profoundly modified by a machine-mindedness. Consequently, we are now overcommitted to a mega-technics, a power-technics. Mumford concludes by calling sleepers to awaken. The effective salvation of mankind requires ''something like a spontaneous religious conversion: one that will replace the mechanical world picture with an organic world picture.'' Only those who have thrown off the myth of the machine will be able to escape the technocratic prison.

Pacey, Arnold. *The Culture of Technology*. Cambridge: MIT Press, 1983.

In this book Pacey disputes the widely held idea that technology is value-free. By the culture of technology he means the "values, ideas, and creative activity" that shape not only machines and processes but also the way in which they are invented and used. Beliefs about the inevitability of technological progress, the culture of technological virtuosity or expertise, and beliefs about resources are highlighted by examining, among other things, nuclear weapons, Third World development, medicine, automation, and industrial decline. The book is a plea for openness, democracy, and diversity in our articulation of technological policy. Open democratic dialogue will stimulate technological innovation in new directions and address the present imbalance between "user needs" and "supplier needs."

Papanek, Victor. *Design for Human Scale*. New York: Van Nostrand Reinhold, 1983.

Papanek begins with a simple declaration: "The average consumer often has no clear concept of what design is all about." How to solve this problem? "One way of getting design and people closer together," Papanek says, "is to design things that make participation by end users essential to the design process." Specific ideas for accomplishing this goal include such diverse suggestions as the curing of product addiction, the humanization of design, and design edcuation. This provocative book is meant for designers and laypersons alike. It is a call to a more humane, ecologically and culturally sound technology.

Papanek, Victor. *Design for the Real World*. 2nd ed. New York: Van Nostrand Reinhold, 1984.

Papanek is an industrial designer, something of a cross between an engineer and an artist. He sets out his design philosophy plainly: "Design must be an innovative, highly creative cross-disciplinary tool responsive to the true needs of men. It must be more research-oriented [in all disciplines], and we must stop defiling the earth with poorly-designed objects and structures." Papanek is an exponent of designing in a "social context." His view contrasts with the view of design that focuses only on the "machine" itself without regard to its ultimate purpose in and effect on various cultures. This book is "must" reading for engineer-designers, but it also provides laypersons with interesting and readable insights into design.

Pirsig, Robert M. *Zen and the Art of Motorcycle Maintenance: An Inquiry into Values.* New York: Bantam Books, 1974.

In this book Pirsig develops an interesting parallel: "The study of the art of motorcycle maintenance is really a miniature study of rationality itself. Working on a motorcycle, working well, caring, is to become part of a process, to achieve an inner peace of mind. The motorcycle is primarily a mental phenomenon." In working out this parallel, Pirsig sets the reader on a course toward the discovery of "quality"—that elusive something in machines that cannot be described in typically Western scientific terms. Pirsig's approach is decidedly Eastern in orientation and provides a refreshing, appropriate counterpoint to a highly rationalized approach to technological design. Although this is a serious book that is sometimes heavy going, it provides the general reader with an entertaining yet thoughtful approach to the subjective character of the machines man designs, fabricates, and maintains.

Ravetz, Jerome R. *Scientific Knowledge and Its Social Problems.* New York: Oxford University Press, 1971.

In this thoughtful and incisive book, Ravetz—a historian and philosopher of science—argues for a "critical science," one in which science, technology, and politics are intimately involved. The "academic science" of the recent past and the "industrialized science" of the present are inadequate to expose in detail and principle the sterile and dehumanized common-sense in which our science and technology are currently conceived. Although this book emphasizes the art of scientific research, it provides an invaluable discussion of the relationship between science and technology.

Schumacher, E. F. *Small Is Beautiful.* New York: Harper & Row, 1973.

The title of this book should have been *Intermediate Is Beautiful;* the subtitle *Economics as if People Mattered* gives the best clue to its perspective. Schumacher rejects the conventional view that greed and envy are to be accepted and utilized as the motivating forces of the economy, science, and technology. He was one of the early critics calling for an economics and technology of permanence instead of regarding the maximization of throughput as the highest good. What he refers to as the "logic of production" (that more and bigger is better) ought not be the logic of life and society. His concern for the poor, for biblical norms in economic life, and for the place of the "common man" in the decisions that affect him all lead Schumacher to champion an intermediate technology as an alternative to the mindless pursuit of large-scale technology and limitless economic growth. Against the hegemony of economic measures of progress, Schumacher argues that consumption is only one means to well-being and that logically, as a means, it ought to be minimized, not maximized, in the pursuit of maximum well-being.

Schuurman, Egbert. *Technology and the Future: A Philosophical Challenge.* Trans. H. D. Morton. Toronto: Wedge Publishing, 1980.

Originally published in Dutch, this book provides a detailed and nuanced critique of a basically European philosophy of technology from a neo-Calvinist, reformational approach. Written by an engineer-philosopher, the book is divided into four parts: (1) an analysis of the structure of modern technology; (2) a discussion of transcendentalist thinkers—F. Juenger, M. Heidegger, H. Meyer, and J. Ellul; (3) a discussion of positivist thinkers—N. Wiener and the neo-Marxists K. Steinbuch and G. Klaus; and (4) an articulation of a liberating perspective for technological development. In the last section the author develops his own Christian view concerning the creational *meaning* of technology.

Stanley, Manfred. *The Technological Conscience: Survival and Dignity in an Age of Expertise.* Chicago: University of Chicago Press, 1978.

Stanley, a professor of sociology at Syracuse University, analyzes the problem of technicism in this book. He believes that industrial societies have allowed technological metaphors and modes of thought to invade their cultural, moral, and political thinking. The solution lies in a recovery of a common language in which human dignity is protected as nonnegotiable. He looks to education as the primary vehicle for social reform.

Weizenbaum, Joseph. *Computer Power and Human Reason: From Judgment to Calculation.* New York: W. H. Freeman, 1976.

This is a thoughtful book about computer technology from a distinguished computer scientist. His main concern is to protect social and human values from what he considers the onslaught of our most prestigious and richly funded modern technology—computers. In his view, computers are the embodiment of scientific rationality. From this perspective, he examines what computers can accomplish as well as what they cannot do or ought not be allowed to do. Weizenbaum builds his argument on the premise that man and machines are different in essence.

Winner, Langdon. *Autonomous Technology: Technics-out-of-Control as a Theme in Political Thought.* Cambridge: MIT Press, 1977.

As a political scientist, Winner is concerned with the literature which argues that technology can no longer be controlled. He focuses primarily on the work of Jacques Ellul, although he also discusses the ideas of Herbert Marcuse, Karl Marx, and Lewis Mumford. Winner rejects the conventional notion that since humans create technology, they also control it. But he also argues that we ought not to conclude that we have no mastery at all over technology. Winner sees the issue in the light of our general loss of confidence in human abilities. He offers no easy solutions to our sense of powerlessness in a complex world, but he stresses that it is a problem that must be solved.